HISTORICAL ENDINGS

Other titles in preparation for the Historical Endings series include:

The Roman Empire by Neil Christie

The Mongol Empire by Charles Melville

Imperial Germany by James Retallack

The Habsburg Empire by Mark Cornwall

The World of Versailles by Patrick Finney

The Post-45 World Order by Saki Dockrill

East European Communism by Robin Okey

THE OTTOMAN PEOPLES AND THE END OF EMPIRE

JUSTIN McCARTHY
Professor of History, University of Louisville

Hodder Arnold

A MEMBER OF THE HODDER HEADLINE GROUP

Distributed in the United States of America by
Oxford University Press Inc., New York

First published in Great Britain in 2001
This impression reprinted in 2005 by Arnold,
Arnold, a member of the Hodder Headline Group,
338 Euston Road, London NW1 3BH

http://www.hoddereducation.com

Distributed in the United States of America by
Oxford University Press Inc.,
198 Madison Avenue, New York, NY 10016

British Library Cataloguing in Publication Data
A catalogue record for this book is available from the British Library

Library of Congress Cataloging-in-Publication Data
A catalog record for this book is available from the Library of Congress

ISBN- 10: 0 340 70656 2 (hb)
ISBN- 10: 0 340 70657 0 (pb)
ISBN-13: 978 0 340 70656 2

5 6 7 8 9 10

Typeset in 10/12pt Sabon by Phoenix Photosetting, Chatham, Kent
Printed and bound in India by Replika Press Pvt. Ltd.

To John Patrick

Contents

	List of maps	*viii*
	Acknowledgements	*ix*
	Pronunciation guide	*x*
1	Introduction	1
2	Reforming the Empire	8
3	The Balkans	38
4	Ottoman Asia	63
5	The Balkan Wars	87
6	World War I	95
7	The peace conferences	113
8	The Turkish War of Independence	128
9	The Balkans after the wars	149
10	Mandates in the Arab provinces	163
11	The Turkish Republic	193
12	Legacy and consequences	216
	Notes	*221*
	Suggested readings	*225*
	Index	*227*

Maps

1.1	Population by religion in 1912	4–5
2.1	The Ottoman Empire in 1800 and 1912	10–11
2.2	Railways built in the Ottoman Empire	29
3.1	Provinces of Ottoman Europe in 1912	41
3.2	Dividing the Balkans by religious group	54
3.3	Macedonia, the Bulgarian view	56
3.4	Macedonia, the Serbian view	57
4.1	Provinces of Ottoman Asia in 1912	64–5
6.1	World War I, theatres of war	100–1
6.2	Eastern Anatolia	105
7.1	Western Anatolia and the Balkans	124
8.1	The war in the west	133
8.2	The war in the east	142
9.1	The Balkans in 1923	150
10.1	The Sykes–Picot Agreement and promises to the Arabs	167
10.2	Syria	172
10.3	Iraq	174
10.4	Middle Eastern railroads	189
11.1	Mortality in Anatolia, 1912–1922	194
11.2	Population living in district of birth	197
11.3	Population by province, 1912 and 1922	198
11.4	Central districts: population by religion, 1912 and 1922	200
11.5	Destruction of agriculture	204

Acknowledgements

Initial research for this book was financed by the National Endowment for the Humanities, with additional support from Dr Turhan Baykan and the University of Louisville. I am especially indebted to Dr Baykan for his vision and generosity. I thank the Library of Congress, the British Library, and the University's Inter-Library Loan. Writing the book was facilitated, as always, by my colleagues and the staff of the Department of History at the University of Louisville, particularly Rita Hettinger, Pat Dalton, Barbara Winsper, Bruce Adams and Thomas Mackey.

My greatest thanks go to my wife, Beth, for her help and tolerance, and to my children – Nick, Cait, Maureen and John – for knowing that their father loves them despite the fact that he so often locks himself in his study to write.

Pronunciation guide

a	soft a as in ‘father’
ay	long i as in ‘kite’
c	j as in ‘jump’
ç	ch as in ‘child’
e	ê as in French ‘être’
ey	long a as in ‘bay’
ğ	lengthens the sound of the preceding vowel, but has no sound of its own
i	long e as in ‘feet’
ı	somewhat like the i in ‘first’ or ‘dirt’
j	like the French g in ‘gendarme’
o	long o as in ‘joke’
ö	like the German ö
ş	sh as in ‘shop’
u	oo as in ‘boo’
ü	like the German ü

1
Introduction

The long life of the Ottoman Empire officially ended on 1 November 1922, when the Turkish Grand National Assembly abolished the sultanate. The last sultan, Mehmet VI, bid farewell to his retinue and palace and left Istanbul. For a brief time Abdülmecid II ruled in the purely religious position of caliph of the Muslims, then on 3 March 1924 the caliphate was also abolished. Six hundred years of Ottoman rule were over.

The Middle East and the Balkans have known much conflict since Mehmet VI boarded a British destroyer, on his way to permanent exile. In the Balkans, Bulgaria fulfilled its irredentist wishes by taking land from Yugoslavia in both World Wars, only to lose it again at each war's end. During World War II, newly independent Croatia was given Bosnia, where both Serbs and Muslims subsequently suffered greatly from attacks by nationalist bands. The Jews of the Balkans were expelled in great numbers when the national states were created, then those who had remained died in Nazi concentration camps. Minorities in Turkey lost heavily through a confiscatory wartime tax that was applied almost exclusively to them. Greeks emigrated from Istanbul. In turn, Greeks persecuted the Turks of western Thrace. Bulgarians expelled Turks in the 1950s and attempted to end Turkish culture in Bulgaria in the 1980s, causing the exodus of hundreds of thousands more.

The dissolution of Yugoslavia loosed ethnic tensions that may never die, even if peoples are permanently divided into separate states. In Bosnia, Serbian mass murder of Muslims and forced dislocation of Muslims and Croats failed to dislodge either people permanently. What was left behind, though, were three small and separate communities, each with new hatreds from new wrongs, real and imagined, to add to long memories of insult to their peoples. In Kosovo, the Albanians were first persecuted by Serbs, who claimed Kosovo as part of their historical patrimony, even though they made up only a small part of the population. Once the Serbs were defeated by NATO bombing, Albanian refugees returned and set about trying to force out the remaining Serbs.

In the Soviet Union, as in Yugoslavia, communist rule managed to suppress nationalist conflict for decades by substituting universal repression in its place. Yet ethnic conflict re-emerged as soon as the Soviet masters had departed: Georgia fought a civil war against Abhazians, the remnants of a community forced from their homes by the tsars; Armenia and Azerbaijan fought over Ngorno Karabagh (Karabag), nationalist emotions forestalling compromise. Armenia occupied a quarter of Azerbaijan. In the final act of a great population exchange that had begun two hundred years before, Turks fled Armenia and Armenians fled Azerbaijan.

In the Middle East, Arabs and Israelis fought their wars. Palestinians fled from homes that had become battlegrounds, and were never allowed to return. Egypt invaded Yemen, and Yemenis fought among themselves. Turkey fought against Kurdish rebels. Palestinians attempted to conquer Jordan. In Lebanon, once considered a bastion of religious tolerance, people began to express their religious differences through warfare. Iraq had to be evicted from Kuwait by Western armies. Syria and Iraq developed into antagonistic states ruled by strongmen. Kings ruled in the Middle East long after they had become anachronisms elsewhere.

The people of the Middle East or the Balkans have not caused a world war or fostered a Hitler, which critics should keep in mind. Nevertheless, something has obviously gone wrong in what was once the Ottoman Empire.

It was not the fault of the Ottomans. When the Ottoman Empire was destroyed it was a state that had lived for more than six centuries. While surely not perfect governors or always just to their subjects, the Ottoman sultans had a record of governing that can stand against any of the great empires in history. The tolerance of the Empire was notable: all the religious groups that were present at the beginning of the Ottoman Islamic empire remained in place when it ended, six centuries later.

The Ottoman Empire was a state in which various ethnic and religious groups lived in close proximity. Map 1.1 gives some idea of its religious diversity. While Muslims were a large majority in all the Asiatic provinces and at least a plurality in all but one of the European provinces, most provinces had significant Christian or Jewish minorities. The map only shows the largest groups in any province, and the actual diversity of the population was far greater than can be seen on it. The Ottomans kept population statistics by religion only, not by ethic group or language. Thus, the Muslims on the map were ethnically and linguistically Turks, Arabs, Kurds, Albanians, Bosnians, Circassians, and many other groups. Jews in the northern parts of the Empire were primarily Sephardic, descendants of those who had been given refuge when driven from Spain and Portugal, but there were so-called 'Oriental' Jews in the Arab world, the first infusion of Zionist Ashkenazi Jews in Palestine, and even Jews in northern Iraq. The Orthodox were, among others, Greeks, Serbs and Bulgarians in the Balkans, Arabs in Palestine and Syria. A profusion of smaller religious and ethnic groups spread throughout the Empire.

The map also says nothing of the actual living patterns of the people. In some areas, ethnic groups were fairly homogeneous: few non-Albanians lived in Albania, for example (although there were Muslim, Roman Catholic and Orthodox Albanians); in west and central Anatolia[1] the population was mainly Turkish; the population of Arabia was Arabic; while the population of southeastern Anatolia and the mountains of northern Iraq was mainly Kurdish. Many other areas, however, had a thorough mix of ethnic groups and religions. In most of Ottoman Europe, villages of one ethnic or religious group lay next to villages of others. Often villages and small towns held a number of ethnic and religious groups.

Despite real defects in governance and periods of civil disorder, the Empire continued its tolerance of diversity until enemies, internal and external, destroyed it. It is not the heritage of Ottoman rule that has been seen in modern ethnic and religious conflict in the Middle East and the Balkans.

In the nineteenth and early twentieth centuries, it was common for European politicians to describe the Ottoman Empire as the 'Sick Man of Europe'. Indeed, as the Europeans depicted it, the Ottoman Empire was not simply sick, but terminally ill: the European Powers, no matter how reluctantly, would soon be forced to do something merciful to put the sick man out of his misery. But this analogy was wrong in many ways. The European Powers were not relatives waiting for an infirm relative to die so that they could divide his goods. They were lions, wolves and bears, waiting for the chance to devour their victim, kept from gorging themselves only by the fear that while they were eating, one of the other animals would in turn gorge on them. Nor was the economy of the Empire in terminal condition. Despite large problems, many of them caused by those same predators, the Empire's economy and its population were both growing. Its administrative system was being thoroughly overhauled and renewed. The numbers of teachers and doctors were growing. Railroad lines, roads, telegraphs and shipping were all increasing at a rapid pace. The Ottomans were making their first tentative steps toward representative government, well ahead of most of the world.

Why, then, did an empire that was rapidly improving first lose so much territory, then die? The answer lies both in the European Powers, who were, to a lesser or greater degree, all enemies of the Ottomans, and in nationalists bent on dividing the Empire. Of the two it was the imperialists who delivered the worst attacks and the final blow. The Ottoman Empire was not sick; it was wounded by its enemies, and finally murdered.

The Ottoman Empire was a medium-sized state coveted by its larger neighbours. The size of the Empire on the map is deceptive. Geographically, the Ottoman Empire was a large state, and indeed until 1878 the Empire did stretch from the Danube to south Arabia. Yet, judged by its population and exploitable land, the Empire was a not very large state. Cultivatable land was intermixed with great regions of mountain and desert. The Empire's

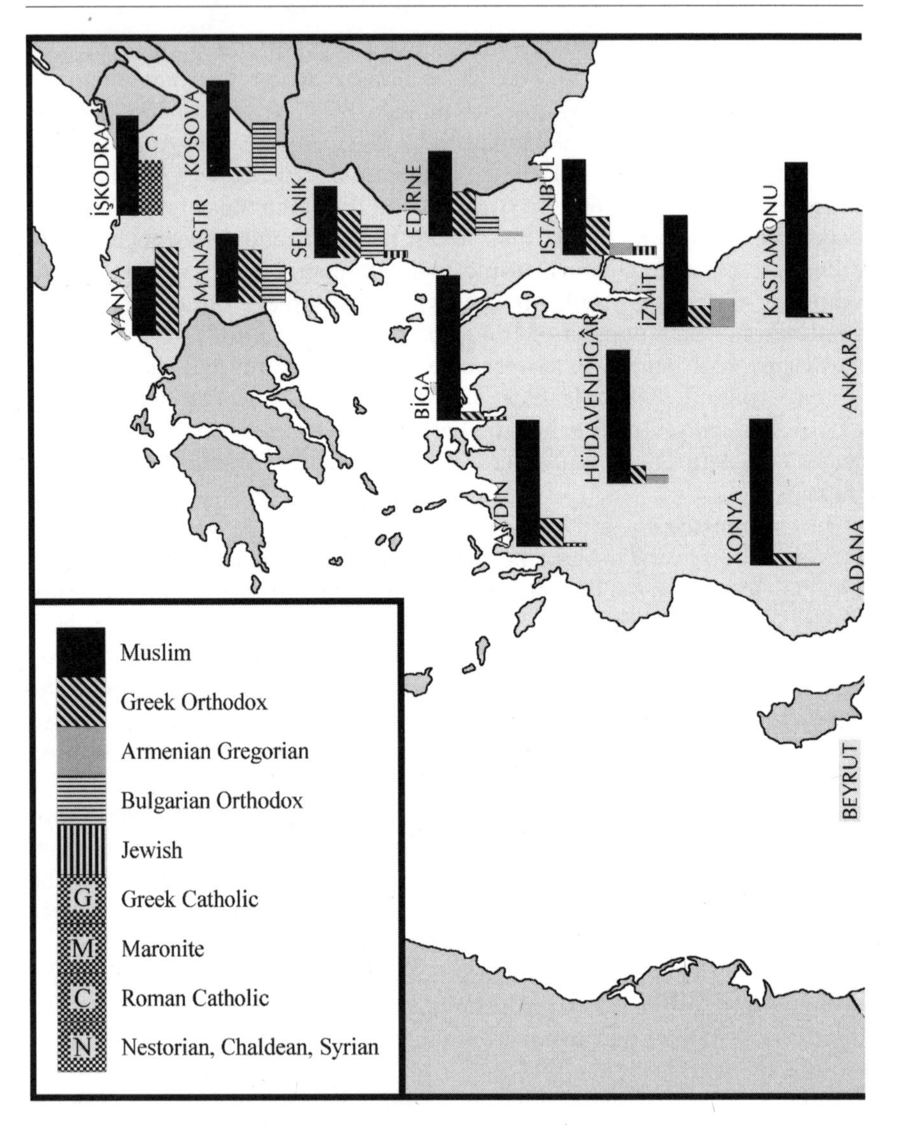

Map 1.1 Population by religion in 1912

population of 32 million (in 1912, excluding provinces in southern Arabia and Africa) was less than a quarter as densely settled as Western Europe. In comparison to its main enemy, the Russian Empire, which had 129 million people in 1897, the Ottoman Empire was a pygmy. All of the major European states had larger populations than the Ottoman Empire.

The vast size of the Empire was not a benefit. It was a hindrance to economic development and governmental control. In most of Europe,

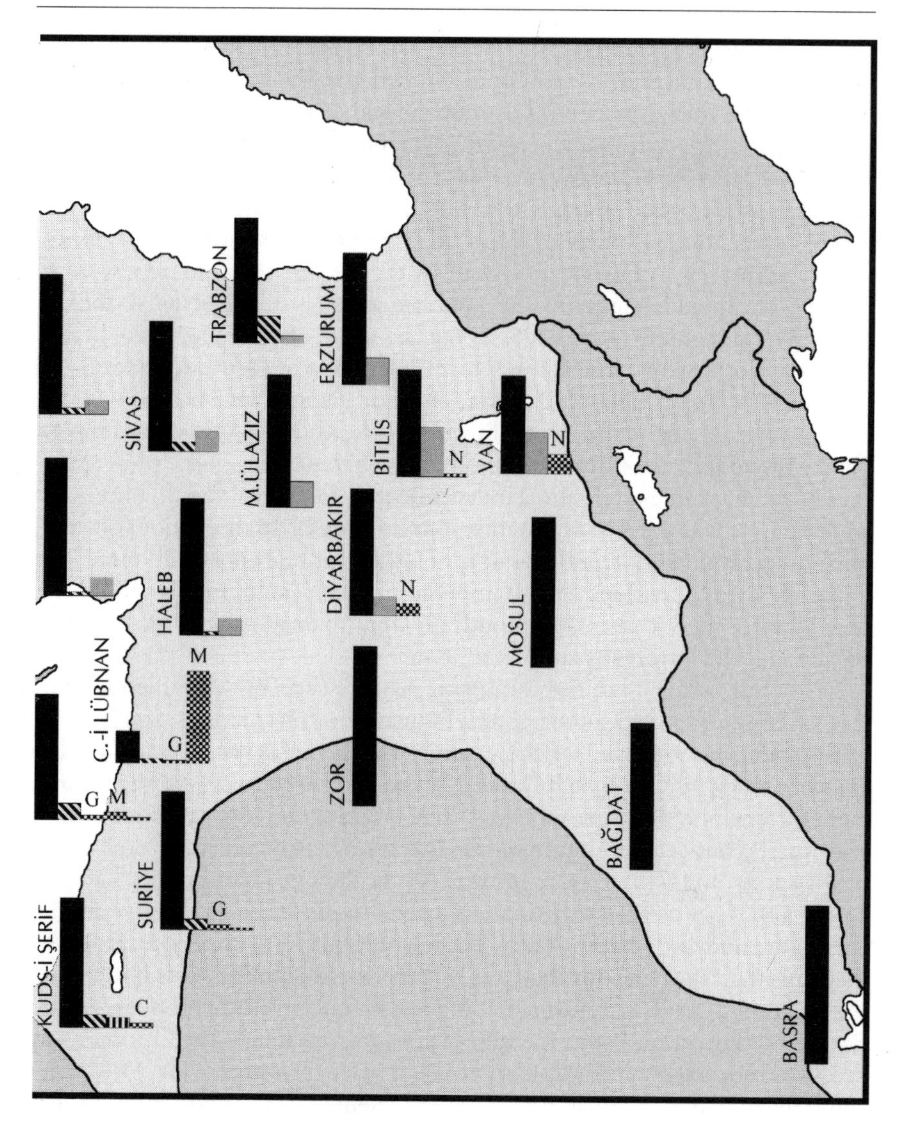

closely packed populations facilitated trade and industry. Population was close to lines of transportation and to supplies of raw materials, making easier the construction of factories and distribution of goods. To connect settlements in the Ottoman Empire, railroads and roads had to be constructed over long stretches of uninhabited land broken by mountains and deserts. Troops and police had to be stationed over huge distances, leaving openings for rebels and invaders. Yet in their final century the

Ottomans did build railroads and roads to connect their provinces. They increased governmental control and civil order in their far-flung provinces, in the process improving both government and economy.

Of course, the Ottoman peoples never became as wealthy as those in England, France or Germany, nor was the Ottoman state as powerful or as rich as the European states. It is not proper to compare them. In the nineteenth century, all the world bowed before the power of Europe. Once-mighty states fell to European power, as the Ottomans ultimately were to do. In order to understand the Ottoman situation, it is instructive to look at a world map from the year 1900, as the last score of Ottoman years began. There were very few countries in which Europeans or their descendants did not rule: Japan, Thailand, Liberia, interior regions of Asia which the Europeans did not want or could not reach, and the Ottoman Empire. Unlike the others, the Ottoman Empire was so desirable a piece of property that it is remarkable it remained independent in 1900. It stood on important trade routes, was the site of the most important Christian religious shrines, and had great potential as a producer of agricultural produce and other raw materials for the markets of any imperial master. The question should not be why were the Ottomans economically and military backward. It should be how did the Ottomans survive so long?

The main factor inhibiting Ottoman progress was not unskilled labour, lack of capital, limited financial and industrial infrastructure, or imperfect government, although all of these surely hampered development. No, the primary enemy of Ottoman advancement was the need to defend the Empire from the enemies that surrounded it. The largest and most ravenous enemy was Russia, but even the supposed friends of the Ottomans took their share of the spoils. In the fifty years prior to 1900, the Ottoman Empire had lost Egypt and Cyprus to the British, Tunisia to the French, Bosnia to the Austrians, and the eastern Black Sea region and northeastern Anatolia to the Russians. More serious than any of these losses, the Russians had forced the creation of Bulgaria, Romania and Serbia out of Ottoman possessions. Earlier the European Powers acting in concert had forced the Ottomans to accept Greek independence. Left to their own resources, the Ottomans could have stood against any internal enemy. They had done so for centuries. But they could not stand against the military attacks of Russia or the economic attacks of Western Europe.

Between 1768 and 1878, the Ottomans fought six wars with Russia, and lost all but the Crimean War. With each loss more territory was taken from the Ottomans. Reparations had to be paid by an already poor Empire. Territories where much capital and work had been expended in modernization were taken, the labour and expenditure lost. The Russians further drained the substance of the Empire by forcing it to feed and support the millions of Muslims that Russia drove into the Ottoman Empire from lands it had conquered.

Were the Middle East and the Balkans better or worse because the

Ottoman Empire was destroyed? The answer depends on the philosophy and assumptions of the respondent. To anyone who believes that Islam should adapt to fit changing circumstances, the survival of the Empire would have been beneficial, for the Islam of the Ottomans was changing significantly. To those who believe that Islam should be essentially unchanging, the end of an Empire that was in its final decades questioning traditional Islamic assumptions can even be viewed as divine judgement. If one considers that imperial domination of weaker peoples can never be just, then European conquest of the Empire must be condemned (as must, for that matter, the original Ottoman conquests centuries before). But to convinced imperialists of the early twentieth century, the end of the Empire was beneficial, because of the common belief that Europeans would necessarily rule better than non-Europeans. The end of the Empire gave those imperialists the chance to expand their empires and spread what they believed to be the benefits of European civilization. To those who believe in nationalism, that each people, however one defines a 'people', deserves its own separate state, the end of Ottoman rule would have to be judged a definite good. Serbs, Bulgars and Greeks had national states that would not have existed if the Empire had survived. Nationalists would naturally be pleased by the division of the Empire. Those who prefer the diversity of many ethnic and religious groups living together would not applaud.

Perhaps more important than any of these factors in judging the dissolution of the Ottoman Empire is its impact on human suffering. The end of the Empire was accompanied by such suffering and mortality that it is very hard to say that on balance all was for the best. Change that leads to the deaths of millions cannot be judged to have been good. It was not the demise and division of the Ottoman Empire in itself that caused this tragedy. The Ottomans did what they could to improve and strengthen their Empire, but this was not enough to save it. The forces arrayed against the Ottomans were too great. It was the method of the Empire's destruction, the putting of imperialist aims and nationalist ideals before either self-determination or human life, that killed the millions, forced millions more from their lands, and led to the conflicts of today.

2
Reforming the Empire

Historians have long argued, and will probably argue forever, over the causes of success of the countries of Europe and North America: the West. Arguments abound as to why it was Europe that went through the Renaissance, the Scientific Revolution and finally the Industrial Revolution. Nineteenth-century Europeans and Americans confidently pointed to Christianity or to European cultural and 'racial' qualities as the cause of their superiority. Later analysts have looked at trade patterns, as well as cultural factors, wisely forgetting supposed racial factors. Whatever the reasons, non-Western societies did not have the benefit of the Renaissance and the changes that followed upon its new way of thinking.

For non-Western societies, the most dangerous result of the development of Europe was imperialism. To those who faced European conquerors there was one really important European superiority – the Europeans had better armies and navies. Neither moral force nor philosophical wisdom was immediately apparent in the European conquests, but superior military force was manifest. Of course, behind the military power of Europe was the European economy and European organizational abilities, and behind these was European education. Military power was grounded in the European way of life, a fact that non-Europeans slowly realized. Countries that wished to compete militarily with the Europeans were forced to emulate that way of life. Their own systems had proven inadequate, as demonstrated on the battlefield. Although it was a process that wrenched traditional culture, countries had to become like the Europeans in order to survive.

The Ottoman Empire was one of the first states to decide to modernize itself along Western models. Few countries outside of Europe were given the chance to make that decision. They were Westernized as part of the process of being conquered and ruled by Western countries. Trying to avoid that fate was what set the Ottomans on the path of reform. As might be expected, changing an entire society was not an easy task.

The Ottomans realized their military inferiority when they were defeated by their enemies. Their defeat in their second attempt to take Vienna (1683) is usually given as the beginning of Ottoman military demise, but this was not apparent to the Ottomans themselves. Hungary and smaller territories were lost from 1683 to 1719. Territories had been lost before, though, only to be regained. Indeed, some of the lands lost were taken back by 1739, even though large expanses had been lost forever. The Ottomans only slowly appreciated that something fundamental had changed. Little was done to adjust to the new world of power until the end of the eighteenth century.

It may seem odd that their precarious situation came largely as a surprise to the Ottomans. Part of the problem was that the traditional Ottoman system was so good. Any governing system that had existed for many centuries must have done something right. Far more flexible than is usually assumed, the Ottomans often adjusted well to changes in European military power. They adopted muskets, for example, and outfitted their forces with them almost as soon as did their European enemies. Muskets, however, could be made in small craftsmen's shops. As technology advanced and factories were needed to make masses of new weapons, the Ottomans fell behind.

Survival of the Empire was aided by the division of its enemies. The Hapsburgs, most dangerous of their seventeenth- and eighteenth-century enemies, were kept busy with religious wars in Europe, conflict with France, and dissension within Germany. Not until Imperial Russia rose to power in the late eighteenth century did the Ottomans meet an enemy that could definitely concentrate its resources on Ottoman defeat, which it did. Peter I and Catherine II began a process of whittling away the Ottoman Empire that Russia was to continue for 150 years.

Once they became threatened from the outside, factors that traditionally had been beneficial began to work against the Ottomans. Although the central authority of the sultan and his government were always the Ottoman ideal, ruling a vast empire in times of poor communications had meant accepting much local control. A system of powerful provincial governors, allowed to function as long as they sent in taxes, provided soldiers when needed, and did not revolt, was an efficient response to political and geographic conditions. The organized decentralization of the Ottoman provinces had allowed them to govern a wide area for hundreds of years. Now it meant that everything from collecting sufficient taxes to policing borders was more difficult in the Ottoman Empire than it was in the states of its more centralized enemies. The *millet* system had made the Empire a state of exemplary tolerance in which differing religious groups had lived together in relative peace and did not threaten the stability of the government. Under that system, each major religious group had governed most of its important affairs. Welfare, schools, and most legal affairs had been left to the individual millets. Christians and Jews were not forced to become either Turks or Muslims. The Empire's peoples remained separated by religion, and liked it that way. However, separatism meant that the Ottomans were fundamentally divided. They could not call upon patriotic

Map 2.1 The Ottoman Empire in 1800 and 1912

RUSSIA
CRIMEA
BLACK SEA
CASPIAN SEA
TRANS - CAUCASIA
KARS
OTTOMAN EMPIRE
ANATOLIA
CILICIA
IRAN
CYPRUS
SYRIA
IRAQ
EGYPT
HIJAZ

support from minority groups. Instead, these groups developed their own individual nationalisms, which was to become one of the main factors in the dissolution of the Empire.

Not all was the fault of fate. The Ottomans had allowed some of their central institutions to degenerate, especially the military. The Janissaries, bloated in number yet poorly trained and ill-disciplined, no longer brought fear to their foes. In the eighteenth century the Ottomans depended more and more on the armed forces of nearly autonomous local leaders, *ayans* ('notables'), whose aims did not always coincide with those of the government. Sometimes little better than bandits, the ayans were often more threatening to the Ottoman population than to the Empire's enemies.

The decay of the traditional military system was evident to the Ottomans themselves. Crusading sultans and grand vezirs (heads of the administration and military) adopted stringent measures to bring Ottoman power back to its old standard. Many a head of the corrupt or inefficient was lopped off, ultimately to no avail. The fundamental problem was not that the Ottomans had become weaker, it was that their enemies had become so much stronger. In order to survive, the Ottoman Empire had to adopt the methods of its enemies.

Reform

Ottoman reform was a 'top down' system of change. In most developing countries, 'the people', in whose name governments were toppled and all reforms made, never had enough education or knowledge of their own political situation to understand revolutionary change. Ottoman subjects were no exception. They understood the effect of invading armies, destroyed homes and crops, and sons taken to war, never to return. They understood increased taxes and illegal payments to rapacious landlords. But they could not have understood what they could do to avert such disasters. Those who had plans to improve the situation were government officials, a nascent western-oriented intelligentsia, and newly educated military men. Like the peasants, they did not always understand the problems, but they had plans and the means to implement them.

Although earlier reform schemes had been tried with limited success, Ottoman Westernizing reform is generally thought to have begun with the reign of Sultan Selim III (ruled 1789–1807). Selim III surely did not adequately understand the nature of the Ottoman problem. He assembled around him a group of reformers who saw the military needs of the Empire, but understood few of the political and economic changes that were necessary to reassert Ottoman power. They set about the reform of the Ottoman military and created a new treasury to pay for military expenditures. Others had attempted to improve the military before by bringing Ottoman forces to their traditional strength and adopting Western weaponry, but with only temporary successes. Selim's reformers realized that what was needed was not a traditional Ottoman army, no matter how dedicated and dutiful, but a European-style army. Only an army like those of the Ottoman's enemies could defeat those enemies.

Selim III created the nucleus of a new army, the Nizam-i Cedid. Men were trained in European methods, including military drill. They wore modified European uniforms, a seemingly inconsequential practice that actually had deep psychological purpose as a commitment to reform. Most importantly, officers and men were organized into a pyramidical chain of command. The traditional confused order of command, in which officers changed often and contradictory commands were all too possible, was replaced by a system in which everyone knew who should be giving the orders. Imported European instructors taught the new army European methods and the use of European weapons. The men trained as a unit, as professional soldiers in the Western mould.

Selim's new army was a military success, but a political failure. It proved its worth on the battlefield, successfully standing against French troops at the battle of Acre (1799). Selim, however, was incapable of using his army to effect radical reform. While he was creating a new army, the old army, led by the Janissary Corps, was left in place. The Janissaries correctly assessed their position in any new order, which was no place at all. The new army must ultimately replace them. Many of the leaders of Ottoman society and politics opposed the 'infidel' changes made by Selim. They foresaw that changing the army could only be a first step to changing society, and the present society was the basis of their power. Ottoman traditional society had existed for centuries; much changed over that time, but changed gradually. Traditionalists feared any radical change, especially change that made them more like their enemies, the Europeans.

In 1807, traditionalists, led by the Janissaries, revolted in Istanbul. Selim could have called in his new army from their barracks outside the city, which would have meant war in Istanbul's streets, or he could have escaped the city, called on supporters in the provinces, and perhaps have eventually defeated the traditionalists. Instead he caved in. His reforming grand vezir was thrown to the mob and torn to pieces. The Nizam-i Cedid was disbanded, and its members were hunted down or escaped to the provinces. This did not save Selim's throne. He was deposed and replaced by his cousin, Mustafa IV (1807–8).

The lesson of Selim's abortive reforms was that the power of traditional elements had to be destroyed before reform could take hold. Traditionalists could complain, even riot, but without an army they could not triumph. Reform, in turn, needed an army and a sultan not afraid to use it. In military matters, the old had to be obliterated before the new could take hold. This principle was largely true in most matters of politics and society, but it would take generations before the implications of radical reform were fully understood. Military reform would necessarily come first.

Sultan Mustafa IV's reign lasted less than two years. Ayans from the Balkans marched on the capital in 1808, intending to rescue Selim III. Mustafa's men reached Selim first and killed him, but Mustafa's brother, Mahmud, escaped to the rebels. They killed Mustafa and took power, naming Mahmud sultan (Mahmud II, 1808–39), but they themselves were soon ejected by the traditionalists. These did not trust Mahmud, who was thought to be a reformer at heart, but they had no choice but to accept him as sultan. All the other adult members of the ruling family had been killed, and traditionalists by definition needed a sultan, the centre of traditional government.

Mahmud II was indeed a reformer, as the traditionalists feared, but he was a wily politician as well. He spent the first eighteen years of his reign building a power base from which he could attack the traditionalists. Mahmud enlarged his personal power in the traditional way – building support by gradually filling the bureaucracy with those who relied on him for their positions. Potential opponents were quite simply bought off. In the provinces, Mahmud proved a master at playing one local lord off against another, all the while maximizing the power of the central government. He also understood the importance of personal image, gaining the reputation of a most pious sultan by building mosques and increasing the pay of religious leaders.

While Mahmud was busy burnishing his own reputation, the Janissaries were busy blackening theirs. In wars against Greek rebels and the Russian Empire they proved to be poor fighters. They were, however, excellent at rioting in cities and terrorizing civilian populations. The people of Istanbul, who had mainly supported the Janissaries when they deposed Selim III, grew tired of them.

Rather than attempt to build a new army as Selim III had, Mahmud slowly built up the power of army corps who for long had been political opponents of the Janissaries. The artillerymen were given special preferment. It had long been accepted even by conservatives that artillery was one part of the military that must be modernized. Mahmud trained his artillerymen and others as secretly as was possible, building a force that could do more than fire cannons. Then, in 1826, he notified the Janissaries that they would be reformed. New, modernized units would be drawn from the best soldiers in the old Janissary corps. As Mahmud probably expected, the Janissaries revolted. This time, however, the sultan was resolute and the people of Istanbul were against the Janissaries. Reliable military corps came into the city and took up positions to defend the sultan. Mobs took to the streets to oppose the Janissaries. When the Janissaries retreated to their barracks to consider their next moves, Mahmud brought up his artillery, bombarded the barracks, and killed the Janissaries. He sent out an imperial order to the provinces disbanding the Janissaries. Those who had hated them for decades began a Janissary hunt. Soon no one could be found who admitted to ever having been a Janissary. The traditionalists were without a military force and reform could commence.

In the final years of his reign, Mahmud set the Empire upon the long path to radical reform. Naturally, reform began slowly. The first census of modern times was taken. A postal system connected Istanbul with the provinces. Secondary schools that offered Western-style training to new military officers were built, although not the new model primary and secondary schools for the masses that were sorely needed. The greatest changes came in the government. Mahmud began to organize the government somewhat along Western lines. His reformers created government ministries with defined responsibilities, and the first steps were taken to create a cabinet to oversee the government. To protect the state, and to be the backbone of reform, Mahmud created a new army. Like Selim's army, it was formed along Western lines. Soldiers were conscripted, a much opposed innovation, but one that provided soldiers that were not part of traditional power structures.

Mahmud's reform set the tenor of future reform in the Empire. It was to be centralizing reform: the new system was always aimed at ending local autonomy and increasing the power of the centre. The new army enforced the change. This was consistent with the Ottoman theory of government, in which all authority theoretically emanated from the sultan. The sheer distance of many provinces from the centre, the persistence of local power structures, and lack of bureaucrats to enforce central decrees had always made the ideal unreachable, even in the glory days of Mehmet the Conqueror and Süleyman the Magnificent. New methods were now to be used to realize the old ideal. Of course, centralization was also the modern form of government in Western Europe. The Ottomans were able to learn from countries such as France bureaucratic techniques that strengthened the central government. Both to learn from the Europeans and to deal with them effectively, in 1833 Mahmud's government began a programme to train diplomats and other officials in foreign languages, especially French, the international language of the time. Bureaucrats trained in the bureau called the Translation Office developed not only linguistic skills but also a Western orientation.

Not all went smoothly. Soldiers could not be trained quickly enough to defend the Empire adequately against the Russians and others, such as Muhammad Ali, the governor of Egypt. With the aid of France, Muhammad Ali had managed to develop a Western-style army more quickly than had the central government and used it against his sovereign. It was the British, not the Ottomans, who stopped him. In the government, bureaucrats also could not be trained quickly enough. Older officials often did not like the new ways and did their best to stymie reform. But reform gradually became the accepted path of the government. By the end of Mahmud II's reign only the most obdurate traditionalists did not expect and accept that change would continue. Some might try to slow its pace, but Westernizing reform would continue and increase.

The Tanzimat

Abdülmecit I (1839–61) succeeded to the throne intent on radical reform. He put the government into the hands of reformers who had been schooled in Mahmud II's new bureaucracy. Their leader was Mustafa Reşit Paşa, an accomplished bureaucrat who had served as Mahmud's foreign minister. Mustafa Reşit had been ambassador to both London and Paris, so he knew Western ways at first hand, at least as well as they could be observed from an embassy. Now, often serving as prime minister and usually as power behind the throne when he was not in office himself, he became the father of the reform period known as the Tanzimat (meaning 'ordering', as in 'putting things in order'). He trained successors, Ali and Fuat Paşas, who continued his reforms after his death in 1858.

The reformers had great obstacles to overcome. Mahmud II had been able to do no more than initiate reforms. The army was improved, but was still not up to European standards. Outside the bureaucracy and the army, education was provided by traditional Islamic and millet schools. Islamic schools concentrated on religious learning, not Calculus, physics, or European languages. Nothing substantial had been done to change the economy. Most of the old political system remained unchanged, but Abdülmecid's men were about to change that.

On 3 November 1830, Sultan Abdülmecit proclaimed the Hatt-ı Hümayun of Gülhane, an imperial declaration of the intent and future actions of the government somewhat like the Queen's Speech to Parliament, with the difference that the intentions were the sultan's own. He declared that his subjects had rights to 'life, honour and fortune' and that their property was inviolate. Specific remedies for past abuses were promised: higher bureaucratic salaries to end bribery, more just military conscription, new laws, and other initiatives. Stating that such things will be done is never enough, and Abdülmecit's intentions proved hard to realize, but the most important point was that the Hatt-ı Hümayun signalled a significant change in the Ottoman theory of government. In the traditional state, all power theoretically emanated from the sultan, who was enjoined by religion and tradition to be a just ruler, but no one spoke of 'rights', unless they were the significant rights guaranteed to Muslims by Islamic Law. Abdülmecit specifically stated that his subjects had secular rights, and that these rights applied to non-Muslims as well as Muslims.

The Tanzimat went a good way toward realizing Abdülmecit's intentions. Although not mentioned in the Hatt-ı Hümayun, the Tanzimat operated under a system similar to the Western idea of the state: the state was to do for its people what they needed and wanted but could not do for themselves. Under the old Ottoman system, the state collected taxes, protected the state and Islam, tried to ensure fairness in government and commerce, and not much else. Most of what moderns expect from the state was provided by the millets – welfare, schools, etc. The sultan and officials had always given much to public welfare, but they were doing their duty as pious Muslim individuals, not doing the state's work. Now the Ottoman government began to be concerned with welfare, schools, laws, public facilities, and other activities routinely overseen by European governments.

Although practice surely did not live up to theory, the effect of this change in governmental philosophy should not be underrated. The new philosophy allowed the Ottoman state to be a changeable system that could adapt to different conditions. All the momentous changes that took place in the Tanzimat and after were based on the assumption that the state had a duty to improve the lives of subjects, not only to protect itself.

The Tanzimat and its successors were most successful in developing the government itself. This should be no surprise, because government was what the reformers knew best. Government was also the area in which a crusading grand vezir, with the support of the sultan, could bring his power to bear in affecting change. Compromise with traditionalists in the bureaucracy was necessary, but great changes were made.

Administrative reform

The two pivotal initiatives of government reform were organization and advice – organizing the administration effectively and creating structures to broaden the participation of subjects in the government. The system of ministries, begun under Mahmut II, was further developed. New ministries did more or less what their names imply to Europeans. The Interior Ministry oversaw police, internal economic development, and provincial government. Taxes, state accounts, and the finances of the other ministries were overseen by the Finance Ministry. The Ministry of Foreign Affairs dealt with, as might be expected, foreign affairs. It also managed relations with consuls and other foreigners within the Empire. Over time, the government created ministries for public works, justice, commerce, education, agriculture, etc. Appointed councils, while not quite legislatures, did propose both laws and state reorganization. A Council of Ministers drew together ministers and other high officials, what might be called the Cabinet, what most mean when they speak of 'the government'. All of this may seem to have been no great reform, until one thinks of what the government must have been like without such organization. In the old system, bureaucrats were normally generalists who were expected to do many jobs during their career. The old description 'Jack of all trades, master of none' would have applied. Now bureaucrats remained in ministries dedicated to one set of activities. They learned their jobs.

The taking of advice as part of government was an old part of the Ottoman system. Indeed, in the traditional Ottoman theory of rule the function of all government was to give advice to the sultan and then carry out his wishes. This was naturally not how it always worked in practice, but the old system did have many outlets for advice-giving, including the Imperial Divan, a body of high officials (*vezirs*) that met under the chairmanship of the grand vezir to debate the Empire's problems and take appropriate action. These consultative bodies were made up of bureaucrats, however, and reflected bureaucratic concerns and approaches. The Tanzimat created councils in which leading members of society advised the government.

Representative government in the Ottoman Empire began slowly during the Tanzimat period of reform. In 1840, the government created advisory councils in some provinces, later expanding to others. Provincial councils were dominated by officials of the government, seven of thirteen members, but the governmental representatives included the head Muslim judge (*kadi*) of the province, and a Christian priest. Six members of local guilds and local notables, large landowners and similar 'men of substance', were also members. Similar councils were begun in local districts. The non-governmental members were chosen by vote of the notables of the districts. Representation was expanded in the Provincial Reform Law of 1864, which mandated elected assemblies at local and provincial levels. The new system was put in place first in the Tuna (Danube) Province in northern Bulgaria, then by 1876 in all the Empire except autonomous provinces such as Egypt, which ran their own provincial political affairs.

Provincial representation was not democratic; the masses were not properly represented, only those with real power in the provinces. The councils could only recommend measures to the government, but this was much more than they had been able to do before. In the provinces, administrative assemblies advised the governors. Good governors had always been close to those who wielded power in local societies. The new councils were an important innovation, however, for they eventually contained members elected from the local population, in practice local notables. Again, this was a small reform when compared to, for example, a state legislature in America, but any election to public office is momentous when there have been no elections before.

Education

Education was also a success, although one that necessarily advanced slowly. Large numbers of teachers had to be trained in new methods before new schools could function, and training teachers took generations. Nevertheless, the Tanzimat began the construction of a public education system. Teacher training schools educated the teachers who went to new middle schools. They in turn trained students in technical subjects and trained more candidates for teacher training. It went slowly. By 1867, only 16,000 students were enrolled in the new-model (Rüşdiye) schools in

Ottoman Europe and Anatolia, which necessarily were creating an educated elite, not educating the masses. By 1913, though, 300,000 were enrolled in state elementary and secondary schools and a like number in millet and foreign, primarily American missionary, schools. The sincerity of the Ottoman effort at educational reform is demonstrated by the government's attitude toward foreign missionary schools. It supported them, despite the fact that they benefited only Christians and sometimes became recruiting centres for separatist movements. Some 23,000 students were enrolled in the schools of the American Board of Commissioners for Foreign Missions in 1913.

The presence of an expanding educated public spurred the production of newspapers and books. Press runs were not large, but books published included histories, economics texts, novels, and books on science and mathematics. Translations from European languages were published. Before the Tanzimat period the only way for a literate person to learn much of science, world history, or most other fields of modern scholarship was to read books in European languages, if they were available.

Finance

Like government activities anywhere at any time, reform was dependent on money. It proved difficult to find enough because of an archaic taxation system. Too much was dependent on collections from tax-farming. Since the days of the Ottoman conquest of the Arab provinces, most of the land there had been in theory the property of the sultan, as was some land in other regions. The sultan had the right to rents from these lands. Other lands were taxed, so that a peasant might not know or care which regime he was under. The tax-farming method of financing government had been developed to collect funds when the government was incapable of keeping the records and finding the number of tax-men that were needed simply to collect regular taxes. Instead, the government auctioned rights to collect taxes on the sultan's land to individuals who paid the government, then sent out agents to collect what they could from the villages. In theory the government made sure that the agents took only what was legally allowed, but in practice agents often cheated the peasants. The government received much less than it should have, and the people suffered.

In the Hatt-ı Hümayun, the sultan had promised rapid dismantlement of the tax-farming system. Tax-farmers would be replaced by bureaucrats who only collected fixed taxes. As in education, good intentions foundered on lack of trained personnel. It took generations to train the tax-collectors. The government needed money, however, so tax-farming could only gradually be abolished. To do that, an accurate register of land tenure was necessary. In 1858, a land registration law was passed, but once again it took long to do the job, which was still not completed in 1914.

Culture

Perhaps the most serious hindrance to reform was cultural. The most facile analysis of Ottoman reform would note that the Ottoman reforms were steadily eroding old traditions and replacing them with European ways. The best reform, therefore, would be to take the medicine at one gulp – to copy Europe in all possible ways, to become European as fast as possible. But that would have been the path to disaster. Islamic traditionalists were repressed, not eradicated, during the Tanzimat. Nothing would have brought the populace, including most of the army, to the side of the traditionalists as would truly radical Westernization. Change had to be slow. Reformers had to be seen as men who wanted to retain as much as they could of Ottoman culture and traditions, making only those changes necessary to defend and enrich the state and the people. This was not a difficult image to uphold, because it perfectly described the men of the Tanzimat. Unlike Turkish reformers of the following century, they had no wish to become Europeans. They planned to understand Europe, to emulate its ways when necessary, but to remain Ottoman.

The burden of imperialism

European imperialism was a constant drag on Ottoman reform. No matter how often they criticized the Ottomans and called for reforms, none of the European Powers wanted the Ottomans to succeed completely. The British, French, Germans and Austrians sold more to the Ottomans than they bought. Ottoman purchases of textiles and other finished goods helped keep the mills of Europe working, so an Ottoman Empire that developed its industry and made its own goods was not desired. The Russians wanted Ottoman land. Up against the limits of their expansion in Europe and Central and Eastern Asia, they viewed the Empire as prime territory for conquest. The acquisition of Istanbul and the Straits (the Dardanelles and the Bosporus), and with them access to the Mediterranean, was the ultimate aim of the Russians. A strong Ottoman state and a capable Ottoman army would not help such Russian plans.

European countries naturally were influenced by their own domestic politics. This sometimes forced them to oppose many Ottoman actions that were in the Ottoman state interest, or even in their own interest, but were unpopular at home. Chief among these domestic concerns in Britain and France was sympathy for the Christian minorities in the Ottoman Empire. It is not too simplistic to say that Europeans did not feel that Christians should be ruled by Muslims. This led to support for minority nationalist movements and approval for the carving of Christian states from the Ottoman Empire. Public opinion could be a potent political force. It led to European military interventions that created independent Greece, Serbia and Bulgaria. It also led to the callous disregard of the murders and forced migration of Muslims when those states were created. The Europeans were in the curious position of demanding reforms and great expenditures by the Ottomans in their provinces, then acceptance of Russian conquest of those same provinces, which made the expenditures useless.

It was those Russian conquests that caused the worst effects of imperialism. The Russians repeatedly invaded the Ottoman Empire, destroying the population and the tax base. The Russians captured Ottoman lands in both Europe and Asia. They forced the creation of independent Bulgaria, Serbia and Romania by defeating the Ottomans in wars forced by the Russians, then demanded reparations for their wartime losses. In the Caucasus, they ejected the native populations of Circassia and Abhazia, forcing the Ottomans to either take in the 800,000 Caucasian peoples the Russians had dispossessed, at great cost in money and in civil disorder, or allow them to die. A further 900,000 Turks were also forced by the Russians into the Ottoman Empire, which had to find food, shelter and farms for them when the existing population was already poor. Much of the financial disaster that constantly threatened the Ottomans was due to the Russians.

Outright conquest was not the only form of imperialism that hampered the Ottomans. Economic imperialism was a significant factor in limiting successful reform. Economists have varying opinions on the utility of tariffs. There can be no doubt, however, that in the nineteenth century protective tariffs were a major force in building local manufacturing in many countries. Faced with the manufacturing dominance of Great Britain and other European countries, one way to develop local industry was to raise customs fees until local manufactures were competitive. Customs duties were also a potentially great source of income to countries like the Ottoman Empire that had few adequate sources of state financing. By enforcing special trade status for themselves through the Capitulations, the Europeans denied the Ottomans the opportunity to raise customs dues and improve their economy.

The Capitulations were first enacted by a strong Ottoman Empire in the fourteenth and fifteenth centuries. In the United States they would probably be called 'most favoured nation status' – reductions in customs dues and special privileges afforded to friends of the Empire. At first only the Italian trading cities and France were granted these benefits, but soon other European countries gained them. The privileges included the right of foreigners to have their own courts, even though the ultimate authority in disputes was still Ottoman law. By the nineteenth century, the Capitulations gave the Europeans the right to customs dues averaging 5 per cent. This was often less than the taxes paid by Ottoman merchants. Instead of assisting domestic manufactures, the customs laws actually hurt local producers. The Ottomans could do nothing about it. Begun as a gesture to friends, the Capitulations were now backed up by European gunboats. Countries such as Britain that generally supported the Ottomans diplomatically would never accept an end to the Capitulations; Ottoman enemies were even less likely to do so. European countries not only paid lower duties, they operated their own courts and postal systems, and Ottoman law was no longer supreme.

By no means were Ottoman financial woes all the fault of the Europeans. Ottoman economic reform suffered from ignorance of commerce and finance. Learning French did not make Ottoman bureaucrats good economists or businessmen. They were particularly unsuccessful in economic matters. Government policies often hindered development. Taxes, for example, were levied on goods transported between Ottoman provinces, an obvious disincentive to economic integration. Exports were also taxed, a disincentive to export. Paper money was issued without enough gold in the treasury to back it. In effect this was a loan to the treasury from those using the paper money. Because this was recognized, the government had to pay interest to those who used its own money. This became such a burden, and the paper money was so untrusted, that the government was forced to borrow from European banks to retire the paper money and return to a pure hard currency system. The Ottomans were poor economists.

Worst of all, the Ottoman government learned to borrow money. At first, it had no choice: the first loan from European banks was taken out in 1854 to fight the Crimean War. Later the Ottomans, like many a developing country after them, borrowed money for economic development (and the occasional palace). The assumption was that money borrowed to improve transportation, help industry, and the like would repay itself when an improved economy generated more taxes. But development never kept pace with borrowing. The Capitulations and lack of an industrial infrastructure meant that economic development went too slowly to repay the loans. So the Ottomans borrowed more and European banks were glad to oblige, at ever higher interest rates. In 1865, for example, out of a loan of £36 million, the Ottomans received only £18 million. The rest was fees and interest paid in advance to the banks. The £18 million they did receive was used to repay earlier debts. They had to pay back the entire £36 million, of course.

In theory, the banks were charging high rates of interest and claiming huge interest payments in advance because the Ottomans were a bad risk. But this was not true, because the banks had silent partners, European governments who would force the Ottomans to pay, even up to the point of invading the country to guarantee repayments. They did this in Egypt in 1882, when the British took over the country as a result of Egypt's default on its debts. The Ottoman Empire was not invaded to collect debts, but in 1881 it was forced to cede important revenues to repay its loans. A Public Debt Commission, operated by Europeans, took the proceeds from taxes on tobacco, silk, fishing, alcoholic spirits, official stamps affixed to legal documents, and the entire tribute payments of Bulgaria, Cyprus, Greece and Montenegro (payments guaranteed by treaty when these countries were separated from the Ottoman Empire). The Ottomans now could not collect either appropriate customs dues or many of their own taxes. This made it hard to finance reform, or even to pay the local policeman.

All of the economic fumbling that characterized the Tanzimat era is understandable. European Powers themselves understood state economics poorly. Like reform of the army or the educational system, economic understanding could only be developed gradually, usually through trial and error. The Ottomans continued to try new methods and schemes to improve state finances throughout the period of reform. Given the economic plagues that were to strike all the developing countries that tried reform in later times, it is surprising that the Ottomans did as well as they did. At the end of the Tanzimat tax farms were still not abolished, but new rules and supervision had made them less onerous to the peasants and more productive for the state treasury. Taxes, a confusing mass of customary duties and temporary impositions at first, had been considerably regularized.

Democracy

The men of the Tanzimat were cautious reformers. They changed government practices, freely borrowing from Europe. In many ways, however, this was a reversion to the old Turkish system of eclectic government. All the early sultans had borrowed extensively from those around them – from Byzantine Greeks, Arabs, Persians, Slavs, and others. Everything from taxation systems to royal architecture to artillery was adapted from systems used by others and melded with Turkish traditions into what was to become the Ottoman system. If it worked, the Ottomans made it their own. What never changed was the purpose of the modifications – to strengthen the sultan's rule and the authority of his close followers, known as the ruling class. The men of the Tanzimat kept to this tradition: they borrowed ideas whenever they thought borrowing would help, but always intended to keep power in the hands of the new ruling class, the bureaucracy, themselves.

The Tanzimat did create what in retrospect were openings to democracy, especially in the provinces. The intentions behind these experiments cannot be viewed as democratic, however. They were practical. Local councils provided much-needed advice on what had to be done in the provinces. They tied provincial power groups to the state, improving the loyalty of what might have become forces of opposition. They were also a small check on the power of provincial governors. It is doubtful if the Tanzimat leaders saw them as any first steps toward democracy. This was not wholly due to a desire of bureaucrats to keep power in their own hands, nor was it unreasonable. An argument can surely be made that economic and educational development were necessary precursors to democracy.

There were those who did plan Ottoman democracy. They were idealists, philosophers, and a mild form of revolutionary – debating societies that often disagreed among themselves and split into ideological factions, but who agreed that some form of democracy was needed if the Ottoman Empire was ever to be truly reformed. Called the Young Ottomans, they were mainly the sons of those who brought about the Tanzimat. Educated in the new Ottoman schools, often with experience of living or studying in Europe, they knew both Ottoman and European administrative systems, but their beliefs about the possibilities of reform were naive.

The ultimate goal of most of the Young Ottoman idealists was the creation of a constitution. Themselves from families of administrators, trained in law and politics, they naturally saw legal change as what was needed in the Ottoman Empire. It was normal for nineteenth-century European reformers to believe in single solution panaceas, whether the cure to a country's ills be a constitution, a republic, a nation-state, or socialism: 'All would be well if only my plan were in place'. A belief of some Young Ottomans was that Islam was at base a democratic system that would be compatible with constitutional government. Another belief, held by most, was that nationalists of the minority groups would come together in a single Ottoman nationality under a constitutional government. True utopians, they neglected many of the uglier realities of the Ottoman situation, such as how the country could stand against Russian attacks or what could be done about the Capitulations. They uniformly underestimated the difficulties of reform. Strangest of all, they considered that Ottoman nationalism would be based on rationalism, when nationalism was by nature an irrational love of country. Why would the people of the Empire suddenly unite in irrational love for an artificial nation? The answer was, 'because they will be democratically governed under a constitution'. But being democratically governed was never a prerequisite or cause for nationalism – witness Hitler's Germany or Mussolini's Italy.

The Young Ottomans could not be called men of the people. The closest they came to the peasants who made up most of the Empire was observation at a considerable distance, and little of that. By Ottoman standards, they were rich, living off family or personal money while they philosophized. They planned democracy without much thought to the wishes of the people, who would surely have rejected it as a strange and alien idea. Concerning religion, their thoughts were progressive but Islamic. The Young Ottomans believed that the Holy Law of Islam was compatible with democracy and reform. They overlooked the important fact that the religious leaders who defended the Holy Law, as well as most believers, did not agree with them.

The reformers joined together in the Young Ottoman society in 1865. A number of them went into exile in Europe, from which they sent newspapers to the Ottoman Empire through independent European post offices, another privilege afforded the Europeans. They argued among themselves over philosophy and tactics. Their motives were not always pure: some had been frozen out of advancement in the bureaucracy; some saw their ideologies as means to personal advancement, and left the revolution behind if they were offered good jobs in government. In other words, they were fairly typical of the European philosophical revolutionaries of their time.

By themselves the Young Ottoman idealists could never have created a state or a constitution. For a radical change in the structure of a state to be successful, there has to be an ideal, an opportunity (usually a present or pending disaster), and the means to effect the change. The Young Ottomans had the ideal, the opportunity would soon arise, but they never had the means or ability to change the state. For that, they needed help from practical men.

The greatest contribution of the Young Ottomans was their success in keeping the constitutional ideal alive. Through their publications they kept constitutionalism in the minds of bureaucrats and the educated section of the populace (newspapers available only in large cities were a poor tool for educating the illiterate rural masses). At first, those in power would never have considered a democracy, even a limited democracy, because it was necessarily a threat to their power. When the powerful came to believe that change was necessary for survival, though, the idea of a constitution would come to the fore. The Young Ottomans were poor revolutionaries, but good propagandists.

The conditions that precipitated political change were military threats to the Empire and the financially disastrous reign of Sultan Abdülaziz (ruled 1861–76). In 1875 and 1876, revolt had flared in both Bosnia and Bulgaria. Thousands of Muslims and Christians had been killed, and the mortality seemed likely to continue. Russia and Austria threatened the Empire's borders. Abdülaziz was ineffective at making needed reforms, but quite effective at borrowing money. When he came to power in 1861 and for the next ten years Abdülaziz was under the control of Mustafa Reşit's protégés, Ali and Fuat, who kept the sultan in check. The Tanzimat reforms of the time were their doing. Fuat died in 1869, Ali in 1871. After Ali's death, Abdülaziz seems to have resolved never to let another power arise in the bureaucracy to threaten the sultan's authority, even if the price was bad government. He therefore changed government ministers often, never letting grand vezirs remain in power long enough either to cement control over the bureaucracy or to do their jobs properly.

The civil wars in Bosnia and Bulgaria and the impending bankruptcy of the state led to Abdülaziz's deposition. As the European press dwelled on the deaths of Christians in Bosnia and Bulgaria, so the Istanbul press dwelled on the deaths of Muslims and the threat to the Empire. Russian military intervention was expected. Abdülaziz and his grand vezir, Nedim Paşa, were felt by reformers, bureaucrats, and even traditional religious elements to be weak, even cowardly, and liable to give in to the Russians. The government was bankrupt, but arrangements negotiated with European bankers were felt to be disadvantageous; popular opinion wanted nothing to do with them, seeing in the agreements yet another loss of sovereignty. Reformers decided that the sultan was too great a hindrance to change. At the same time, fanned by feelings of solidarity with the Balkan Muslims, students from religious schools (*softas*) took to the streets. They too felt the sultan was a threat, because of his conciliation of Europeans. As no one might have expected, the traditionalists and the reformers united in a common cause.

Abdülaziz tried to placate the opposition, taking reformers into the government and rejecting the loan arrangements, but it did no good. Hüseyin Avni Paşa, a reformer who had been named head of the army, committed the military to a *coup d'état*. Soldiers deposed Abdülaziz and he was replaced by his nephew, Murat V (ruled 1876). The reformers were for a short while in a position to produce their constitution. The first choice for a successor to Abdülaziz, Murat V, was favourable to constitutional reform and plans for the constitution began as soon as he took the throne. Murat was mentally unbalanced, however, and was soon replaced by his brother, Abdülhamit II (ruled 1876–1909). The new sultan seemed at first to favour reform also. The new constitution was proclaimed on 23 December 1876.

From the standpoint of true democracy, the first Ottoman parliament was flawed. It was indeed elected democratically, but votes were not equal. To placate the European Powers, districts were gerrymandered to increase artificially the number of Christian deputies. Ministers were responsible to the parliament in that they had to answer parliamentary questions, but they and the rest of the administration were selected by the sultan and his government. Neither the grand vezir nor the other ministers were chosen by the parliament. This was theoretically true in some other parliamentary systems, as well, but in the Ottoman system there was no assumption of routine royal acceptance of the candidates of the leading party in parliament. Indeed, the concept of 'party' in the European sense was foreign to the parliament. Laws passed by the parliament did not take effect unless promulgated by the sultan. The sultan could also change the budgets passed by parliament 'in emergencies' and prorogue the body for as long as he wished. Democracy was real, if flawed; democratic power was not. The constitution was the result of compromise between the reformers, traditionalists in government, and the sultan. Abdülhamit assuredly did not want a strong parliament that would take away his own powers.

Despite its defects, the Ottoman constitution was an important step in reform and democracy. Until it was promulgated, the theory of the Ottoman state was that the sultan was the government. All laws were his laws; all state actions were his doing. This had been less than a reality during the reigns of weak sultans, of course, but even in the nineteenth century a strong sultan could bend the state to his will, as Abdülhamit II was to prove. The theory had now changed. The sultan's prerogatives were only slightly limited by the constitution, but they were limited. Most important was the assertion that law ruled the land, not imperial whim. The radical assertion that popular will, as expressed through elections, should be the basis of government was a most significant change in itself. The failure of this first step at rule by law was not unusual; in most countries the first steps of democracy have been faltering ones. Perhaps the greatest significance was that a constitution was written at all.

In fact, the Ottoman constitution was a failure. If a constitution could be created due to a period of danger to the state, it could also be destroyed during a period of danger. This danger came in the Russo-Turkish War of 1877–78, which the Ottomans lost badly. For the first time there was a parliament to answer to. Parliament complained bitterly about the prosecution of the war, questioning the actions of both the military and the sultan. A number of members of parliament began to demand parliamentary control of the military. Fearing for both his own rule and the safety of an Empire that would speak to Europe with many voices, the sultan dissolved the parliament, as he was empowered to do by the constitution. He did not abolish the constitution; he simply never called a new election for parliamentary deputies. The parliament was not to meet again for thirty years.

The reign of Abdülhamit II

Until fairly recently, the common opinion of Sultan Abdülhamit II was worse than negative. Democrats naturally damned him for terminating the first experiment in constitutional rule. Advocates of liberal reform opposed his almost paranoid fear of opposition and imposition of personal control. To Europeans of his time he was known as the sultan who put down what they considered to be justified Armenian nationalist revolts. The Ottoman military felt that his lack of expenditure on military preparedness endangered the Empire. On the other hand, Abdülhamit's reign has been called the 'culmination of the Tanzimat', furthering centralizing reform and physical development. Islamic traditionalists have characterized him as a pious sultan who cared for Muslim values, which other reformers had neglected or opposed. All of the opinions were correct.

Abdülhamit was a follower of many of the principles of the Tanzimat – reform of the governmental system, improving government efficiency, and centralization of power. The power was to be in his hands, however, not in those of the bureaucracy. On the negative side, Abdülhamit so greatly feared opposition that he damaged effective government to keep personal power. Due to his treatment of the constitution, his assessment of the opinions of democratic reformers was surely accurate. His fears led to creation of a *de facto* secret police that watched over bureaucrats and military men. Spies and informers were to be found in all areas of government and many parts of civil society. As might be expected, their omnipresence was much exaggerated in the popular imagination. The spy system does not seem to have had much effect on efficiency or corruption, but the spies were looking for disloyalty, not malfeasance in office. They created a climate of fear which, while not to be compared to that of later totalitarian states in Germany and Russia, cannot have been conducive to loyal dedication among civil servants.

As had been the case with the Tanzimat reformers, Abdülhamit's worst problems were financial. Early in his reign, in 1881, the sultan had eased the threat of bankruptcy that had helped bring down Abdülaziz. Through deals with European creditors a Public Debt Commission had been created to oversee repayment of government debts. Important state revenues, such as taxes on silk, alcohol and tobacco, were conceded to the Commission. Abdülhamit had no choice, and the deal was the best the Ottomans could have expected, but it left the state much weakened financially. Taxes that would have supported schools or the military now went to European bankers. As a result, salaries were often in arrears, and bureaucrats took to bribery to make up their personal deficit.

Where Abdülhamit shone as a ruler was in the physical development of the Empire. His government accurately assessed the need of the state and the economy for modern systems of transportation and communication. Railroad track in the Empire increased threefold during his reign. All-weather roads increased sixfold. Government buildings proliferated, including extensive construction in parts of the Arab world that had previously received little attention.

It was not only the economy that benefited from the building programme. The power of the state was carried on the new railroads and roads. Troops and officials could travel quickly to far-flung regions of the Empire. Orders arrived in provincial capitals soon after they were issued in Istanbul. The railroads, roads and telegraph lines went far toward unifying the Empire and were to have great effect in the future. The Ottoman Empire could not have fought as well as it did in World War I, nor the Turks win their Independence War, were telegraph lines, roads and railroads not in place beforehand.

The Young Turks

The Young Turks, opponents to Abdülhamit II, were less philosophical, more pragmatic, and politically more mature than the previous generation of Ottoman revolutionaries, the Young Ottomans. Their concerns were social and economic reform and the influence of the European Powers on the Empire. They accepted the reality of an Empire in which members of Christian minorities had developed their own nationalisms, and put forth a Turkish nationalism to take its place among them. In exile during Abdülhamit's reign, they met with and even agreed on common goals with minority revolutionary groups. Nationalism was never their prime focus, however. Their focus was on developing the Empire economically and militarily. They believed Abdülhamit II was acting too slowly on the economy and endangering the Empire by neglecting the military. Like the Young

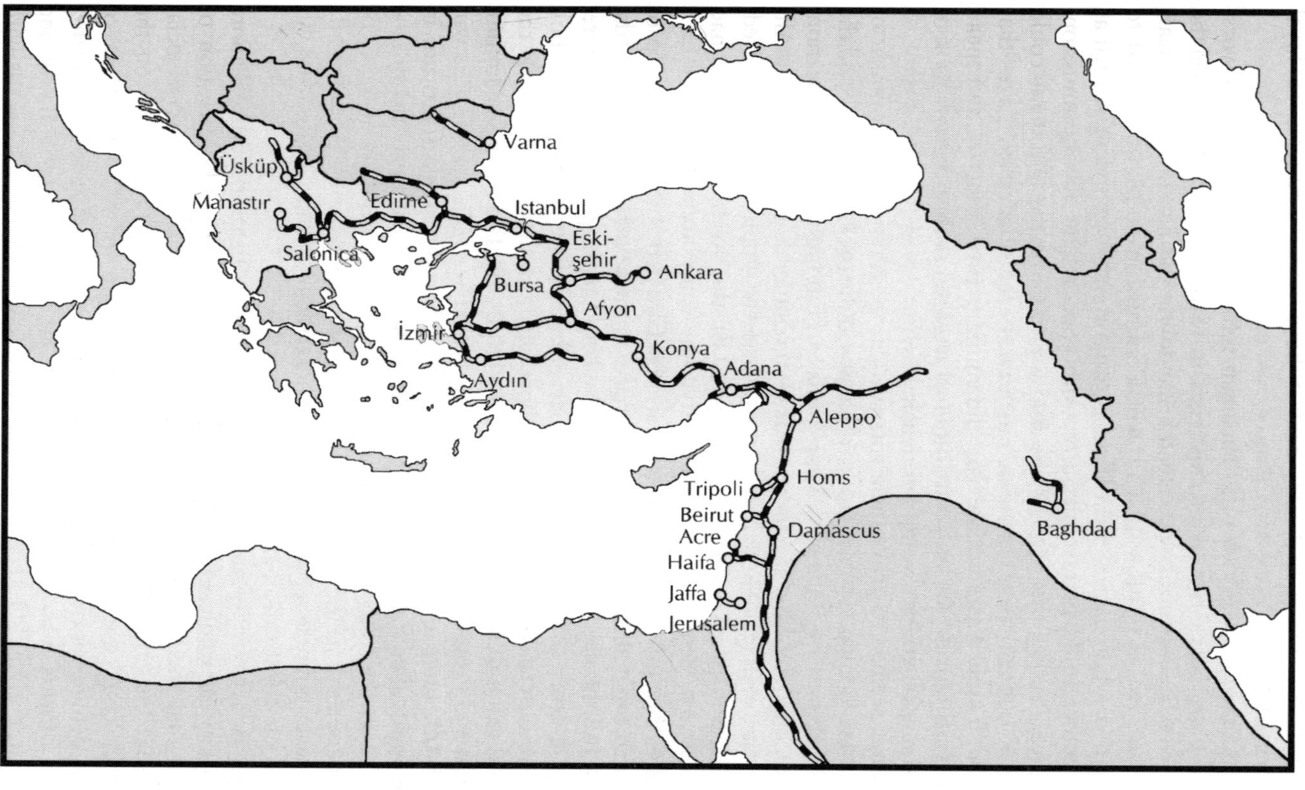

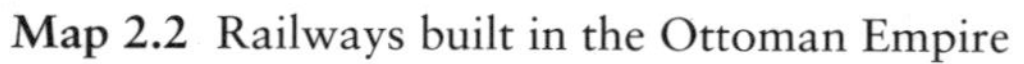

Map 2.2 Railways built in the Ottoman Empire

Ottomans, they believed that democracy and a functioning constitution were the means to their ends. Less naive than the Young Ottomans, they still believed that democracy would draw together the disparate groups in the Empire.

The Young Turks' revolution began in the military schools. Cadets in the military medical school organized the Committee of Union and Progress (İttihat ve Terakki Cemiyeti, CUP) in 1889. Learning from the systems of European revolutionaries, the CUP organized its members in cells so that each member could betray only a few others if caught. The organization soon spread to the other schools and into the regular army and the bureaucracy. The opposition of the military arose from the belief, largely justified, that Abdülhamit was starving the military of needed material and manpower, fearing it as the only institution that could depose him. Yet, they believed, a strengthened army was needed before it was too late. Events in Macedonia seemed to prove them correct.

The Macedonian troubles (to be discussed in the next chapter) were the result of actions by Bulgarian, Greek and Serbian nationalist bands, each intent on claiming Macedonia for their own countries. The Ottoman army was in the middle, charged with protecting the populace, with limited resources. Europeans, especially Austria and Russia, blamed the troubles on the Ottomans, demanding, in effect, that the army keep the people safe somehow, but not pursue too zealously the Christian rebels who did the killing. To cap it all, the soldiers were not being paid. In 1907, due to a poor harvest and the need to pay European bankers first, soldiers' salaries were months in arrears. The army was, it believed, kept from doing its job by a lack of resources and men, European meddling, and the low morale that is a natural result of not being paid. This was the moment for the Committee of Union and Progress. It was time for revolution.

In 1908, units of the Ottoman Third Army, the army stationed in Macedonia, called for a restoration of the constitution. Agents of the sultan, sent to quiet the soldiers, were killed. Many soldiers, members of the CUP and others, took to the hills, themselves forming rebel bands. Abdülhamit, ever a clever politician, saw his peril and adjusted to it. On 23 July 1908, he restored the constitution and called elections.

The military was by no means united in support of the CUP revolutionaries. Many old soldiers felt that the army should stay out of politics. Others believed that the CUP leaders were upstarts who had no appreciation of traditional Ottoman ways, which was at least partially true. The usual notion of 'class' does not fit the Ottoman Empire well, but if the 'upper class' is defined as the families of high bureaucrats, religious leaders and military officers who had led the Empire for centuries, even during the Tanzimat, and 'middle class' is defined as those with education and perhaps money, but not of the traditional ruling group, then many of the CUP leaders were from a 'middle-class' background, the children of lesser bureaucrats or businessmen. They were the first generation of this middle class who aspired to political power, and they were resented.

Because of these divisions the CUP was not able to function at first as a political party. It was also caught off guard by Abdülhamit's 'conversion' to democracy. It would take time to transform a group of revolutionary cells into something resembling a political party. The CUP as such, therefore, did not contest the election of 1908. Nevertheless, delegates sympathetic to the CUP won a majority of the seats in the new parliament. A new grand vezir, Hüseyin Hilmi Paşa, a man favourable to the CUP, took office.

The new government set out to reform the old system by sacking bureaucrats and saving money. Of course, those not sympathetic to the reformers were the first to go. They joined with traditionalists, men of religion, many older military officers, and virtually anyone with a stake in the old system in opposition to the government and hatred of the CUP. In parliament, a far from loyal opposition centred around the Liberal Union. Philosophically, the Liberal Union, which took many names over the next ten years, was more favourable to European interests and philosophies than was the CUP. The Liberals were not much concerned with philosophical consistency, however. Some of the philosophers who had been in exile under Abdülhamit, those imbued with the ideals of European liberalism, did indeed join the party. High bureaucrats committed to authoritarian reform, richer Muslims and Christians, and others who had no faith in liberalism also joined. Not overly concerned with the fears of the CUP that European conquest was imminent, the Liberals seemed to be mainly concerned with taking power for themselves by opposing the CUP. That was the glue that held them together.

On 13 April 1909, traditionalist officers and men of religion staged their own revolution. Religious students and soldiers under the command of traditionalists marched on the parliament and killed pro-CUP military officers and two deputies. The Liberal Union and the sultan supported the rebels and formed a minority government. But they had erred. The remaining pro-CUP deputies fled toward Macedonia and the protection of the Third Army, which came by train to meet them. The commander of the Third Army, Mahmud Şevket Paşa, had commandeered trains to defend the elected parliament. Istanbul fell to them on 24 April. On 27 April the parliament deposed Abdülhamit, replacing him with his brother Mehmet V (ruled 1909–18), who was to be a figurehead. For a while, democracy had triumphed.

It was too much to expect that true democracy would take hold overnight in the Ottoman Empire. Few of the conditions of a successful democracy were in place: no one had experience in even the forms of parliamentary government, the populace was largely illiterate and without any understanding of democracy, and the times were perilous ones; few would trust fractious parliamentary debates at a time when the country might be attacked at any moment. What evolved in the Empire was to be the form of democracy. In reality, military rule was followed by what is today called a 'one-party state'.

The CUP now organized itself as a political party. Although its members were fractious and often divided among themselves, the CUP had a clear majority. Two groups stood in opposition – the Liberals, who had been outlawed after the coup, but simply changed names and leaders, and religious conservatives. Once again a military disaster led to political crisis. On 5 October 1911, Italy invaded Libya, the last region in Africa actually ruled by the Ottoman Empire. (Egypt, nominally Ottoman, was under British control.) Coastal Libya was quickly lost, leaving a guerrilla war against the Italians in the interior. Parliament objected. Led by the Liberals, but joined by members of the CUP party, the parliament might have voted no confidence in the government. But Sait Halim Paşa, the grand vezir, thwarted them by calling a snap election. The balloting itself was relatively fair, and the CUP would surely have won without tricks, but they could not resist temptation. Press censorship and even threats of violence were used against opponents. The 1912 election resulted in a large, but tainted, victory for the CUP. The victory did not last long. A group of military officers threatened the government with revolution, the cabinet resigned, and parliament was dissolved (5 August 1912). After a brief caretaker government, the Liberals returned to lead an unelected government.

The Liberal government presided over military disaster. In 1912 Montenegro, Serbia, Greece and Bulgaria invaded the Ottoman Empire. The first Balkan War began and ended in rapid defeat (Chapter 5). Such faith as had ever existed in the Liberal government faded. Finally, the CUP seized power on 23 January 1913. A Liberal attempt at another coup soon after failed. Elections in 1913 returned a majority of CUP deputies.

From 1913, all the forms of government continued. Parliament met, debated, and had much influence over laws. Actual governing, however, was in the hands of the CUP. Sait Halim once again became grand vezir. The strongest forces in the government, however, were the three leading members of the CUP, known as the Triumvirate – Cemal Paşa, minister of the navy and later governor of Syria,[1] Talât Paşa, minister of the interior, and Enver Paşa, minister of war. The government was by no means a classic dictatorship, run by executive order. Instead, the CUP was evolving into a political party that represented the local interests of its members and influential constituents. CUP representatives brought these interests to the government. Power shifted and realigned itself before major decisions were made. The very fact that there were three leaders with sometimes conflicting views made for a less dictatorial political system.

The Ottoman Empire immediately before World War I could not be called a democratic state, although it may have been on the road to democracy. It was a one-party state, with many of the trappings and some of the realities of democracy. The foremost sign of democracy was that the Empire had some time before begun to listen to a significant portion of its population, voices that before had seldom been heard, and to include the wishes of much of the populace in its governmental decisions. Although not truly democratic, the Empire had become representative.

Economic development

Economic development of the Empire was not a great Ottoman success, except in the one most important criteria of success. From 1878 to 1912 the population of Ottoman Anatolia increased at a rate of 0.015 per year, only slightly less than the rate of growth of the Turkish Republic immediately before World War II (0.017) and as high as could be expected, given prevailing standards of health and sanitation. Increase in the Arab provinces was only slightly slower. More than any other statistic, this indicates the success of Ottoman reform. It must be kept in mind that before the reforms population had stagnated or, in time of war, actually decreased. There were no major epidemics and, except for a brief successful war with the Greeks, no wars between 1878 and 1912, but this would not explain much of the increase, a few per cent at best. Availability of medical care was improving, but was still mainly available only in cities, so was not much of a factor. What accounted for the increased life expectancy of the people was an improvement in civil order. Crops were less likely to be stolen by rapacious ayans or governors collecting illegal taxes, and the crops could get to market on safer roads. The increase in population of the late Ottoman period is a symbol of a general improvement in life at its most basic level: the people were safer and better fed.

One can assume that local manufacturing must have improved as people had more to spend, but evidence of this was not collected. The craftsmen who made wagons, saddles and textiles for local use did not figure in official statistics.

Fairly accurate figures for production of farm products did not become available until the 1910s, but export data on cash crops indicates a sizeable increase in production. Between 1878 and 1912 cotton exports nearly tripled, as did exports of silk and silk cocoons. While such exports were affected by the efficiency brought to the market by Europeans working for the Public Debt Commission, they also indicate more work for the Ottoman subjects who were producing the goods.

Unfortunately for the economy, with the improvement in living standards in the Empire also came a desire and need for foreign goods. Imports always outpaced exports by a large margin. This could not be avoided. Modern machines were needed, so the Ottomans imported 200 times as many machines as they exported. Chemicals and other tools of modern manufacturing also had to be imported. With the Capitulations in place it was impossible for the Ottomans to develop needed new industries or even to protect the ones they had. As seen above, the Empire exported much cotton, but it imported twice as many finished textiles as it exported.

Once-flourishing domestic textile manufacturers had been bankrupted when they could not compete with British mills.

The true economic disaster for the Ottomans continued to be debt. Military expenses were always great, but unavoidable. Previous debts had to be paid. Yet more money always had to be found if roads were to be built, railroad tunnels dug, and ports improved. Without those expenditures the economy would not improve. Therefore, new money had to be found, usually by borrowing even more at higher rates. The Ottomans were not good economists and the economic system dominated by the Europeans was against them, as it was against all who were not part of it. When the burden of the Capitulations was added, the Ottomans had little chance of economic survival. Nevertheless, they did manage to lay railroad track, hang telegraph line, rebuild ports, and greatly improve the economic infrastructure of the Empire. Much of what they built – the improvements in the infrastructure of Ottoman Europe – they were not allowed to use; soon after it was built it was taken by their enemies.

A reformed Empire

In the years of reform the fundamental concept of Ottoman government had changed. From a system of 'The sultan protects; you pay for his services; all the rest is up to you', to the new system of active government intervention into society and economy meant crossing a great gulf. Before the Tanzimat, Ottoman rulers had indeed intervened in society and economy, but on a selective, sometimes capricious, basis, not as a matter of state duty. Now the state defined itself as the body that provided for subjects what they needed but could not easily provide for themselves. This brought the Ottomans into line with the theory of government in the West.

The relationship of subject to ruler was also changed fundamentally. The Hatt-ı Hümayun declared as surely as the American Declaration of Independence that humans had rights – personal rights that any just government must accept. The Ottoman Empire never was the 'oriental despotism' of fantasy, but the subject of human rights had never been at the forefront of political thought in the Empire. The concept that drove Ottoman political philosophy was the duty of the government to ensure justice, and justice was applied mainly to groups or to all subjects collectively. Recognition of the individual as a political entity with rights was another step toward a Western idea of government.

Closely tied to the concept of individual rights were the beginnings of democracy in the Empire. The framers of the Ottoman constitution failed to make their constitution the real law of the land. But not even Abdülhamit II, with the power of the state more firmly in his hands than any sultan for 100 years, could completely defy the idea of the constitution. Throughout his reign, Abdülhamit kept the constitution intact in law, even if not alive in spirit. The idea was simple but powerful: everyone was bound by civil law. The sultan had always been bound by Holy Law, but the penalties had been otherworldly and proved difficult to enforce on earth.

It is also notable that the Hatt-ı Hümayun proclaimed that rights adhered to all the sultan's subjects: 'These imperial concessions shall extend to all our subjects, of whatever religion or sect they may be; they shall enjoy them without exception'. The Ottoman Empire was always an Islamic Empire. In such an empire, Christians and Jews were allowed to live, and even prosper, but did not take part in the running of the state. The Ottoman government of the later nineteenth century changed that. If Christians could vote, they could and did take up leadership positions in the parliament. More notably, Christians took positions in the bureaucracy. The Foreign Ministry was most notable in this regard, with non-Muslim numbers reaching above 25 per cent. Other ministries had smaller, but significant, non-Muslim representation: more than 10 per cent in the Ministry of Justice, and more than 5 per cent in the Ministry of Interior. From 1880 to 1912, 7 per cent of the graduates of the School of Civil Administration, which trained the future leaders of the bureaucracy, were non-Muslims. These numbers are, of course, much lower than the proportion of non-Muslims in the population, but it must be remembered that much more lucrative career opportunities existed for Christians outside of the Civil Service. The highest position taken by a Christian was foreign minister, and it is doubtful if a non-Muslim would have been made grand vezir or minister of war. Nevertheless, the important fact is that the Ottomans had opened the government to non-Muslims, a radical change in the state apparatus.

The government was also opened to those who were not part of the traditional Istanbul ruling class. The bureaucracy was opened to the middle class, sons of merchants and craftsmen. Nearly 20 per cent of the officials in the Foreign Ministry may have come from this group (the numbers are very imprecise). The School of Civil Administration graduates from 1908 to 1912 included 28 per cent from Anatolia, 32 per cent from the Balkans, and 11 per cent from the Arab provinces.[2] This spoke not only of an opening of what had been a fairly closed bureaucratic society, but of the success of the new schools in educating potential leaders of the government.

The rulers of the constitutional state after 1908 were representatives of the changes in the composition of the Ottoman state. The CUP members were unquestionably the new men, less fettered than others by ties to traditions. They were the first government leaders who arose from the educated section of the general populace, not from the class of bureaucrats. Many of the notables of the CUP, such as Cemal Paşa, had worked their way up the military structure. Some were medical doctors. Talât Paşa's family could be called poor; he had been a teacher and post office worker. Mehmet Cavit, minister of finance, was the son of a merchant. Enver Paşa was the son of a minor bureaucrat. The middle class had risen to places of power.

Although for obvious reasons not publicly described as such at the time, Ottoman reform struck at the heart of traditional Islam. Islamic toleration was always based on the superior position of Islam and of the Muslim community. Rule was never to pass from Muslim hands. In legal proceedings non-Muslims held an inferior position. Socially, there can be no doubt that Muslims felt superior. The Hatt-ı Hümayun violated these traditional Islamic principles by stating that subjects were to be equal before the law. The Hatt went further, declaring that a new penal code would be written, one that applied to all subjects. To understand the momentous change that this involved one must remember that a penal code already existed in the Sharia (Sharī'a, Şeriat), the Holy Law of Islam. The Holy Law was fundamental to Islam, recognized by all Sunni Muslims as the divinely sanctioned guide for human interactions. In theory, it held answers to all legal questions. In fact, early Ottoman sultans had created administrative laws (*kanun*) that were in fact new legislation, but they had always obtained judgements from Islamic jurisconsults (legal experts) stating that the new rules were in accordance with the Holy Law. None would have admitted that new laws were being made.

Ottoman reformers made new laws. True, the reformed codification of laws, the Mecelle, was based on Islamic Law and modernized, but 'based on' was not a principle accepted in Islamic jurisprudence. Nor were the new secular courts instituted by the Tanzimat in accordance with Islamic principles. Trials in new mixed courts that treated Muslim and non-Muslim testimony equally went against the Islamic principle that Muslim oaths were given precedence in court. New commercial codes were not even based on Islamic law; they were in essence European codes, translated to fit Ottoman circumstances. Judges became independent state employees. Appeals to court decisions were decided by higher judicial courts and councils, agencies of government. In short, the Law, the basis of Islamic living, was no longer the Holy Law. Muslim courts and law still existed, but were increasingly marginalized.

The very idea of a constitution was an innovation in Islam. By definition, an ultimate law of the state was a contradiction of the religious belief that the state was to be ultimately guided by the Holy Law. The Ottoman constitution enshrined the legal realities of the final period of the Tanzimat. It did not create a separation of Church and State, which would have been asking too much, but there was no question as to which was the master.

The government of the CUP carried secularization much further. It took control of the Holy Law, the pious foundations, and even the Muslim schools out of the hands of the *ulema* (Muslim religious scholars and judges) and put them in the hands of state ministries. The Ministry of Justice paid Islamic judges, making them state officials. Judgements of the religious courts were subject to appeal to secular appeals courts, unquestionably putting the state above religion. Muslim pious foundations had in theory been under control since the Tanzimat, but the government had delegated the Şeyhülislam (head of the Ottoman Islamic institution) as the official in charge. The CUP put the foundations in the hands of secular officials. All of these changes were accepted by high Islamic officials, although the actions seem to have been direct contradictions of Islamic precedent. The cynical might note that Islamic legists were paid by the state and had no wish for unemployment. There was, however, a definite reformist strain among even members of the ulema.

These changes in the Ottoman system were neither small nor cosmetic. From the time of Mahmud II the Ottoman Empire had undergone radical changes in government and political life. Human rights, a constitution, Christians in high office, a parliament, the middle class in charge of the state, the power of Islam eroded – who could have foreseen such dramatic changes from the Ottoman Empire of 1826? By all the standards of its time the Ottoman Empire was much improved. Unfortunately for the Ottomans, the forces arrayed against them were powerful, and had little respect for what the Ottomans had achieved. The factor that was to decide the fate of the Ottomans was not their success in reform, their increasing openness to human rights, or the modernization of their system of government. Their fate was to be decided by the military power of their adversaries.

3
The Balkans

In no country or time has the 'nation' been anything other than a potent shared idea. The more who believed in the nation, the more powerful the idea. Nevertheless, it has never been more than an idea. A state can be defined by its laws or its borders. Ethnic groups, although harder to delineate, can at least be understood statistically as the proportion of a population that dances the same dances, eats the same foods, speaks the same language, and gathers together to engage in those activities. The nation is different. It cannot be absolutely or statistically defined, because it only exists in the minds of nationalists. This has not kept nationalists from asserting that their nations actually exist as other things exist, that they are not just a shared opinion. At first nationalists spoke of 'common blood'. This did not fit well with biological knowledge, although nationalists continued to speak of their nations in quasi-genetic terms. The more common belief was that the nation was spiritually real – an indefinable spiritual connection that made people French, Bulgarian, or German in their souls. Writings and speeches of nationalists leave no doubt that they believed the nation to be such a spiritual state, or perhaps a shared emotion. (Obviously, this was a changeable spirit, since migrants to the Americas began as members of the Italian or German nation and mystically changed nations as they debarked in new homelands.)

The terms nation and nationality are subject to some linguistic confusion. In English, the question 'What is your nationality?' is usually answered by naming the state of which one is a citizen. This objectively has nothing to do with the idea of the nation, but it does confuse discourse. The old European idea of 'race' is closer to defining what the nineteenth and early twentieth centuries felt to be a nation. Scholars and politicians then spoke of an 'English Race', a 'German Race', a 'French Race', and assumed all would understand what was meant. Race was no more identifiable than nation. In the absence of scientific evidence, however, both necessarily were described in spiritual terms. Herder, Fichte, Hegel, von Ranke and their myriad followers were not embarrassed to write in terms such as the 'Spirit of the Nation'.

The primary assumption of nationalism was that there were separate peoples, *Volk*, groups whose members existed within the common soul of the nation, the *Volksgeist*. Thus the tie between members of the nation was mystical, by definition beyond logic, an article of belief. Like religion, nationalism promised that faith and dedication would bring rewards. In the case of nationalism, not heaven but good government, prosperity, and shared victory over others were promised. As was the case with heaven, a good deal of faith was demanded before the goal could be achieved.

Nationalism naturally affected the actions of rebel movements and governments alike. In what might be described as a functional theory of government, a state should act to ensure a good life for those who are its citizens and, given a measure of altruism, for others as well. But nationalism was not about that. Nationalism was about ensuring the triumph of the nation. Nationalists might each have had a different vision of what defines their nation, even of who was a member, but they united in declaring that there *was* a nation and that it deserved a state of its own. In the eyes of most nationalists, their nation also deserved to stand above other nations. The corollary was that nationalists were willing to die and even more willing to kill for their nation.

Practically, the two most obvious identifiers of a nation were language and a common history. Neither had been very important in the political operation of the traditional Ottoman Empire or earlier states. In a tradition that extended back to antiquity, differences among languages and customs in the Balkans and Middle East were of course recognized, but the categorization of differences was most often religious. Religious separation and identity can be considered the normal state of the traditional Middle East and Balkans. The Ottoman Empire, drawing on both local traditions and Islamic practice, divided its subjects into millets, religious groups certified by the state as representatives of their group of believers. Each millet then provided courts, schools, assistance to the poor, and other services, as well as more purely religious functions. Although there were many religiously mixed villages and many mixed neighbourhoods in cities, co-religionists tended to live and work together. Ethnic divisions were not considered, at least not administratively, within millets. For example, the largest millet, the Orthodox, included Greeks, Romanians, Serbs, Bulgarians, Arabs and others.

All this began to change in the nineteenth century, gradually being replaced, or at least augmented, by nationalism, an identity that transcended religion. It is important to note that in the Ottoman Empire nationalism never supplanted religion as a focus of personal identity. Nationalism was truly only a force among the intelligentsia and the political and economic elite. For the mass of the people of the Empire, religion was still the primary self-identifier. In practice, religious identification did not much conflict with the ideals of nationalism. Radical intellectuals, who were not themselves necessarily religious, were willing to use religion as a unifying force as long as it suited their purposes.

Nationalism came to the Balkans from its birthplace, Western Europe. In the eighteenth century commercial contacts between the Ottoman Balkans and Western Europe increased. Balkan Christians conducted the majority of this trade, relying on commercial networks with representatives in both the Ottoman Empire and European states. In addition, Christians filled the important place of middle men in the trade of Europeans, who knew neither the languages nor the commercial customs of the Empire. This Christian merchant class was the natural conduit of nationalist ideas into the Ottoman domains. Many merchants spoke European languages and had extensive contacts with Europeans from outside the Ottoman Empire, including periods of residence in foreign countries. These contacts, which transmitted nationalist ideas beginning in the eighteenth century, must necessarily be simplified here. The important point is that literate, entrepreneurial members of Ottoman minority groups saw foreign systems and learned European ideological fashions and political philosophy.

What was learned was a simple and powerful idea: peoples were divided and identified by their language and their history. Germans might be Lutheran, Calvinist or Catholic, but they were primarily Germans, tied together by the spirit of the German nation. French Catholics and German Catholics or Hungarian and German Protestants might hold the same religious tenets, but were not tied together in the most important way – they were not members of the same nation.

Language was only the most obvious mark of common nationality, not its primary definition. What was essential was a shared 'racial' history. Crudely put, as it usually was, members of the nation descended from the same ancestors; they 'shared the same blood', 'shared the same soul', or simply were 'of the same stock'. Of course, no one then or now could identify their ancestors beyond a limited number of generations, especially not in a region that had been invaded by the gene pools of so many conquerors. This was not much considered by Balkan nationalists. The important point was whether one believed that common ancestry existed. That was enough. It was not necessary for individual members of the nation to be conscious of their membership, or even to want to be included. Intellectuals and politicians defined who were members of the nation. Thus Pomaks, Bulgarian-speaking Muslims, were considered by Bulgarian nationalists to be part of the Bulgarian nation, whether or not they wished to be. The Greek nation avowedly included Greeks in Greece proper, who spoke Greek, Greeks in Albania, who spoke Albanian, Greeks in Anatolia, who spoke Greek or Turkish, and even Slavic-speaking Macedonians, who had no wish to be Greek. Many of those who considered themselves to be Albanians were 'Albanian-speaking Serbs' to Serbian nationalists. There were to be difficulties when the same groups were claimed by different

Map 3.1 Provinces of Ottoman Europe in 1912

nationalisms. In Macedonia, as will be seen, inhabitants were considered to be Greeks, Serbs, Bulgarians or Macedonians, depending on who described them. Being fought over was not a happy experience for the Macedonians.

The nationalism of the Balkans was similar to that of Germans such as Heinrich von Treitschke. Members of the nation were destined to be in that particular nation by spirit or biology. Whether they knew they were part of the nation or wished to be part of the nation made no difference. They were to be taught or even forced to accept their rightful place.

The first rebellions

Defects in the Ottoman governmental system contributed greatly to the development of national feeling and rebellion in the Balkans. At the turn of the nineteenth century, the Ottomans were too militarily weak to control their European territories. While the Ottomans could field an army capable of defeating most outright rebels, they could neither find nor pay for a sufficient number of troops to police the Empire. The nucleus of the army, the Janissary Corps, had degenerated into a poor fighting force. It was, however, strong enough to terrorize sultans and bureaucrats and to make the life of peasants and city-dwellers hell. Effective power in the provinces was held by ayans who ruled their territories and sent tribute to Istanbul. The government needed them, for they were the most effective fighters in the Ottoman forces.

Many of the local rulers, especially in Anatolia, were truly local, respected leaders whose families had held high positions for decades, even centuries. Others, especially in the Balkans, were little more than very successful bandits. In order to quiet them somewhat, to integrate them into the Ottoman system, and because they could do little else, the Ottoman government often named the most powerful bandits or local leaders as governors of provinces. This did not lead to effective rule. There were other bandits, as well. Christian as well as Muslim bandit gangs had sprung up wherever there were mountains in which they could hide. Among the Christians, the bandits often took on a protective colouring as defenders of their own people. Not quite Robin Hoods, they did not spread their gains among their own, but they were at least more likely to rob and murder others. To the peasant of the Balkans the distinction between bandits in the mountains and bandits in the governor's mansion must have been minimal. Both stole whatever they could.

Serbs had a great and fully justified complaint against the Janissaries and ayans who exerted control over Serbia. The Janissaries were more an occupying army of plunderers than an efficient military force, and the local lords were in fact bandits, although often bandits who had been awarded government titles and offices in the hope that they would settle down. Muslims, Jews and Christians shared an antipathy to their masters. The central government shared the desire of the Serbs to be rid of ayans and Janissaries. In the 1790s, Sultan Selim III granted some autonomy to Serbs of the province of Belgrade, including the right to bears arms and to have Serbian tax-collectors. In 1797, he ordered Ottoman troops to cooperate with a Serbian militia to defeat the Janissaries and their ayan allies, but Ottoman forces were too weak and the rebels triumphed. Making the best of it, Selim III named the most powerful of the rebellious ayans, Osman Pasvanoğlu, as governor of Vidin and allowed the Janissaries to act as before in Belgrade Province. The inevitable Serbian revolt against the situation came in 1804. At first, the sultan's army and the Serbs cooperated, but the Serb war against the Janissaries evolved into a rebellion against all Ottoman power. The rebels occupied Belgrade in December 1806.

At this point Serbia became embroiled in international politics. From 1806 to 1878, Serbian independence and Serbian borders were to be decided by Russia actions against the Ottomans. Russia was to manipulate the Serbian situation to fit its own ends, in the process making Serbia independent. The question of rebellion, nationalism and national independence in the Balkans would never again be disconnected from greater European politics. The division of the Ottoman Empire and creation of new Balkan states was to be decided in European chancellories. Imperialism and nationalism were to be cooperating forces in the destruction of the Empire.

The Ottoman Empire went to war with Russia and England in 1806. England withdrew from the war in 1809, but Russia and the Ottomans continued to fight until 1812. Under the terms of the Treaty of Bucharest the Ottomans lost Bessarabia to the Russians. They would have lost much more, had Napoleon not begun his plans to march on Russia, forcing the Russians to disengage with the Ottomans. The Russians promised aid to the Serbian rebels, but delivered little. The Ottoman army then moved into Serbia to defeat the rebels. In 1810, however, the Russians finally delivered supplies, weapons and ammunition to the Serbs, along with Russian officers as advisers. This saved the Serbs for a time, but the Russians abandoned them once again when they made peace with the Ottomans.

The Ottomans retook Serbia in 1813. Prompted by the Russians, they adopted a conciliatory attitude toward Serbia, allowing much local autonomy. Muslims were forcibly evicted from Serbia and, according to the Convention of Akkerman of 1826, only Ottoman garrison troops remained in the province of Belgrade to symbolize imperial authority. As a condition of the peace that followed the next Russo-Turkish War (1828–29), Russia forced the Ottomans to make Serbia become formally autonomous under its own prince, actually independent. Russia had carved a new state from the Ottoman Empire. Serbia was enlarged, again due to Russian pressure, in 1833. The Serbs were set upon a policy of national expansion that was to continue to the 1980s.

The Greek revolution was another case of European intervention creating a separatist state. It began in 1821 with attacks on tax-collectors, and Greek peasants and bandits joined in what was to become a general war on all things Turkish. Approximately 25,000 Turks of the Morea (southern Greece) were killed. The only Turks who survived had escaped to Ottoman military fortresses or out of the region. In March 1821 the Greek revolution spread to Ottoman Romania. Once again, the character of the rebellion was primarily religious, Christians against Muslims. Once again, Turks were slaughtered as the first act of rebellion. The rebellion failed in Romania. The Russians, who had been confidently expected to intervene, did not act. They had other plans for Romania.

In Greece the Ottomans proved to be too militarily weak to defeat the rebels with their own forces. They called on a nearly independent vassal, Muhammad Ali of Egypt, to defeat the rebels. He did so, but the outcome of the Greek revolution was to be decided in Europe, not in battles with rebels in Greece.

A wave of philhellenism swept European countries when the Greeks rebelled. The Europeans did not see the realities of the rebellion, which were as much murderous acts against Muslims and hatred of tax-collectors as they were idealism. Instead, Europe, where the upper classes were steeped in Classical learning, saw the Land of Socrates, Plato and Aristotle fighting for its freedom. Many saw a war between Christianity and Islam, and knew which side they were on. They intervened. Without justification or any declaration of war, a joint English, French and Russian fleet destroyed the Egyptian and Ottoman fleets at Navarino (1827). Russia invaded Ottoman Europe, defeating the Ottomans in the war of 1828–29. The Ottomans were forced to recognize an independent Greek kingdom and autonomy for Serbia and Romania (Wallachia and Moldavia).

The revolts in Greece and Romania cannot be viewed as nationalistic. The Greeks who were preponderant in the revolt intended to create a Greek state as the Byzantine Empire had been a Greek state. Greek culture and religion would be dominant, but the new empire's subjects were not to be defined ethnically. They were to be Orthodox Christians, not Greeks. Thus it seemed completely reasonable that the revolt should start in both Greece and Romania.

Further dismemberment of the Ottoman Empire, 1875–1878

European military power had created independent Greece and virtually independent Serbia and Romania out of Ottoman Europe. In both Serbia and Greece revolts had been aimed at more than independence: the rebels intended to eject local Muslims from their new states. In Serbia, this had been accomplished with limited bloodshed, the result of treaties forced by Russia. In Greece, migration had been forced by mass murder. The end was the same in both. Greece and Serbia were ethnically homogenous states in which nationalism would grow. The same patterns were to be followed in the civil wars of 1875–76 and the Russo-Turkish War of 1877–78: a powerful Russia was to defeat the Ottomans; the defeat would result in the creation of a new state, Bulgaria, and the aggrandizement of Serbia and Greece; local Muslims would again be killed or forced from their lands.

The 1875 rebellion in Ottoman Bosnia began as a protest against rapacious landlords and high taxes. At first, the rebellion was not particularly nationalistic in character. Most of the rebels were Bosnian Serbs, but they had sympathy in other communities. Many, no matter what their religion or ethnic group, welcomed attacks on tax-collectors. Soon, however, nationalist Serbs from Bosnia and Serbia itself changed the character of the rebellion. Guns, money and men arrived from Serbia and Montenegro, with support from Russian pan-Slavist elements (see below). Instead of government officials, Serbs began to attack Muslim villages. The change was significant: instead of fighting against perceived oppressors to gain a better life, Serbs were fighting for their nation against what they perceived to be another nation. Muslim villagers, who knew little of nationalism but much of revenge, responded with attacks on Serbs. Bosnia degenerated into intercommunal war.

As was often the case, European governments demanded that the Ottomans make concessions to the rebels to end the fighting. As was not often the case, the European demands were reasonable. In December 1875 the 'League of the Three Emperors' – Russia, Austria and Germany – demanded that the Ottomans end tax-farming, lower taxes, and make other reforms. The Ottomans complied. The reforms answered many of the initial complaints of the rebels, but the rebellion had become a nationalist revolt with aims that went well beyond economic welfare. The Serbian rebels would be satisfied with nothing less than joining Bosnia with the Serbian kingdom, and so they continued their revolt. At that point the Ottoman army put down the rebellion by force.

Serbia, thwarted in plans for expansion in Bosnia, declared war on the Ottomans on 2 July 1876, but was easily defeated in August. The Serbs regrouped, but were defeated once again in September. At this point the Russians intervened and threatened to invade the Ottoman Empire if it attacked into Serbia. The Ottomans withdrew.

In Bulgaria, meanwhile, another group of nationalist rebels attempted to take advantage of the Ottoman concentration on Bosnia. Previous attempts at nationalist rebellions in Bulgaria had failed quickly. Organized and stationed in Serbia and Wallachia (southern Romania), guerrilla bands crossed into Bulgaria, attacked Ottoman outposts, and attempted to foment nationalist revolt among the Bulgarian peasants. All their attempts foundered because of lack of popular support and the power of the Ottoman military. The Ottoman army had benefited greatly from recent reforms. It was not strong enough to stand against Russia or Austria, but it could easily defeat rebels within the Empire. In 1876, however, the army was away in Bosnia. The rebels saw their chance.

On 2 May 1876, rebellion flared in the towns of Panagiurishte, Koprivshtitsa and Klisura. The rebels were mainly local nationalists from the commercial class and from outside the Empire, with only minimal support from the peasantry. However, their initial actions led to a downward spiral of violence and eventual Russian intervention. They began their revolt by slaughtering the Muslim villagers in the surrounding region. Approximately 1000 Muslims were killed. The Ottomans, with few regular troops to call on, called upon local Muslims, called *bashi bozuks*, and Circassians to put down the revolt. They did so with ferocity, killing the rebels and, inevitably, large numbers of innocent Bulgarians. The Circassians, who had been expelled from their homeland by the Russians with great mortality, were especially violent and resisted Ottoman orders. Some Circassians and bashi bozuks were tried and executed for their actions. Nevertheless, the overall effect was to escalate violence. Some 1000 Muslims had died initially; now between 3000 and 12,000 Bulgarians were dead. Once Serbia was defeated, the regular army moved into Bulgaria and ended the unrest.

The Ottomans had successfully put down rebellions in Bosnia and Bulgaria and had defeated the Serbian kingdom. Internal nationalist rebellion had proven to be impossible. None of this mattered, however, because the Russians had decided to intervene.

European prejudice did much to affect coming events. For its own benefit, chiefly to keep the balance of power in Europe, Britain had long been a diplomatic force on the side of the Ottomans. In the Crimean War, Britain and France had joined the Empire against the Russians. But the events in Bulgaria and Bosnia made continuation of this policy impossible. In British newspapers, the deaths of the Bulgarians, styled the 'Bulgarian Horrors', were reported and greatly exaggerated. Muslim deaths went unmentioned. Serb depredations against Bosnian Muslims were likewise ignored. William Ewart Gladstone organized a mass campaign in Britain against the Turks, partly from his evangelical Christian convictions and partly to discomfort his political opponent, Benjamin Disraeli, the prime minister. British public opinion became ardently anti-Turkish. Overcome by public opinion, Disraeli, who wished to commit to the Ottomans against the Russians, could only advise the Ottomans, not stand behind them.

Although the tsars were not known for paying much attention to public opinion, Russia too had been affected by the unrest in Bosnia and Bulgaria. Pan-Slavist sentiments were fashionable among the Russian intelligentsia at the time. Pan-Slavism was a collection of vague beliefs that ranged from affection for brother Slavs to the belief that all Slavs were really one nation that should be led by Russia. Pan-Slavists were inflamed by the Slavic losses. Support for the Serbs was especially strong. The tsar was expected to do something to help the Slavs. More concretely, the Russians had no wish for a resurgent Ottoman state in the Balkans.

The Ottoman government gave in to Russian sentiments when it could. It agreed to sign an armistice with Serbia on 31 October 1876, just as total Serbian defeat was imminent, and would have accepted other plans for reforms in the Bulgaria, as it already had in Bosnia. What it could not accept was the Russian plan to divide Ottoman Europe into autonomous Christian states. Russia expected, and the Ottomans understood, that such states would be clients of Russia, and would soon become completely independent. The Russians were in fact demanding the dissolution of the Ottoman Empire in Europe. The Ottomans refused. Russia went to war.

The Russians first covered their flank by dealing with Austria. In the Budapest Convention of 15 January 1877, Austria agreed to remain neutral in the coming Russo-Turkish War. Her payment was to be Bosnia – something for nothing.

Russia declared war on 24 April 1877, crossed the Danube, and invaded Ottoman territory on 22 June. By the middle of July, Russians held all of northern Bulgaria. They were stopped at the fortress city of Plevna until 10 December. After Plevna fell, however, most of the rest of Bulgaria was taken quickly. The Russians moved into eastern Thrace, taking Edirne on 20 January 1878. Istanbul was now virtually undefended. In eastern Anatolia the Russians had taken Kars and surrounded the Ottoman garrison in Erzurum. The Ottomans were forced to capitulate.

The Ottomans signed an armistice on 31 January and the Treaty of San Stephano on 3 March 1878. Under its terms, a Greater Bulgaria was to be created, stretching from the Black Sea to Albania and south to the Aegean Sea. By now, however, fickle British public opinion had changed, this time against the Russians, rightly seen as threatening British interests in the Near East. Austria was also upset by the creation of a new Balkan rival, Greater Bulgaria. Germany offered its good offices as mediator. The ensuing Congress of Berlin forced Russia to accept a much smaller Bulgaria, and even that was divided into a Bulgarian kingdom, in the north, and Eastern Rumelia, a practically autonomous part of the Ottoman Empire. They were to be joined together in 1885. Serbia was granted the region of Niş (from which all but 10 per cent of the Muslims were evicted or died). Montenegro received a small amount of territory, as well. Greece was given a small slice on its northern border, Thessaly and Epirus, after negotiations that ended in 1881. Russia itself was forced to settle for land in northeast Anatolia (the Batum–Kars–Ardahan region), and southern Bessarabia.

Mortality and forced migration

For the people of the Balkans, the wars that created Bulgaria and increased Serbia led to what was to become the characteristic mark of nationalism in the Balkans and Anatolia, the massive dislocation of peoples. An unknown number of Bulgarians left Macedonia for Bulgaria when Macedonia was returned to the Ottomans. It was, however, the Muslims of the Balkans who suffered most from the Russian conquest.

Few of the cities and only a small part of the countryside in Bulgaria were scenes of protracted battle, so civilian losses due to battle were relatively few. Nevertheless, 17 per cent (262,000) of the Muslims of Bulgaria died during and immediately after the 1877–78 war. Some 515,000 surviving Muslims, almost all Turkish, were forced from Bulgaria into other areas of the Ottoman Empire, never to return home. They were victims of a combination of local Bulgarian rapacity and what later generations would call state terror. When Russian troops entered part of Bulgaria, Bulgarian revolutionaries, Russian soldiers, especially Cossacks, and Bulgarian peasants began a programme of rape, plunder and massacre. The result was the flight of the Bulgarian Muslims. Some 55 per cent of the Muslims of Bulgaria, mainly Turks, were either evicted or killed.

As agreed with the Russians, and confirmed by the Congress of Berlin, the Austrians took Bosnia. They maintained the fiction of Bosnian autonomy by accepting Ottoman overlordship for Bosnia until 1908, when they annexed the province. Due to mortality in the 1875–76 wars and emigration, the Muslim population declined from 694,000 to 449,000, a loss of 35 per cent. The number of Serbs in Bosnia declined by 7 per cent.

The rebellions in Greece, Serbia and Bulgaria set the standard for nationalist revolt in the Balkans. The states to be created or enlarged were to be ethnically homogenous – unitary states that were insofar as possible devoid of their principal minorities, Muslims. National states in the Balkans were to be states for 'the people' alone, defined as members of only one ethnic group. This was to be the continuing definition and practice of Balkan nationalism.

The spread of nationalism

The spread of nationalism was the result of actions by states and politicians who saw benefit in asserting it. Nationalism was intended to be a political force, a tactic that would increase the size and power of Bulgaria, Serbia and Greece. The fact that nationalism was a tactic does not mean that it was a callously used fiction to its practitioners. No, they believed in their nationalistic purpose. To them, the advancement of the state, the nation, and their own political fortunes were the same.

With the possible exception of Serbia, the states hewn from the Ottoman Empire by European intervention cannot be considered to have initially been national states. Their peoples were not much animated by nationalist ideologies. This would change as nationalists set upon their duty to create national feeling within the new kingdoms and without.

The chief weapon of nationalism in the new states and within the Ottoman Empire was education. The nationalist mission was to spread national consciousness among those members of the nation who did not yet possess it. Schools were the main agents of this proselytism. The new states – Bulgaria, Serbia and Greece – all instituted nationalist curricula in their schools. From the standpoint of the nationalists, the intent was to open the people's mind to their true identity. A more cynical interpretation might call it indoctrination. However it was defined, it was successful.

The nationalist schools operated in both the newly independent states and the Ottoman Empire. In this they took advantage of the Ottoman policy of allowing each religious group to educate its own students. So committed were the Ottomans to this policy that they, probably foolishly, allowed even those known to be spreading sedition to continue to operate schools.

Bulgarian national schools in the Ottoman Empire began in opposition to Greeks. The autocephalous (autonomous; only accepting the authority of the Patriarch of Constantinople in theory) Bulgarian Church had been closed in 1767 at the instigation of the Greek Patriarchate, and Greek bishops were increasing their hold on Bulgarian dioceses. Education, in the hands of the clergy, was in Greek. To counter Hellenization, the Bulgarian merchant class founded and operated Bulgarian schools. When the Bulgarian Church was re-established (1870) it took over most of the schools. Bulgarian sources estimated that by the turn of the century there were approximately 700 Bulgarian schools in the Ottoman Europe. This figure is many times the number of such schools registered with the Ottoman government and must include many small church schools and a good amount of exaggeration, but the effort was obviously sizeable. Many of the schools provided a good education. All taught Bulgarian separatism.

The Greeks claimed 1400 schools in Macedonia, a ridiculously inflated number, but indicative of another massive effort at spreading a nationalist message. The University of Athens was founded explicitly with the idea of carrying Hellenism to those outside Greece, as well as educating the Greeks of Greece. The University and other schools trained teachers who went out of the Greek kingdom to educate 'unredeemed' Greeks in nationalist ideals, as well as providing a better education than had been available previously.

Serbian schools were never as numerous or as successful in spreading their message, probably because so few in Macedonia felt themselves to be Serbs and because education in Serbia itself was of a low standard.

As independent states, the Balkan countries had new tools to spread nationalism in the Empire. Greeks were especially adept at using their consular system to spread Greek nationalism. They awarded Greek citizenship to many local Ottoman Greeks, thus creating dual subject status, which in fact was loyalty to Greece while holding Ottoman papers. The consuls also acted as agents of a resurgent Greek culture, bringing in Greek newspapers and books. For many Ottoman Greeks, brought up under the millet system, their personal identity was already Greek, even though this was religious identity. It was a short step to Greek nationalism.

Religion and nationalism

Religion, the traditional self-identifier of Ottoman subjects, was turned to the purposes of nationalism in the new states. This occurred despite the initial opposition of most of the Orthodox hierarchy. Men of God naturally felt that one's primary allegiance should be to religion, not to a secular faith. The Orthodox Patriarchate and its bureaucracy were indeed Greek, and they attempted to spread the Greek language and religious tradition among all the Orthodox Christians of the Ottoman Empire. They viewed themselves as the caretakers of the Greek tradition of the Byzantines. But this was a tradition in which people of different languages and cultures were to be brought together through belief. Nationalism could be seen as a violation of the Church's ecumenical mission. The creation of separate national feeling would also lead to the demand for separate clergy and separate authority structures, which was a more concrete threat to the Patriarchate.

The nationalist solution was to create exactly those national churches that were feared by the Patriarchate. The reasoning of the nationalists was that the Patriarch of Constantinople was under the thumb of the Turks. He was to be afforded respect, but his orders were not to be followed. The Greeks themselves were the first to break from his authority. The Greek Church of the Greek Kingdom was unilaterally declared to be autocephalous in 1833, although this status was not accepted by the Patriarch of Constantinople until 1850. From that point the Church of Greece was a national church that supported nationalist aspirations.

Bulgarians long fostered a deep resentment of the Greek Orthodox. In the early 1800s, Bulgarians within the Ottoman Empire protested, even revolted, against Greek bishops. Episcopal venality and increased Church taxes were one cause of the mutiny, but the Bulgarians also wanted priests and bishops who spoke the same language as the people. The best friend of Bulgarian episcopal autonomy turned out to be the Ottoman government. Bulgarian men of affairs in Istanbul had the money and position to affect change and did so. In 1848, they convinced the government to support acceptance of the first Bulgarian Church, in Istanbul. In the 1860s, Bulgarians began to refuse to accept Greek bishops, creating a situation that might lead to further rebellion, but the Istanbul Bulgarians convinced the Ottomans that acceptance of Bulgarian ecclesiastical independence was the path to civil order. Bribes were not a small part of the process. The Bulgarian Exarchate, an autocephalous Bulgarian Church, was recognized in 1870. It was still in theory under the Patriarchate and its jurisdiction extended only over northern Bulgaria and adherents in Istanbul, but it was to spread. Dioceses were allowed to vote to become members of the Exarchate, which they did.

Far from leading to civil order, the conflict over religion in Bulgaria was a strong factor in uniting the Bulgarian Christians and stressing their separateness. Bulgarians within and without Bulgaria had come together and stressed the nationality of religion. After 1878, an independent Bulgaria was to use the Church to spread the Bulgarian nationalist message, especially through its schools.

The Serbian Orthodox Church had been autocephalous under the Patriarch of Peč until 1766. It had long been a centre for dissatisfaction with Ottoman rule and Serbian subservience, but was especially disliked by the hierarchy of the Greek Orthodox Patriarchate of Constantinople. It was the Greek Orthodox who engineered the downfall of the Peč Patriarchate. As with the Bulgarians, the Greeks then began to Grecify the Church, with similar results. The Patriarch was finally obliged to accept autocephalous status for the church in Serbia in 1879.

Whereas the Constantinople Patriarchate had stood for a universal religious dominion, even if it was a dominion that spoke Greek, the national churches were just that, national. They stressed national schools, national pride and national saints. The Church was now an instrument of the advancement of the nation.

The reasons for the success of nationalism

How much the masses of people of the Ottoman Balkans believed in nationalism as an idea will never been known. No opinion polls were taken. From all evidence it seems extremely unlikely that nationalism could have been prominent as a reason for the Greek War of Independence, for example. The idea of nationalism had simply not developed very far at that time. In their revolt, Serbs may have felt the sort of ethnic identity that at least was a precursor of nationalism. Bulgarians, however, showed little support for nationalism before 1878. The nationalists who attempted revolt in Bulgaria were too poorly supported for that to have been true. Why, then, were the revolts successful, if most of the people were not initially nationalists?

First of all, it must be remembered that none of the nationalist rebellions were successful on their own. In Greece, Serbia and Bulgaria rebellions only succeeded because of intervention by one or more European powers. Greece, Serbia and Bulgaria were created by the European Powers, especially by Russia.

There were also many reasons for rebellion other than nationalism. Those who rebelled had their own reasons for their actions. It is certain that members of religions often scorned or disliked members of religions other than their own. This extended to animosity between Christian groups, not only between Christians and Muslims. Religious belief facilitated feelings of separation and alienation between Muslims and Christians. How much these feelings might have contributed to rebellion cannot be known, but they were definitely a factor in the Greek revolution.

One factor in revolt may have been a very human feeling of dislike for those in power, especially if the powerful were conspicuously different in religion and language. The tax-collector had indeed always been the enemy. There was the perhaps naive belief that members of one's own group would be less rapacious, more honest, caring masters. Ottoman rule in the eighteenth century had provided many reasons for this feeling. The ayans who controlled much of the Balkans until the 1820s were truly oppressive masters who usually showed little concern for any of the people they controlled. The fact that they defied the Ottoman government and tyrannized Muslims as well as Christians would have meant nothing to those who suffered their depredations. Memories of the days of the ayans would have lasted long after the Ottomans had destroyed their power and greatly improved the quality of life. Memories in the Balkans are long.

Revolt promised more concrete benefits, as well. In the Balkans, nationalist revolt always resulted in the expulsion or death of many who were not of the nation – Muslims and Jews high on the list. These people had farms, animals, houses and businesses that they would not be using any longer. For poor people, this was a prodigious benefit.

Finally, rebellion was plainly the path to power and reward. The European Powers, who would ultimately decide all matters, supported it. Even those who might have supported the continuation of Ottoman rule, if only for their own benefit, could see the path that history was taking. The Powers would support small nation-states in the Balkans, but all expected that they would eventually force the dissolution of the Ottoman Empire. Because this was ultimately true, nationalism became realism.

Once the national states were formed, nationalism gained adherents, not the least because it had succeeded. Further success was expected, so nationalism became a force on its own. For believers, nationalism was not only a true description of ethnic and political reality, it was the future. European states had succeeded as nations. Now Balkan nations would follow in their success.

Dividing what remained

All Balkan nationalists had their plans to divide the Ottoman Empire. In order to evaluate their plans, it helps to consider what a properly divided Ottoman Empire might be.

If, at the beginning of the twentieth century, one were set on dividing Ottoman Europe into separate ethnic states, it might have been possible to divide the region more or less rationally. The primary criteria for creation of new states would necessarily have been religion. Muslims and Jews unquestionably identified themselves primarily by religion. A Bosnian Muslim, an Albanian Muslim and a Turk might speak different languages, but no one can question that they felt that religion was a bond that brought them together. Christians divided by religion and language group: Greeks, Bulgarians, Serbs and Romanians were all Orthodox Christians. Unlike the Muslims, however, language and ethnicity divided co-religionists. Their theoretical states, therefore, would have to be divided into major ethnic groups as well as religion.

Map 3.2 draws hypothetical states from Ottoman European territory as it was in 1911. The states are based on religious affiliation – Muslim, Bulgarian Orthodox and Greek Orthodox. Wherever possible, the states have been adjusted to fit into natural boundaries such as mountain ranges or rivers. In other words, these are the states that would have been 'natural' in the Balkans, given religion as the primary affiliation of the people. Bulgaria would have extended far to the southwest; its territory would have included the present-day Republic of Macedonia and surrounding areas. The Muslim territories would have been divided by the Bulgarian territory into two parcels of land. The eastern territory, which would have included all of Thrace and eastern Macedonia, would have been primarily Turkish-speaking. The western territory would have been primarily Albanian-speaking, with large communities of Turks and Slavs. Serbia would not have expanded at all; the demographics were against it. Greece would have expanded only slightly.

Whether such states would have been viable is unknowable, although it can be argued that they could not have turned out worse than the states that were ultimately created by military conquest, with little regard for the real differences in the population. Sadly, rational division of the Ottoman Balkans was never a possibility. No one was willing to consider anything but their group's maximal claims. And they all claimed the same land. Nowhere was this as true as in Macedonia.

Macedonia

Macedonia was not an Ottoman administrative designation. It was generally described as the Ottoman provinces of Selanik (Salonica), the southern half of Kosova Province (the Üsküp or Skopje region), and western Manastır Province (Map 3.1). Bulgarian, Greek and Serbian nationalists all claimed part or all of Macedonia, based on their assertions as to the true identity of the Christians of the region. They naturally did not agree. Given the nationalists' propensity for including factors such as borders of long-dead kingdoms or 'national soul' as a defining characteristic of nationality, no matter what the people felt themselves to be, agreement was impossible.

The question 'Who are the Macedonians?' never arose in the Ottoman

Map 3.2 Dividing the Balkans by religious group

government, which only identified people by religion. But it was a very important question for Bulgarian, Serbian and Greek nationalists. It is also a fine example of the sort of absurd question that defined nationalist conflict. The truly important question was: 'What do the people of Macedonia want for themselves?' No one wanted to ask that question, perhaps for fear that the answer would be: 'We just want to be left alone'. The only choice the Macedonians had made themselves was the choice to join the Bulgarian Church. Under the Ottoman law that created the Bulgarian Exarchate in 1870, seventeen dioceses that had demanded a Bulgarian Church had been made part of the new Church. If Christians in other Macedonian dioceses voted by a two-thirds margin, they too could join the Bulgarian Church. As seen in Table 3.1, they did so overwhelmingly. This can be taken as a clear sign that the Macedonians did not wish to be Greek. It cannot be taken to mean the Macedonians wanted to be known as Bulgarians. A Macedonian Church was not given as an option. Most Macedonians probably only wanted a liturgical language that was more understandable than Greek; they were not making a political statement. One can speculate that some Macedonian-speaking Christians thought of themselves as Bulgarians, some thought of themselves as Macedonians, and some did not care.

It should be noted that Bulgarian-speakers were present in Macedonia. Members of the Bulgarian Church in Macedonia were not all linguistically Macedonian. There were also a small number of linguistic Macedonians who remained with the Greek Church. If it were not confusing, it would not have been Macedonia.

Maps 3.3 and 3.4 give an indication of the Macedonian claims of Bulgarian and Serbian nationalists. The maps were taken from the American Carnegie Commission's investigation into the Balkan Wars.[1] The Commission felt that they represented the thinking of Bulgarian and Serbian nationalists. In fact, the maps were more moderate than many Bulgarian and Serbian claims.

The Bulgarian map is absurd. On it, virtually everyone who is not a Greek or a Turk is automatically a Bulgarian, and indications of Greek or Turkish population are limited to areas in which they were an overwhelming majority. There are no Serbs on the map. The Bulgarians assumed that all Slavic-speaking Macedonians were Bulgarians.

Although many Serbian nationalists dispensed with logic and claimed that the Macedonians were 'South Serbs', the more reasonable among them could not bring themselves to claim that the Slavic-speakers of Macedonia were Serbs. The Macedonians spoke a dialect that, while a distinct language, was closer to Bulgarian than to other Balkan languages. Moreover, the Macedonian Slavs were mainly members of the Bulgarian Orthodox Church, which most of them had elected to join once they were given the choice. Therefore, the Serb map identified the Macedonians as a separate people. The alternative would have been to call them Bulgarians.

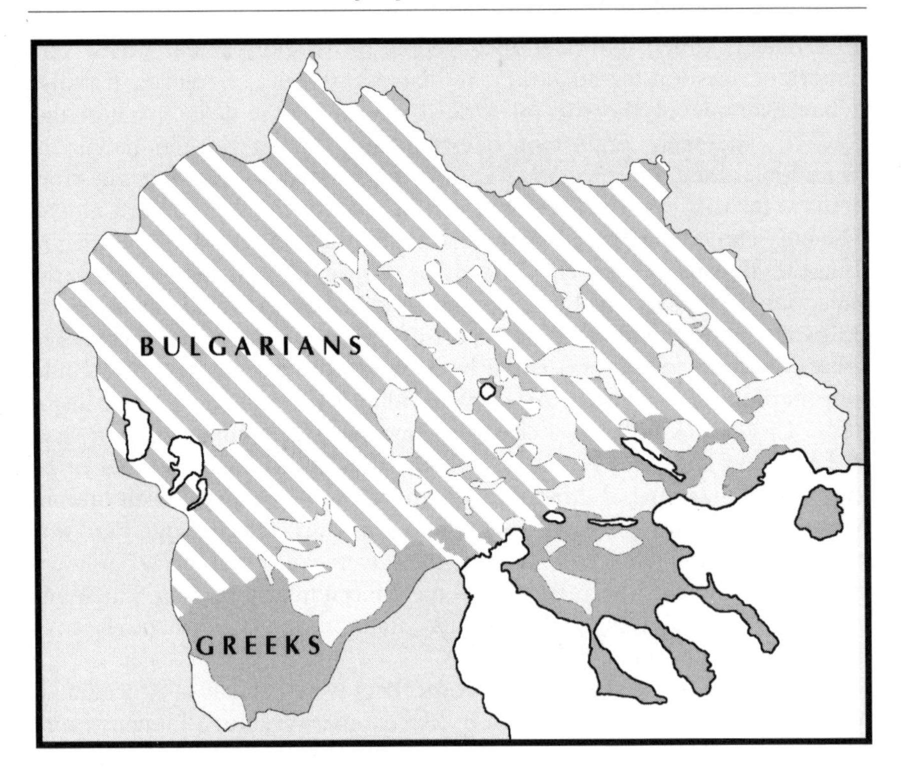

Map 3.3 Macedonia, the Bulgarian view

Instead it was the Bulgarians who disappeared from the map. All the Bulgarian-speakers in Macedonia were listed as Macedonians, divorcing them ethnically from the Bulgarians in Bulgaria. Areas with large numbers of Greek, Turkish, Bulgarian and Albanian-speakers were also identified as either Macedonian or Serb. (More rabid Serbian map-makers simply listed all the Christians and many of the Muslims of Macedonia as 'South Serbs'. After the Serbs conquered the largest section of Macedonia in the Balkan Wars this view triumphed. Macedonians as such then disappeared as a separate people on Serbian maps and in Serbian statistics.)

Serbian nationalists saw the main enemy of Serbian expansion to be Bulgaria, which could claim with some justification that the Macedonians were Bulgarian. Although they claimed 'racial brotherhood', the best Bulgarian justification was religious. The Macedonians were mainly Bulgarian in religion. Like the Orthodox in Bulgaria proper, they had accepted the authority of the Bulgarian Exarchate. This religious identification was never accepted by Serbian statisticians, who preferred 'ethnic' distinctions that they themselves defined. But Serbs also made claims by religion. Albanian-speakers of Orthodox religion were identified, despite all

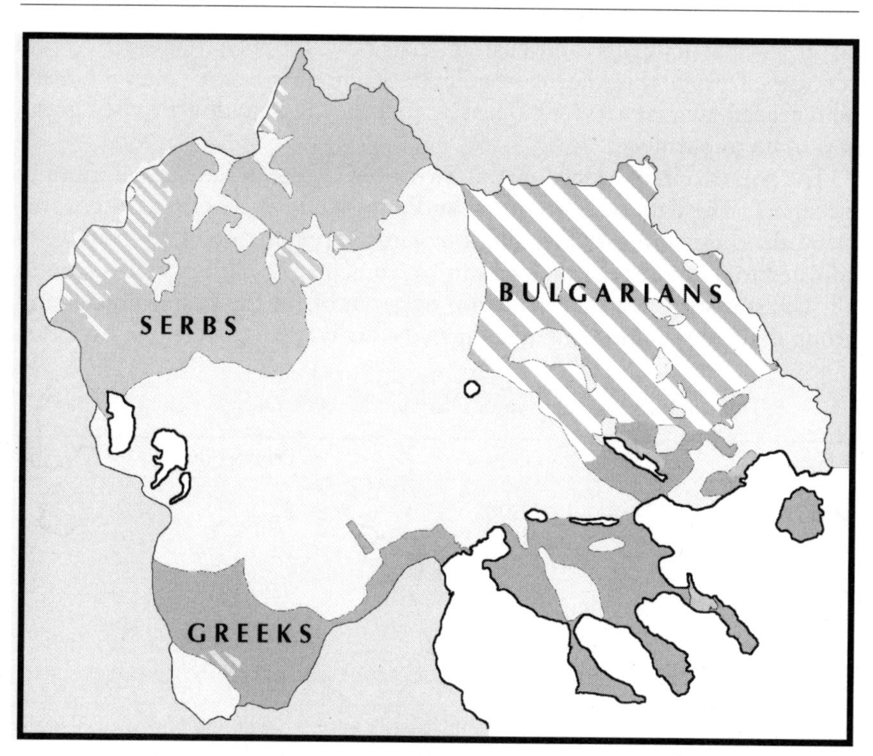

Map 3.4 Macedonia, the Serbian view

historical evidence, as 'Albanian-speaking Serbs'. Of course, the real criteria was 'race'.

The Serbian identification of peoples was later to facilitate the creation of a Greater Serbia, later Yugoslavia, in which different Slavic linguistic groups would be brought together under Serbian leadership or domination, depending on who was describing it.

There is no need for a map of the Greek view of Macedonia, because Greek claims were not based on contemporary ethnicity. The Greek claims were almost totally based on history and racialism, with a small portion of religious identification. In classical times, Macedonia had been tied to Greece or perhaps one could say that under Philip and Alexander Greece was part of Macedonia. Such arguments carried weight in Western Europe and America, but not on the ground in Macedonia. No one with any knowledge of contemporary Macedonian language or culture would have believed the Macedonians to be Greek. Religiously, those who dwelled in Macedonia were either Bulgarian, Muslim or Jewish, with Greek Orthodox concentrated only in the far south and east of Ottoman Europe. Therefore, the Greeks fell back on racial criteria. The Macedonians were supposedly

Greeks whose language and customs had been forcibly changed over the centuries. Despite this, they were still Greeks 'in their hearts', even if Greeks who needed language lessons. The fact that they had no desire to be Greeks was of no importance.

The population of Macedonia, drawn from Ottoman statistics, is given in Table 3.1. The data were recorded and published by the Ottoman government, the only authority actually to count the population. They have been adjusted to allow for the undercount of women and children that is seen in all such statistics, but the correction does not affect the proportion of any group in the population; all are adjusted equally.

Table 3.1 The population of Ottoman Macedonia by religion, 1911

Religion	Population	Proportion (%)
Muslim	1,012,000	42
Greek	514,000	22
Bulgarian	774,000	32
Other	84,000	4
Total	2,384,000	

Source: Justin McCarthy, 'The Population of Ottoman Europe Before and After the Fall of the Empire', in Heath W. Lowry and Ralph S. Hattox (eds), *Proceedings of the Third Conference on the Social and Economic History of Turkey*, Istanbul, 1990, pp. 275–98.

Because Macedonia was not an Ottoman administrative designation, population figures do not fit it perfectly. In any case, no one could agree on the borders of Macedonia. The numbers in the table are for the Ottoman province of Salonica and the sub-provinces (*sancaks*) of Manastır, Dibre and Üsküp. If these hypothetical borders of Macedonia had been advanced north they would have included more Bulgarians, south would have brought in more Greeks, and west would have included more Muslims. No reasonable expansion of the borders much changes the demographic picture – a Muslim plurality, with Bulgarians the largest Christian group.

The real demographic picture of Macedonia was not one the nationalists wished to see. They realized that Ottoman population data carried weight, because they were not self-serving estimates, but actual counts of the population. The nationalists therefore falsified the Ottoman numbers to justify their own claims. Confident that few would ever see real Ottoman statistics, Greek and Bulgarian nationalist and governmental sources published 'Ottoman statistics' to bolster their case that their group was dominant in the population. Strangely, the supposed Ottoman data were completely different depending on who published them. Ottoman data printed by Greeks showed them to be in the majority, while Ottoman data published by the Bulgarians showed the opposite. Data published by different groups supporting the same cause even came up with different numbers for the same year, as if the Ottoman census bureau had taken away a few Greeks or added some in different editions of the same census. Of course, they all were fakes, and all quite different from authentic Ottoman population statistics (Table 3.2).

Table 3.2 Bulgarian, Serbian and Greek statistics on the population of Macedonia

	Bulgarian statistics	Serbian statistics	Greek statistics	Actual population
Turks[a]	499,000	231,000	634,000	1,112,000
Bulgars	1,181,000	57,000	332,000	774,000
Greeks	229,000	201,000	653,000	514,000
Serbs	1,000	2,048,000	—[b]	—[b]

Sources: Carnegie Endowment for International Peace, *Report of the International Commission to Inquire into the Causes and Conduct of the Balkan Wars*, Washington, 1914; Justin McCarthy, 'The Population of Ottoman Europe Before and After the Fall of the Empire', in Heath W. Lowry and Ralph S. Hattox (eds), *Proceedings of the Third Conference on the Social and Economic History of Turkey*, Istanbul, 1990, pp. 275–98.

Notes:
[a] 'Racial' categories as listed, except for last column, which is by religion. The 'Turks' entry there is for Muslims.
[b] Listed under Greeks (i.e. by religion) in the fourth column, probably deliberately excluded in the third.

In the European press and in European chancellories the 'Macedonian Question' was always discussed as a matter of Greeks, Bulgarians and Serbs. The question was which group would get how much of Macedonia. But one searches in vain through reams of diplomatic documents for any mention of the Muslim population and its wishes for Macedonia. The Muslims were in fact the largest religious group in Macedonia. As shown on Map 3.2, a division of Ottoman Europe that respected demographic realities would have awarded much of Macedonia to its Muslim inhabitants.

Nationalism and population

Conflict over Macedonia illustrates one geographic dilemma of Balkan nationalism – everyone wanted the same territory. The nationalists were not willing to accept language, religion, or self-identification of the people who lived in Macedonia as the criteria that would decide their political fate. They knew it was theirs, no matter what opposition might be heard from the inhabitants. However, had the nationalists turned rationalists and decided to adopt a set of identifiable criteria for Macedonia, a major demographic hurdle would still exist.

The great difficulty for any nationalist division of Macedonia or the other regions of the Ottoman Balkans was that the Balkan ethnic groups were not unified geographically. Problems of ethnic identification and settlement in the Ottoman Balkans were actually much more complicated than Serbian, Bulgarian or Greek nationalists admitted. The use of ethnic maps and indeed the whole question of ethnic 'possession' of any region were suspect. The Ottoman Empire in Europe was not neatly divided into ethnic enclaves in which populations were homogenous. Ottoman peoples lived with and among each other. Bulgarians lived in what today is Bulgaria, Greece, Macedonia, Turkey and elsewhere. Greeks lived in all of those places, as well. The Ottoman Balkans were a demographic stew of Bulgarians, Greeks, Serbs, Macedonians, Jews, Vlachs, Albanians and Turks. If the various peoples had ever dwelled only among their own, centuries of migration in a multi-ethnic empire had thoroughly mixed them.

European government intelligence reports and travellers' guidebooks of the Ottoman Balkans described what one might find on roads while riding through the region: 'Turkish village, Bulgarian village, Greek village, Turkish village, mixed Bulgarian and Turkish village, Bulgarian village . . .'. This sort of ethnic and religious intermingling was spread throughout the Ottoman Balkans. There were cities and rural regions that had Greek, Bulgarian or Muslim majorities, but very few totally Bulgarian cities, Greek cities or Muslim cities. Ottoman Europe was a polyglot, multi-ethnic, multi-religious region, often with mixed populations down to the village level. In 1911, before the Balkan Wars, Muslims were probably a slight majority in Ottoman Europe; Ottoman statistics indicated a 51 per cent Muslim population. Even if this was somewhat in error, Muslims were definitely the largest single religious group. Ethnically, the Muslims could be divided into two large non-Slavic groups – Turks and Albanians – and smaller Slavic-speaking groups. There can be no question but that the Balkan Muslims would have chosen to remain within the Ottoman Empire. They were never given the choice. Nationalist expansion did not accept the plebiscite as an expression of the true will of the people. Such matters were to be decided by war.

The intermixing of peoples was the main moral predicament of Balkan nationalism. England, Germany or Italy could become nations by asserting the identity of the mass of people in each country. They spoke the same language. While there were cultural differences by region, the differences were much less than those between the people and those in other countries. English subjects in London, York and Bristol might vary in accents, foods and folklore, but they differed much more from Parisians or Romans. How could national states be created when the different 'nations' did not live apart, but were mixed? The sad answer would be that they could not.

Imperialism and nationalism: Crete

Until the Balkan Wars at the very end of the Ottoman Empire, Balkan nationalism was never able to stand on its own. Assistance from the Great Powers was necessary for national revolution to succeed. Events surrounding rebellion on the island of Crete portray well the interrelation of nationalism and imperialism.

From 1824 to 1840 Crete was ruled by Muhammad Ali, who had received the independent governorship of Crete as payment for his actions in the Greek Independence War. Its population was mainly Greek, with a large Muslim minority. When the British forced Muhammad Ali out of all his governorships except Egypt in 1840, Crete once again became a regular Ottoman province. The success of the Greek revolution had affected Crete, and nationalist uprisings became frequent. An Ottoman law of 1858 gave the Cretan Christians special status and release from many ordinary obligations concerning taxation, to no avail. Further concessions, including the use of Greek as an official language on the island, an advisory assembly, and naming of Greek officials came after revolts in the 1860s. In 1878, reeling from its disastrous war with Russia, the Ottoman Empire was prevailed upon by European pressure to cede effective control of Crete to an elected assembly. The sultan was forced to choose a Christian governor. This too did not end civil disorder. Sultan Abdülhamit II then attempted to stiffen his rule, naming Muslim governors and curtailing the powers of the assembly in 1889.

For a while the Ottoman show of resolution kept relative peace on the island, but the Powers stepped in once again. They forced the sultan to name yet another Christian governor and return power to the local assembly. The situation remained calm until mainland Greece stepped in.

Greek nationalism and irredentism were inseparable from the Greek government. The National Society (Ethniki Hetairia), founded in 1894 to foster the expansion of the Greek state, included among its members three-quarters of the officers in the Greek army. It smuggled arms and fighting men into Crete in preparation for an uprising. Massacres of Cretan Muslims began in February 1896, followed by massacres of Christians. Full-scale rebellion and civil war between the Greek and Muslim communities erupted.

The sultan wished to put the rebellion down with troops, but was willing to make concessions. The Powers, as might be expected, would not allow the military repression of the rebellion, but favoured the concessions. The sultan agreed in August 1896 to give the island much autonomy under a Christian governor, who had to be acceptable to the European Powers. Again, all was to no avail. Aided by agents from Greece, rebels began to fight on Crete once again in 1897. Muslims were attacked and forced to flee from interior villages to the coasts, where they could be protected by Ottoman soldiers.

Feeling in Athens was strong for intervention. The government gave in to it and sent 1500 Greek soldiers to invade Crete. In Europe, especially in England, public opinion, fed by a Grecophile press, came down against the Ottomans. The Powers called on the Ottomans to accept absolute autonomy for Crete and on the Greeks to remove their soldiers from the island. The Ottomans accepted; the Greeks refused. The Greek government said that it would only accept annexation of Crete by Greece as a solution. The Powers then declared a blockade of the island and landed a small number of troops. The rebellion continued, the rebels now fighting European troops.

In Greece itself war fever took over the government. A plan was set afoot to invade the Ottoman Empire. The Greeks would march north and take land including Macedonia. Members of the National Society were armed and sent across the border to act as shock troops. On 17 April 1897 the Greek army attacked the Ottoman Empire.

Militarily, the war of 1897 was a disaster for the Greeks. The Ottomans easily defeated them. Within a month the Greeks were routed; the Greek army collapsed and the Ottomans invaded Greece. The Europeans then stepped in yet again. If the Greeks had won, there can be no doubt that the Ottomans would have been forced to cede territories in Europe, but the Ottomans were to be allowed no such victory. Under European threat, the Ottoman army was required to stop in its advance into Greece. In the ensuing peace treaty, the Ottomans naively demanded territory in Greece. But the Powers had other ideas: in the peace treaty they dictated the Ottomans gained virtually no land and but a small indemnity. The principle of the Europeans was plain: the Ottomans were allowed to lose land, never to gain it.

The Powers still were embroiled in Crete. They dissolved their intervention by demanding the withdrawal of all Turkish troops from the island and naming a new high commissioner to rule Crete, Prince George of Greece, son of the Greek king. In 1908 Crete formally became part of Greece. All of the Muslims of Crete had been expelled.

The Ottoman sultan had given in to the Powers on every point throughout the Crete crisis. He had, it must be admitted, no choice but to abandon the Muslims of the island and had done so. The Greeks had attacked the Ottoman Empire without cause, and had been defeated. The Ottomans had then lost the land that had been the cause of the war. The Ottomans would have lost land if they were defeated in war. They also lost land if they won. In reality, the Ottomans were not only fighting to defend their territories against nationalist separatism and invasion by their neighbours. They were fighting against the European Powers. It was a war the Empire could never win.

4

Ottoman Asia

With the exception of Arabia, nowhere was the Ottoman state as weak as in southeastern Anatolia and northern Iraq. The mountainous terrain, the distance from the centre of the state, and the unwillingness of the peoples of the east to submit to central authority had made governance of the region difficult long before the Ottomans appeared.

The Muslim population of the southeast was primarily Kurdish. Kurds formed a compact population in the Dersim region (southwest of Erzincan), the Van Province, the Diyarbakır Province, and the Mosul Province (northern Iraq), with large groups of Kurds in regions bordering those provinces. The Kurdish population was mainly semi-nomadic tribesmen, answerable only to their own chiefs, but many Kurds were settled farmers and city-dwellers.

The Kurdish tribes were not accustomed to following orders from the government. From the time of Süleyman the Magnificent (ruled 1520–66), when many of the Kurds had been brought under Ottoman suzerainty, the main Ottoman effort had been to keep the Kurds from causing trouble. The government was content to let them alone as long as they did not attack settled areas or disrupt trade. The Ottoman army was only used if Kurdish chiefs revolted and disrupted the east. This had happened most recently in the 1870s. Kurdish tribes were the main factor in civil unrest in the southeast. Never truly under government control, raiding settled populations had long been part of their way of life. Armenians and settled Muslims were the primary victims of Kurdish raids and revolts. Kurdish landlords oppressed both Muslim and Armenian populations.

The Ottoman state attempted to expand its control over remote areas after the 1877–78 Russo-Turkish War. Sultan Abdülhamit II attempted to impose authority over traditionally autonomous Kurdish tribes by an ill-advised attempt at turning their belligerency to the purposes of the state. He created the Hamidiye cavalry in 1891, which was made up of regiments of Kurds, provided with arms, uniforms, and some training by the government. This proved to be the equivalent of a mayor today arming a local

Map 4.1 Provinces of Ottoman Asia in 1912

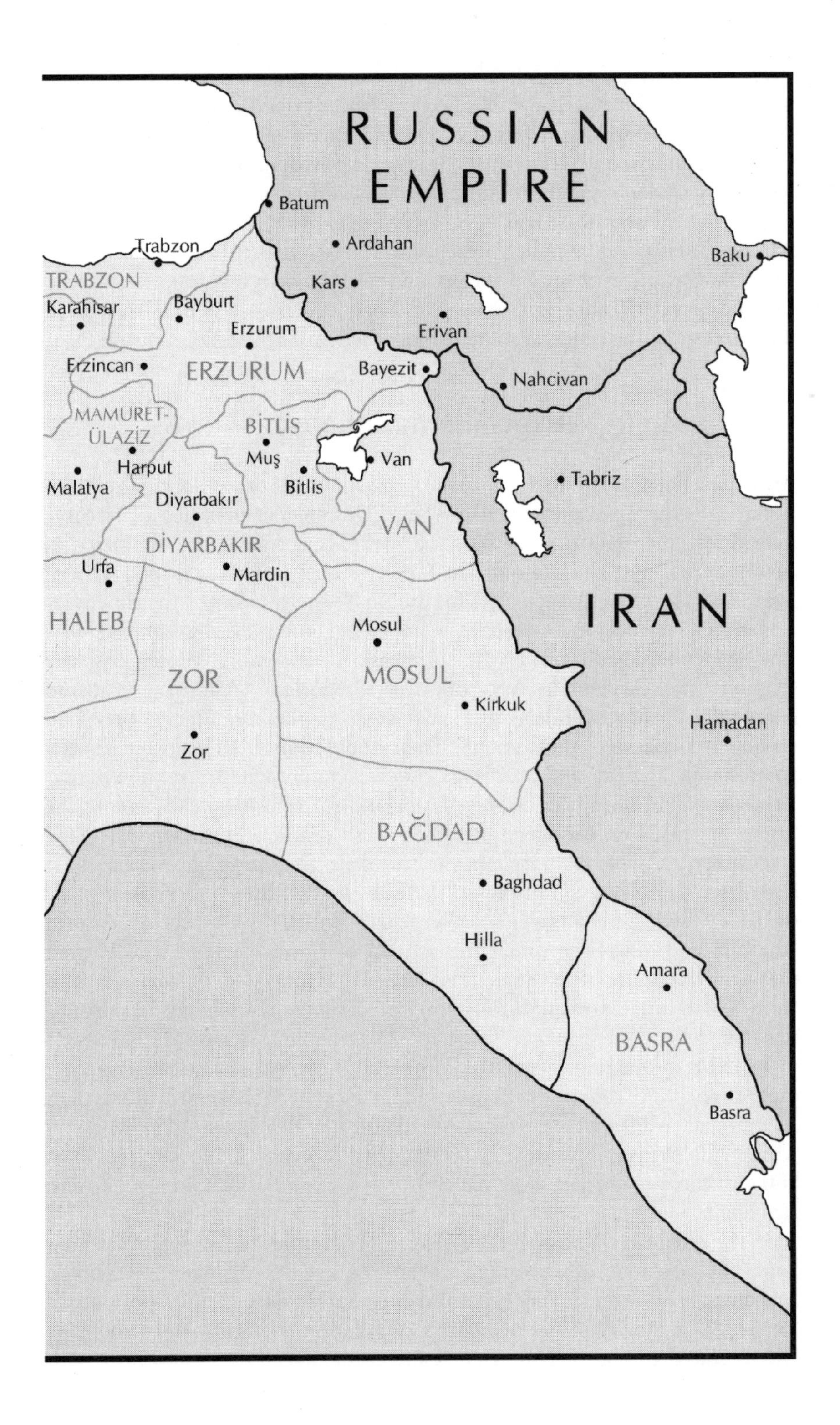

RUSSIAN EMPIRE
Batum
Ardahan
Kars
Erivan
Baku
Trabzon
TRABZON
Karahisar
Bayburt
Erzurum
Erzincan
ERZURUM
Bayezit
Nahcivan
MAMURET-ÜLAZİZ
BİTLİS
Muş
Van
Harput
Malatya
Bitlis
Tabriz
Diyarbakır
VAN
DİYARBAKIR
Urfa
Mardin
IRAN
HALEB
Mosul
ZOR
MOSUL
Kirkuk
Hamadan
Zor
BAĞDAD
Baghdad
Hilla
Amara
BASRA
Basra

street gang and giving them colourful clothes in the hopes that they would become good citizens. The tribes became better armed but no less independent. When Abdülhamit was deposed the experiment was dropped. The CUP government adopted a more practical approach, bringing the Kurdish regiments under regular military control (and of course changing their name), but the southeast was never truly controlled.

Lack of an effective police presence in the east was to work in favour of Kurdish disruption of settled society and of Armenian revolutionaries, who found it easy to organize and smuggle in weapons. It was also to work against the interests of the peaceful population, whether Christian or Muslim.

Armenian nationalism

Armenian nationalists had a difficulty unknown to other national revolutionaries – there were too few of them. Despite the presence of sizeable minorities, the majority in Bulgaria were Bulgarians, the majority in Serbia Serbs, and the majority in Greece Greeks. This was not true of Armenia. The term 'Armenia', a fixture on Western maps of the time, was a historical statement or perhaps a hope, but not a demographic reality. The Armenians had lived in the southeast for millennia. United by their religion (the Armenian Apostolic or Gregorian Church, considered heretical by the Orthodox) and protected by the mountains, they had remained a cohesive ethnic group. Their population distribution in eastern Anatolia in ancient and medieval times is unknown. It is known that Armenians had been leaving their homeland for centuries, even before the Turks appeared on the scene in the eleventh century. Some left to escape civil disorder. The primary reason for their migration, however, must have been the bleak conditions in the east. It was, then and now, a place of rocky soil and inhospitable weather. Politically, much of eastern Anatolia had long been under the control of Kurdish tribes, who treated the Armenians no better than they treated anyone else. It was a region from which inhabitants naturally emigrated. There were better opportunities elsewhere.

In 1911, in one province of the southeast, Bitlis, Armenians were slightly more than 30 per cent of the population; in another, Van, slightly more than 25 per cent. All the other provinces had considerably lower proportions of Armenians. Muslims were a large majority in every Anatolian province. Some of these majorities were Kurdish, most were Turkish, but none were Armenian.

In the northeast, across the Aras River, lay another traditional Armenian land, the province of Erivan (Yerevan), today the Armenian Republic. Armenians had been leaving Erivan so constantly that by 1800, if not much earlier, the majority of the province's population was Turkish. Armenians had migrated and become merchants and craftsmen all over the region, with concentrations of Armenians in Batum and Baku, on both sides of the peninsula, and in other cities.

So what were nationalists to do under such adverse circumstances? The first necessity was to apply force to compel the majority to accept creation of a minority state. The force must come from outside, because a relatively small minority could never hope to come to power on its own. Then there would have to be an expulsion of Muslims and an in-gathering of Armenians. Because there were more Muslims in the area claimed by the Armenian nationalists[1] than there were Armenians in all the world, the expulsion would necessarily be much greater than the gathering.

For outside force the nationalists must necessarily look to Russia. Russian power had forced the creation of independent Serbia, Romania and Bulgaria. Russia was, moreover, the only power whose army was large enough and close enough to defeat the Ottomans in the east. Many Armenian nationalists would have preferred Britain and France, far more progressive states, as a guarantor of their independence, but it had to be accepted that their intervention would be primarily diplomatic. Russia unfortunately gave little indication that it was truly in favour of Armenian independence. When Russia took Erivan in 1828 it did expel Muslims and gather in Armenians, but it insisted on ruling them itself. Nevertheless, Russia could be expected to favour Christians, as it always did, and it was the only hope.

By 1880, the antagonistic separation of the Muslims and Armenians in eastern Anatolia was already well advanced. The original acts in the tragedy that was to unfold between the Armenians and the Muslims had little to do with nationalism. As in the rest of the Middle East and the Balkans, self-identification of peoples was by religion. The concept of 'nation' was unknown. Religion was a sufficient cause for separation, as all the Armenians in the eighteenth and early nineteenth centuries were Armenian Apostolic Christians. Many obviously felt an affinity with Russians, brother Christians. The Russians played on this brotherhood in the region they called Transcaucasia (the region across the Caucasus mountains from Russia, a Russo-centric term that is used here only because of its common currency). Armenian secular and religious officials cooperated with the Russians in their conquest. Armenians fought on the side of the Russians against their rulers in both the Ottoman and Persian empires. They were especially important as spies for the Russians. Correspondingly, Muslims of Transcaucasia and Anatolia fought for the Ottomans and acted as their spies. The sides were being drawn.

The Russians began to conquer Transcaucasia in the late eighteenth century. They annexed the kingdom of Georgia in 1800. In wars against the Persian and Ottoman Empires from 1804 to 1829, they took the regions that today are the Azerbaijan and Armenian Republics, aided by local Armenian forces. Ottoman Armenians assisted the Russians in their invasions of Anatolia in 1855 and 1877. When conditions of peace treaties forced the Russians to leave some of their conquests, tens of thousands of Armenians followed them out of the Ottoman domains. They were replaced by even larger numbers of Muslims forced out of the new Russian conquests. A great forced exchange of population was transpiring. In each war and each forced movement of peoples, hatred and fear of the other increased.

Hatreds in the east were exacerbated by the Russian expulsion of 1.2 million Muslims (the Circassians and Abhazians) from the western Caucasus in the 1860s. One-third of these Muslims were killed or died as a result of their refugee status. The Muslims of the east began to expect that similar treatment was to be expected for them if the Russians took their land. Those viewed as Russian sympathizers were not only considered to be traitors, but potential murderers of Muslims.

Armenian separatists were disappointed by the results of the 1877–78 Russo-Turkish War. During the war, Russia had conquered much of the region called Armenia. In the Treaty of San Stephano, imposed on the defeated Ottomans in 1878, the Russians had claimed northeast Anatolia (the Kars–Ardahan–Batum region) for themselves, with no accommodation of Armenian national claims within the new Russian territories. The Armenian Patriarch of Constantinople, Nerses, had asked the Russians to create an Armenia, but had come away empty-handed. In the treaty, the Ottomans were only enjoined to put in place 'reforms' in the east. The Treaty of Berlin, which superseded the San Stephano agreement, gave back some territory in the east to the Ottomans, but gave none to the Armenians. Obviously, depending on Russian action alone would not give Armenian separatists what they wanted.

The answer was to organize an Armenian revolution that would draw in the Powers and create an Armenia, or at least take it from the Ottomans.

Support for the revolution

Revolutionary nationalism of Christian peoples in the Ottoman Empire always drew significant support from Western Europeans and Americans. The Western public seldom knew any of the details of life or politics in the Ottoman Empire, but they believed that Christians should never be ruled by Muslims. Centuries of prejudice against Muslims had its effect, as did newspaper accounts that always told one side of a complicated relationship among Muslims, Christians and the government. However, this affection for Christian nationalism seldom translated into effective support for Armenian revolution. Religious groups in the West were to wring their hands at Armenian suffering, ignoring completely suffering caused by Armenians. Governments were to demand, somewhat half-heartedly, Ottoman reforms in the east. None sent guns or ammunition.

True support for Armenian nationalist revolution came directly only from the Russians and indirectly from American missionaries. The American Board of Commissioners for Foreign Missions sent its first missionaries to the Middle East in 1819. Conversion of Muslims and Jews to Christianity proved impossible. Orthodox Christians, with few exceptions, refused to adopt Protestant belief. Only Armenians accepted Protestantism in any number, despite strong opposition from the hierarchy of the Armenian Gregorian Church. Even the majority of Armenians, never to become Protestant, were willing to take advantage of the one practical benefit brought by the missionaries: a good education. The Ottoman government was willing to accept foreign schools, even those that educated only Christian minorities, in the hope that improved educational methods would filter through to the entire society. Missionaries from the American Board, mainly Congregationalists, increased from 2 in 1819 to 34 in 1845, 146 in 1880, and 209 in 1913. By 1913 they were educating 26,000 students in 450 schools, mainly Armenians in Anatolia. (Other missionaries, from the Presbyterian Church, were active in Syria.)

American missionaries provided the education of Ottoman Armenians. Few Armenians went to state schools; the education in the American schools was superior. This naturally emphasized the separation of the Armenians from the other communities in the Empire. The improved American teaching methods, which included commercial training as well as academic subjects, built Armenian mercantile expertise and, ultimately, wealth. The missionaries sponsored Armenian students in America and facilitated Armenian migration to America, from where immigrants sent money home. Improvements in their opportunities helped to raise the Armenians above the Muslims economically, which also aided separatism.

The missionaries did not preach Armenian nationalism; their proselytizing was directed at different ends. Indeed, they were aghast at the violent actions of the revolutionaries. The missionaries nevertheless contributed greatly to the development of nationalism. They unquestionably taught Christian superiority. Missionary writings make it obvious that they firmly believed that Christians would not only be the ones who were saved but also would be better businessmen, thinkers, and of course rulers. The provision of an American education to Armenians, but not to Muslims, did make the Armenians more literate and more educated, which cannot but have heightened feelings of superiority. The American schools also became gathering places for revolutionary students, the backbone of any revolution.

The other missionary contribution to the cause of Armenian nationalism and revolution lay in missionary propaganda in the Western nations. The missionaries were in complete sympathy with the aims of Armenian nationalism. Throughout the nineteenth and into the twentieth century, missionaries and their supporters flooded the English-speaking countries with pro-Armenian, anti-Turkish propaganda. This became a great contribution to feelings against the Ottomans in the West. Again, missionary writings leave no doubt that they felt it morally wrong for Christians ever to be under non-Christian rule. (It should be noted that few missionaries felt that self-rule was necessary, just Christian rule. Therefore many accepted Russian imperialism. This separated them from outright Armenian nationalists.)

Russian intent in supporting Armenian revolutionaries is obvious. The tsar's government was in disagreement with almost all of the avowed principles of the parties. The parties' socialist orientation (described below) was surely anathema to the Russian government. The Russians had no intention of ever accepting an independent Armenia, either in Transcaucasia or in Anatolia. The Russians' treatment of Armenian nationalists was thus ambivalent, sometimes arresting them, at other times providing arms. Russian support was directed against the Ottomans. It involved more than a bit of hypocrisy. At the same time as they were demanding national self-expression for the Ottoman Armenians, for example, the Russians were closing the Armenian schools in their Empire. But any disturbance in eastern Anatolia could only benefit Russian long-term plans to annex the region to their Empire, so the revolutionaries could usually depend on the Russians to at least look the other way as they organized and smuggled guns. The Russians knew that the Armenians would be useful allies in the war that the Russians were sure would come. The Hunchak programme, for example, stated that the best time for Armenian revolution was when the Ottoman Empire was at war. This could only have brought joy to the Russian Ministry of War.

Revolutionary societies

In the 1860s and 1870s Armenian revolutionary groups had begun to appear in the east and in Istanbul. While unsuccessful in their primary goal, they did raise the 'revolutionary consciousness' of Armenians in the east. Attempts were made to gain Russian financial and military support for Armenian communities, particularly in Van and Zeytun (a mountainous region in which the Armenians were virtually autonomous). Except in Zeytun, where the Armenians held off an Ottoman army sent to assert state authority, nationalist activities before 1878 had little effect. More effective revolutionary organizations began to form after the Armenians' disappointments of 1878.

Three Armenian revolutionary parties were to take the lead in organizing revolution. The first, the Armenakan Party, was founded by young Armenians in Van in 1885. Avowedly revolutionary, its programme stressed the need for nationalist organization and arming its adherents.[2]

The second group, the Hunchakian Revolutionary Party (Hunchaks) followed a time-tested method of organization – creating an organization among students and émigrés in Europe, then exporting the revolution to Anatolia. The founders were all Russian Armenians. None had ever lived in the Ottoman Empire. Founded in Geneva in 1887, the Hunchak programme chose terror as the essence of the organization. The programme called for the assassination of both Turks and Armenians who stood against the nationalist cause, as well as terrorist acts that would weaken Ottoman control and convince the Armenians that the cause would be successful. Although the revolution was to begin in Ottoman Armenia, the Hunchaks distrusted the Russians and specifically warned that Russian imperialism was a danger to the movement. This was unique among the Armenian revolutionary movements, and it naturally cost them Russian support. The party was Marxist, much affected by Russian revolutionaries who were in contact with the Hunchaks. It aimed at a democratic and socialist Armenia. From Europe, Hunchak organizers were sent first to Istanbul, where they had considerable success among young educated Armenians, then to the cities in the east.

The third and ultimately most successful of the revolutionary parties was organized at first among the Armenians in the Russian Empire. A number of Armenian nationalist organizations were founded among the Armenian intelligentsia in Russia. Moscow, St Petersburg, and cities in Transcaucasia, places where there were Armenian students, became centres of organizations that ranged from debating societies to armed insurgents. The Dashnaktsuthian Party (Dashnaks, the Federation of Armenian Revolutionaries, after 1892 the Armenian Revolution Federation) was founded in Tiflis in 1890 as an umbrella revolutionary organization by members of earlier parties. After disagreements with the Hunchaks and with more conservative revolutionaries, the Dashnaks finally became an officially socialist revolutionary organization, a member of the Second International. The Dashnak programme dedicated the group to the importation of arms and men into the Ottoman Empire and to the use of terror and the looting and destruction of Ottoman government installations to further the revolution. The programme was not much different from that of the Hunchaks in fact, although Dashnak public statements were more moderate.

The Armenian revolutionaries were much affected by the recent events in Bulgaria. There a small group of revolutionaries had killed large numbers of Muslims, drawing retaliation and an even greater number of Bulgarian dead. Finally Russia had intervened, causing mass expulsion and death among the Bulgarian Muslims and the creation of a new Bulgarian state. This was seen as an effective plan, if one that regrettably necessitated the loss of a number of Armenians. The most well known expression of this plan was recorded by the American missionary educator Cyrus Hamlin, no friend of the Turks:

> One of the revolutionaries told Dr. Hamlin, the founder of Robert College, that the Hentchak [Hunchak] bands would 'watch their opportunity to kill Turks and Koords, set fire to their villages, and then make their escape into the mountains. The enraged Moslems would

> then rise, and fall upon defenceless Armenians and slaughter them with such barbarity that Russia will enter in the name of humanity and Christian civilization and take possession.' When the horrified missionary denounced the scheme as atrocious and infernal beyond anything ever known, he received this reply: 'It appears so to you, no doubt; but we Armenians have determined to be free. Europe listened to the Bulgarian horrors and made them free. She will listen to our cry when it goes up in the shrieks and blood of millions of women and children. . . . We are desperate. We shall do it.'[3]

The demographic and geographic differences between Bulgaria and eastern Anatolia seem not to have entered into the plan.

At first, the plan seemed to be working. Armenians of the Sasun region had real grievances against Kurdish chiefs, who had long collected illegal tribute from them. Hunchak revolutionaries took advantage of Armenian feelings to organize the populace, and a guerrilla war ensued. In 1894 Armenian bands expanded their activities to attack Ottoman tax-collectors and other officials. The Ottomans responded with the army, which pursued the Armenian bands. As the bands withdrew, they slaughtered the Muslim inhabitants of the villages in their path. The army and especially the Hamidiye Kurdish irregulars then slaughtered Armenians. In 1895 the Hunchak Party led another rebellion, this time in Zeytun. It spread throughout the region of Zeytun and Maraş. The Armenian leader of the rebellion claimed an exaggerated 20,000 Muslims had been killed by his rebels. The Ottoman army defeated the rebels with much difficulty, killing uncounted numbers of rebels and civilians. In an Armenakan-led revolt in Van in 1896, an estimated 400 Muslims and 1700 Armenians died.

Assassinations and attacks on government offices in the east further inflamed the Muslim populace, but without the results seen in Sasun and Zeytun. An Armenian attack on the Ottoman Bank in Istanbul, an Armenian bombing campaign in the capital, and subsequent riots resulted in more Armenian deaths than Muslim. The attempted assassination of Sultan Abdülhamit II in the same year killed twenty police guards, but led to no attacks. The revolutionary plan had failed.

All had gone according to the revolutionary script except for European intervention. The British and the Russians had both protested at Muslim actions against Armenians, forgetting as always the deaths of Muslims. The kings and prime ministers were in general agreement that Sultan Abdülhamit II should be forced from the throne. Many felt it to be the time for dissolving and dividing the Ottoman Empire. Their protests remained diplomatic, however. They simply did not trust each other. The British put forth plans to sail their fleet through the Dardanelles, depose the sultan, and accede to Armenian demands. Russia felt it had great influence on the Ottomans and did not wish to see it replaced with British, French, Austrian or international control. The Russians had their own pending plans for

Istanbul, plans which did not include the British putting a sultan friendly to the British on the throne. Russia might have been willing to agree to an occupation of Istanbul, but only if she were left with effective control of the Straits, something the British were unwilling to concede. The Austrians, seeing nothing in it for them but strengthened enemies, were opposed to any action. France was afraid that a British–Russian dismemberment of the Ottoman Empire would leave nothing for her. European banks, especially French ones, had heavy and lucrative commitments in the Empire, which they did not wish to see lost. In the end, none of the European powers was willing to go to war with the Ottoman Empire or each other. Bulgaria in 1877 had been a different matter: Austria had been bought off by possession of Ottoman Bosnia; Britain had been constrained by the 'Bulgarian Horrors'. In the 1890s, Russia had little to offer Austria, Britain or France for their cooperation. Russia was still seen as the main potential danger to the European balance of power. Not until the next decade would increasing German power cause the British to look to Russia as an ally.

Perhaps the mistake of the Armenian revolutionaries had been to believe the rhetoric of the Europeans. They *may* have believed that the European Powers sincerely cared about the situation of the Armenians and were committed to Armenian independence. But 'may' is the operant word, because it is hard to understand how anyone could have observed Russia's past actions and still believed in her altruism. Public opinion in Europe was indeed concerned about the Armenians, but the governments were far more concerned with the balance of power and their own interests.

Ottoman Muslims and nationalism

Understandably, Muslim peoples were the last to be touched by nationalism. Nationalism flourishes when groups feel that they are not empowered. The Muslims of the Empire had for centuries been considered to be the First Community by themselves and the government. Until the very end of the Empire they had not held much actual power, but nationalism is a thing of perception, not reality. Bulgarian, Serbian or Armenian nationalists did not wish to be ruled by Turks. This was not a problem for Turks.

The glue holding the Muslims of the Empire together was Islam. The Ottoman Empire was an Islamic Empire, the last in a long line of religious states extending back to the Umayyads. Loyalties and self-identification of the people, whether Muslim, Christian or Jewish, were primarily religious. To develop an Arab or a Turkish nationalism would be to turn one's back on history and religion. Nevertheless, there were some tentative attempts at Arab and Turkish nationalism. They had little effect on the Empire, but their influence was to be felt later.

It is easy to see expressions of ethnicity among Turks, Arabs or Kurds and call them nationalism, but in fact there was very little true nationalism among the Muslim linguistic and ethnic groups of the Ottoman Empire. It is important to make this distinction. As nationalism has been used here it is the belief that a 'people', however defined, should have a state, and the willingness to do something about it. Have linguistic revival, ethnic identification, etc. often led to active nationalism, i.e. revolution? Yes. The nationalisms of the Christian groups of Ottoman Europe began with literary revivals and study of historical myths and folk customs, then gradually evolved to revolutions. Is such an evolution to revolutionary violence preordained and unstoppable? No. If that were so, countries such as the United States, with their myriads of much-loved ethnic traditions, could never exist. It is possible to love one's own religion, language and literature, ethnic food, folk dance, and music, yet still be content to be a part of a state that has no particular interest in those things.

Turkish nationalism

The Ottoman Empire was known as Turkey in America and Europe long before that name was ever used by the Turks themselves. The people called 'Turks' by Europeans and others were often actually non-Turkish Ottoman Muslims. In fact, the Europeans had it backward. The Ottoman Empire was not Turkish in the way France was French or Germany German. Members of the traditional Ottoman ruling class could definitely be called Turkish only in that they knew Ottoman Turkish, itself a literary and court language quite different from the 'common Turkish' spoken on the farms of Anatolia. They might be from any of the varied ethnic groups of the Empire – Turks, Arabs, Bosnians, Albanians, etc. The governmental system was also Turkish in that it identified itself with a history that traced back through the Seljuk empires to Central Asia. This was not an ethnic, and surely not a nationalistic, identification. In the nineteenth century, Christians who took high office in the government, including foreign minister, were never thought of as Turks, although they were surely dedicated Ottoman subjects.

Recognizing the benefits of nationalism in organizing a state and claiming the loyalty of its peoples, the Tanzimat government made attempts to create an Ottoman nationality. The Young Ottomans followed in aspiring to make such an identification the basis of loyalty to a constitutional state. It never worked. The non-Muslims of the Empire were used to identifying themselves separately, first by millet, then by nation. They had no wish to partake of an artificial Ottoman nationalism. Christians might be loyal subjects, but not because of emotional commitments to an Ottoman Nation. Those who could be said to be 'patriots' were mainly Muslims, and their loyalties were to Islam, as embodied in the Islamic Empire.

As the Empire became less formally Islamic, the loyalty of the Muslims might have been expected to change, but this was not the case. Most Muslims could have had little realization of changes in the character of government. The judicial system was less Islamic, but villagers settled their disputes themselves, seldom resorting to any kind of formal law. Pious foundations were now governed by secular officials, but for the masses the only concern was whether the foundations still operated soup kitchens for the poor and saw to the upkeep of mosques. To the people it was still an Islamic Empire.

Turkish nationalism arose slowly among the literati, those who had contacts with European thought. Initial impetus came from non-Turkish European scholars who began the study of Turkish language and history, sometimes with a decidedly racialist strain to their work. They began to write of a Turanian people, a racial grouping that included Turks in the Ottoman Empire, Central Asian Turks, Mongols, and often Hungarians and Finns. Central Asian Turks, refugees to the Ottoman Empire from Russian domination, carried with them the idea that the Turks were brothers, separated by politics and history, but the same people. This ideology, pan-Turkism, began to have a cachet in Istanbul literary circles in the late nineteenth century. Histories and dictionaries that emphasized purely Turkish history and language began to appear. The effects of this on the mass of the people and the state were slight. Istanbul literary fashions did not carry far beyond the large cities of the Empire. Abdülhamit had little time for an ideology that would separate some of his subjects from others. His efforts were more toward pan-Islam, which held up his own position as caliph and spiritual leader of even those Muslims he did not rule.

Nationalism played a part in the Young Turk secret society, although the ideology of the Committee of Union and Progress was generally Ottoman, rather than Turkish. This began to change as fortune turned against the Empire in the Balkan Wars. Typical of the times, Ziya (later Ziya Gökalp), the philosopher of Turkish nationalism, joined the Young Turk movement in 1896. He did not originally see any conflict between Ottomanism and Turkish nationalism, but began to stress 'Turkism' much more after the defeat in the Balkans. Differing considerably from most Balkan nationalisms, that of Ziya was not racialist. He believed one became a part of the nation through education in its values, not through 'blood' or 'spirit'. While refreshing intellectually, this belief was potentially dangerous to the beliefs and identities of non-Turkish nationalists in the Empire. Racialist nationalists held that one either was or was not a part of the nation, based on ancestry. Ziya's nationalism allowed the expansion of the nation, just as the early Turks had expanded their ethnic group, by adoption. Ziya and his followers did not press this issue, although Arab nationalists surely knew it might someday adversely affect them. Rather they began to identify and 'purify' the Turkish element. They advocated the Turkification of language, using Turkish words, not Arabic or Persian, and the culture of the Turks of Anatolia, not the high culture of Istanbul. Society was to be changed to emulate real or imagined customs from the Turkish past. This meant a good deal of real reform – real democracy and political participation, completely secular courts, equality for women, including an end to polygamy, and a nationalized Islam reduced to basic principles and then merged with Turkish customs and language.

Ziya was a member of the executive council of the Committee of Union and Progress and a widely respected educator, the first professor of sociology at Istanbul University. His opinions carried weight and drew adherents within the CUP. There was a natural appeal in a Turkish nationalism to match the nationalisms of others. In 1912, Turkish Hearth Societies began to appear in the Empire and soon greatly multiplied in schools and government bureaux, aided by elements of the CUP. These taught the purified Turkish and the Turkish values of the nationalists, bringing to the hinterland what had been essentially an ideology of the intelligentsia. However, the Ottoman Empire was still a multi-ethnic empire, even after the losses of the Balkan Wars. Kurds, Arabs and many smaller ethnic groups made up half the population. Nationalists within the CUP were always constrained by the need not to alienate non-Turks. Nevertheless, the state did pass some nationalist initiatives, especially during World War I when the use of the Turkish language in government and education was expanded.

The period of CUP rule experienced a confusion of ideologies, none of which adequately identified the government or the ruling party. It was a time during which the bases of Ottoman political ideology were being rethought. Ottoman nationalism, Turkish nationalism, pan-Islamic beliefs, and practical politics all existed side by side, often two or more in the same head. After the Balkan Wars the CUP government definitely took action against adherents of nationalisms that they viewed as threats to the state. Some of these actions were very hard-edged: a boycott of Greek businesses in western Anatolia was accompanied by threats and coercion that forced the emigration of Greeks; Arab nationalists were hung during World War I. Other actions were long needed, such as the abolition of the Capitulations in 1914, when the Europeans were too busy with their war to take action, and the state fostering of Muslim businesses. Such actions were not so much Turkish nationalist as pro-Ottoman. It does not take nationalist ideology to persecute perceived enemies or advance the cause of friends. The government fostered intellectual expressions of Turkism, but the leaders of the state were no ideologues. They were practical men who viewed political and economic success as their ideology.

Turkish nationalism is sometimes portrayed as the driving force behind Turkish actions in World War I. This is not even a half-truth. It is true that Enver Paşa and others harboured fanciful plans to unite with Turks under Russian rule, but these were in no sense the reason the Ottomans went to war (see Chapter 6). Nor was nationalism the emotional force that sustained Turks in battle. The Ottoman army did not cry 'Glory to the Nation' or 'Turks Forever' as it went into battle. It cried 'Allahu Akbar' ('God is Great'), as had the Muslim armies before it. Nevertheless, nationalism has commonly been forged in an atmosphere of conflict with adversaries demonstrably different from oneself – 'us versus them'. The Ottoman Empire from 1912 to 1922 was surely a place of conflict between Turks and others. It would be strange indeed if this did not lead to the development of nationalism among the Turks.

The Kurds

Nationalism was not an understood concept for the second largest ethnic group of Anatolia, the Kurds. Those Kurds who were under the leadership of tribal chiefs felt loyalty to those chiefs and to leaders (*sheikh, şeyh*) of mystical religious sects. A long history of revolt against central authority demonstrates that these Kurds felt little loyalty for the sultan and none at all for the government. Like the Arabs of the desert, to be seen below, Kurdish tribal leaders opposed the centralizing efforts of the CUP government. They had no wish to lose their authority to the government. This did not cause them to unite with other tribes in a common goal. Kurds in other tribes were occasional allies, occasional enemies, but no more. To speak of any sort of nationalism, or even ethnic identity, in such circumstances would be absurd.

The other Kurds, those of the cities and those villages more or less independent of tribal control, were much like Turks in their relation to the state. Loyalties were to the sultan and religion. Some Kurds, like the immigrants to Istanbul who set up a school for Kurds, identified with their home region and ethnic group even after being integrated into Ottoman urban society. This was also true of other ethnic groups, such as the Circassians or Muslim Georgians, as well as for Turks who organized themselves by their region of origin when they came to the city. Such organization indicates no particular disloyalty (or loyalty) to the state.

Nationalism in the Arab provinces

It is difficult to speak of Arab nationalism within the Ottoman Empire. The self-identification of the Ottoman Arabs was based on religion and locality. First was religion. As with other Middle Easterners, Islam provided the primary identity of most Arabs. Arabs of other religions felt the separation from the dominant community and if anything felt even more identified by the beliefs. Next came locality. Self-identification was local, from village to city. Since few people were mobile and most lived close to their birthplace, the question of identification seldom arose. When it did, the answer was religious or local. An Arab might consider himself 'a Muslim from Damascus', for example, not a Syrian, an Ottoman subject, or even an Arab. The Ottoman Arabic-speaking Middle East could have been divided by economic sub-units centred on Damascus, Aleppo and Baghdad, for example, but these were not units to which the inhabitants owed a particular loyalty. Tribes also held the primary allegiance of many, and not only the bedouin of the desert. Not even Islam was a completely unifying force. Sunni Muslims were a majority, but there were also Shia Muslims and groups considered heterodox by both Sunni and Shia.

Through most of Ottoman history, Arabs had been largely autonomous within their own provinces. The Ottomans did send out governors to rule and Janissaries to enforce the governors' authority, but this authority did not run very far. In practice, outside of major cities real authority was in the hands of local notables. In the cities, Ottoman authority was constantly being subverted by the assimilation of imperial forces to local power structures. In eighteenth-century Damascus, for example, the Janissaries had settled down, begun businesses, and become one faction in local power struggles. Their sons became Janissaries, inherited their fathers' power, and perpetuated the Janissaries position in the local power structure. Such 'imperial' troops were not representing the wishes of the Istanbul government.

For the government the most important question in the Arab provinces was the delivery of taxes. Much could be tolerated as long as the funds needed to pay for wars against Austria and Russia arrived in Istanbul. Imperial attention was necessarily focused on imminent danger to the survival of the state. Only if autonomy turned into rebellion would the state attempt to take definite action, and this did not often work. Through much of the eighteenth and early nineteenth centuries Syria and Iraq remained in the hands of virtually independent, sometimes entirely rebellious governors.

It was not until well into the nineteenth century that Ottoman military reforms gave the central government enough power to reassert its authority. Even then, most local matters were settled locally. Ottoman reformers undoubtedly would have liked to have intervened more definitely into the Arab provinces, but they were busy elsewhere with wars and with the first applications of reform in the European and western Anatolian provinces. Correspondingly, until late in the nineteenth century Arab notables were not much represented in Istanbul. The traditional Ottoman system, with its emphasis on an almost hereditary bureaucracy and military, did not afford many openings to power in the capital. At home, however, Arab notables held real power. The weak beginnings of Arab nationalism came when the Ottomans appeared to be asserting central authority beyond the traditional level.

Most Arabs had good reason to wish for the continuation of the Ottoman state. For Muslims, it was the Islamic Empire. They might be displeased at the Empire's increasing secularization, but it remained the only significant Muslim state and the only possible bulwark against domination by Christian Europeans. Interestingly, the Empire had appeal for many Arab Christians precisely because of its secularization. They could foresee that an Arab state would be a much more orthodox Muslim land, with fewer opportunities for non-Muslims. With the exception of the Maronites in Lebanon, the Christians were not numerous enough to have any hope for their own state. All Christian denominations together made up less than 20 per cent of the population of Ottoman Syria, and they did not like each other well enough to cooperate, in any case. Iraq's Christian population was even less significant.

Before World War I, true Arab nationalists, those who wished to carve an Arab state from the Ottoman Empire, were very few. There was, however, a drive among Arab intellectuals for what might be called cultural autonomy. Arabism, as it has been called, had various manifestations. Some stressed loyalty to Islam and its Arab roots. Others, including Arab Christians, looked to the greater body of Arabs as a people whose history, culture and language deserved respect. Still others were loyal to their regions, such as Syria. Nearly all of the Arabists saw no contradiction in being both Arabists and Ottomanists.

Syria

As in other regions of the Empire, Tanzimat centralization ended much of the *de facto* autonomy in the provinces of Ottoman Syria. Improvement in communications and in the state's military power made governors less independent. State schools began to take the place of traditional education, their graduates becoming bureaucrats and others whose education afforded them power independent from the traditional authority of the Arab notables. At the same time, with the arrival of more bureaucrats from Istanbul, imposing new rules, the government became more noticeably 'Turkish'. The new state schools taught in Turkish, and cases before the new courts were tried in Turkish, necessitating translators for Arabic-speakers. Newly arrived officials often did not speak Arabic well. While this little affected the mass of the Arab subjects of the sultan, it did create tension within the new politically minded intelligentsia, often the graduates of the new schools.

American missionaries provided a notable, if largely unintended impetus to Arab nationalism. The schools operated by Presbyterians afforded an excellent education to Arabs in their own language. At the university level, the missionaries taught Muslims as well as Christians. Many of the founders of a nineteenth-century literary revival of the Arabic language were employed by the American missionaries or encouraged by them. The printing press brought by the Americans was a source for the dissemination of Arabic literature and history that had faded from popular memory. As such, it advanced the consciousness among Arabs of the worth of their culture, a precursor of nationalism. Many of those who were to be at the forefront of Arabist movements were graduates of the American schools.

Like nationalist movements in the Balkans, the beginnings of Arab awareness of their separate character can be said to have begun with a literary renaissance. It stressed the greatness of the Arab past and, although often unstated, the inferior place of the Arabs in modern times. This was necessarily a movement of the educated elite, some of whom translated this feeling of Arab separatism into a call for more political autonomy for the Arabs. Beginning around 1880, very small groups began to meet in ephemeral secret societies that went further, calling for Arab independence. What seems to have been the first of these nationalist secret societies was made up of graduates and students of the Syrian Protestant College (later the American University of Beirut). In keeping with the tradition of nationalist groups, Arab separatists also organized in Europe. All of these movements, however, were small and seem to have had little impact on Arab society as a whole.

The reign of Abdülhamit saw little expression of Arab separatism, perhaps because the image of Abdülhamit as a pious sultan had its effect in the Arab world, as did his espousal of pan-Islam, the doctrine calling for unification of the world's Muslims. The sultan also gave attention to the economic needs of the Arabs. While the Hijaz Railway was a symbol of the power of the Empire and the importance of Islam, it also was an economic boon for Syria. Abdülhamit's administration supervised transport construction such as had never been seen before in the Arab world – more than a thousand kilometres of rail line and hundreds of kilometres of new and modernized macadam roads in Syria, and modern ferry services on the Tigris and Euphrates in Iraq. Increased military protection from bedouin and bandits allowed a tremendous increase in cultivated land. Modernized ports such as Beirut, Haifa and Iskenderun (Iskandarun) and an improved economy allowed exports from cities on the Mediterranean coast to rise by 50 per cent. Abdülhamit also had the good fortune not to fight a major war that drew Arab soldiers to fight away from their homes, a thing that caused disaffection both before and after his reign.

The government of the Committee of Union and Progress did not enjoy such goodwill. Much of the complaint was directed at symbols. Under the CUP government, Turkish was made the official language of the Empire. Even though Ottoman Turkish had always been the administrative language in fact, the symbolism irked many. Government schools taught in Turkish, which they had under Abdülhamit and before, but now it became an irritant. Some bureaucrats (the percentage is unknown) did not speak Arabic, but again this was as it had always been. Perhaps the fact that there were more bureaucrats in the new system caused rancour. For Arabs who had supported the CUP before its revolution, the results of the revolt were unsatisfactory. The CUP leadership never allowed them into its inner circles of power. A feeling of Turkish superiority was easily detected among the CUP leadership. The organization of the Turkish Hearth Societies across the Empire after 1912 signalled that Turkish nationalism was on the rise. Such happenings would probably have led to conflict if the Empire had survived. As it was, too little time remained for much opposition to develop.

It is doubtful whether most Arabs much cared about any of this. A significant group of intellectuals, however, began to express their ill feeling. Arabist newspapers multiplied, enjoying a fairly wide circulation. Public societies began to call openly for increased autonomy, including the required official use of Arabic and more local authority. Secret societies, almost surely of very limited membership (although, being secret, their numbers were unknown), agitated for substantial autonomy, even independence, to little effect. More prominent were Arab members of the 1908 Ottoman parliament, many of whom opposed the CUP. They were concerned by what they perceived as government laxity with Zionist settlement in Palestine and wanted more cultural and linguistic autonomy for Arab provinces, but not independence. The Arabists within and without the parliament were also worried about the dangers of European domination. They saw recognition of cultural autonomy and limited political autonomy as actions that would make the Empire stronger against its adversaries.

Were the stirrings of Arabism true nationalism? Very few of them. Unlike the Bulgarian or Armenian nationalists and the few in Arab secret societies, the Arabists called for differing degrees of autonomy, not independence. Few seem to have been willing to express even those feelings. What they wanted was responsive government and improved status within the Empire. Their main interests were the use of Arabic in schools and administration, local government in which more of the officials were Arabs, and an end to a military policy that moved Arab conscripts to other parts of the Empire. When they opposed 'Turkism', both real and imagined, they were likely to wish to replace it with Ottomanism or Islamic solidarity within the Empire. Though Arabists might oppose use of Arab soldiers in 'foreign' wars, Arabs volunteered and were conscripted in both the Balkan Wars and World War I without mutiny.

During World War I Cemal Paşa, the CUP leader who had become the governor-general of the Syrian provinces, adopted a carrot-and-stick policy toward Syria. The carrot was construction of schools and roads. It was not a time, though, when such things were properly appreciated. More important concerns occupied the Arabs, specifically conscription of their men for the Ottoman army, always a sore spot, and the possibility that the Ottomans would lose and the Empire be finally divided. Many Arab officers in the Ottoman army organized into a secret society that at least contemplated Arab independence. Arab notables also began to meet to consider their options. Some went so far as to communicate with the British and French and with the rebel sharif of Mecca. To them this was undoubtedly prudence. Planning what to do if the Empire dissolved was not the same as acting to hasten the Empire's demise. To Cemal Paşa it was treason. It is hard to see how else he could have defined it, but he most likely exaggerated the danger. He applied the stick: in 1915, 11 were hanged in Beirut and a number were arrested and banished to Anatolia; in 1916, 22 were hanged in Damascus and 200 were imprisoned. Some of those who had led movements for autonomy before the war were also executed or imprisoned, sometimes with little real justification. Given the lack of subsequent revolt, Cemal Paşa's actions may have led rebels to rethink their plans. It is more likely that there never were many rebels.

Maronites

The exception to the general lack of separatism among the Arabs was the Maronites of Lebanon. The region called Lebanon today was a grand mixture of millets. The largest single group was probably the Maronite Christians, who were uniate Catholics (i.e. they accepted papal authority, but kept their own liturgy and clergy). There were also Greek Orthodox, uniate Greek Catholics, Sunni Muslims, Shia Muslims, Druze,[4] and other groups. The region was largely mountainous, which facilitated autonomy. Struggle between local notables was common, but not religiously motivated; sides were drawn with Christians and Muslims on each. The Ottomans exerted little control.

In the eighteenth century traditional power relationships in Lebanon began to break down. The cause was both demographic and religious. For unknown reasons, the number of Maronites began to expand. Maronites correspondingly began to expand their area of settlement south into regions controlled by Druze landlords. At the same time, the Maronites had begun to become clients of the French. A typical method of expanding European power in the Ottoman Empire was to attach a European country to one millet as 'protector'. The Russians claimed protectorship of all their Orthodox co-religionists, but there were few Catholics for the French to protect. The Maronites, the only compact group of Catholics in the Ottoman Empire, offered an opening for the French. Some Maronite notables even took Napoleon's side against the Ottomans when the French invaded Syria.

To the south of Lebanon, Maronites worked for the Druze landlords, but resented it. They were supported by their clergy, which stood against the Druze. Peasant revolts broke out in the 1840s. The Ottomans with great difficulty brought order. Maronite peasants seem equally to have resented traditional landlords in their own lands, again supported by the clergy, who saw the landlords' power as opposing their own. In 1858, Maronite peasants revolted against the landlords. The rebellion spread south, where it became an intercommunal war between Maronites and Druze. The Druze won, killing thousands and creating up to 100,000 Maronite refugees. Attacks on Christians in Damascus, Aleppo and elsewhere followed, killing an estimated 5000–10,000 people. At that point the French intervened.

Napoleon III, emperor of France, and French public opinion felt France could not stand by while her clients suffered. The fact that Ottoman troops had already restored order was of no consequence. The French forced the Ottomans to create a largely independent land for the Maronites. It was smaller than Maronites might have wished, encompassing only Mount Lebanon and neighbouring areas, not the fertile Beqaa valley to the east or the coastal trading cities of Beirut, Tyre and Sidon. A Christian governor was to be appointed and a council made up of Christians, Muslims and Druze advised him. Maronites made up a large majority of the population.

One cannot speak of nationalism of the Maronites at this stage. Their identification was undoubtedly religious. The antecedents of nationalism were surely present, however. There was separatism and a view of others as enemies and one's own compatriots as the only ones to be truly trusted. Nationalism developed as the nineteenth century progressed. On Mount Lebanon and in nearby cities the Maronites drew continually closer to France. The primary agents of this were French missionary schools. Unlike the American missionaries, the French were conscious agents of their nation's interests in Syria. At first, their schools taught only in French, only adding Arabic instruction when the Americans, who taught mainly in Arabic, successfully competed with them for students. The French unhesitantly advanced nationalism among the Maronites through their educational system and through economic preferment of the Maronites. Maronite intellectuals, the ruling elite, religious leaders, and a significant part of the populace identified themselves not as Arabs, and surely not as Ottomans, but as Maronites, members of their own national group.

The Hijaz

The bedouin of the Arab desert were far from being Arab nationalists, nor were they Ottoman loyalists. Their position concerning the Ottoman government can be summarized as 'Protect us from the foreigners, and then leave us alone'. They had no plans to pay taxes, submit to conscription, or obey Ottoman laws unless forced. This naturally caused conflict with the government. Husayn ibn 'Ali, who became sharif (*amir*) of Mecca, was as independent-minded as the desert nomads. Both he and the bedouin resisted any imposition of central control from the CUP government.

The worry of the Hijaz leaders was that the Ottomans would extend their control over the region. The Hijaz Railway was seen as the prime agent of Ottoman power, as indeed it was intended to be, and tribes had attacked the railroad as it reached Medina. Opposition from the tribes and the sharif had kept the track from advancing beyond Medina, but the Ottomans did not give up their intention to bring the railroad to Mecca. This would allow them to transport troops quickly to the heart of the Hijaz. Troops would be the first step; tax-collectors and conscription would follow. Both the government and the bedouin knew this.

Sharif Husayn seems to have had no particular loyalty to the Ottomans, although he had lived for many years in Istanbul and was an Ottoman official. He conspired with Syrian Arab nationalists before and during World War I, but never adopted their ideology. His concern was the continuation of traditional Muslim culture, his own rule, the succession of his family to power, and keeping the Ottoman tax-collector and conscription agent at bay. When World War I broke out he seized his opportunity for independence and allied himself and his bedouin followers with the British. He was promised an Arab kingdom under his rule, but he was no Arab nationalist.

Husayn's son, Faysal, was to become the focus of true Arab nationalism when he attempted to hold the World War I Allies to the wartime promises they had made to his father (Chapter 10).

Iraq

Arab nationalism was a slight factor in Ottoman Iraq. Iraqi tribal leaders and notables had always enjoyed a considerable degree of autonomy. Throughout the Empire's reign Iraq had simply been too far away to be ruled effectively from Istanbul. It had not developed the type of new intelligentsia that led the call for Arabism or Arab nationalism in Syria. Local feelings were centred on more concrete matters. One of these was fear of British encroachment in Iraq. With its near monopoly on trade in the Indian Ocean and Red Sea, Britain naturally sought to expand its trade in Iraq, and this brought it into competition with Iraqi merchants. They complained to the central government that concessions to the British would lead to disaster. First the British would invest, then they would have to protect their investments, and eventually they would take over Iraq in the same way they had taken Egypt. Dislike of the British had the effect of bringing together the merchant class and much of the populace, not in opposition to the Ottoman Empire, but in opposition to Britain. This proto-nationalism would surface again and begin to develop into real nationalism when the British did indeed conquer Iraq.

Arab nationalism and the West

One factor that differentiated Arab nationalism from the nationalisms of the Ottoman Christians in the Balkans and the Armenians is the lack of European support. Feelings of superiority had been fostered among the Christian minorities by commercial preference given them by Europeans. Nationalist revolutionary groups had met freely in Europe. Most importantly, the European Powers had shown that they would force the creation of new national states militarily. Except for the Maronites, none of these were true for the Arabs. No British societies formed to press the case of the Arabs. Arab interests were not a subject of concern for either Western governments or the Western public. Christian movements were supported partly because they were Christian, and most of the Arabs were Muslims. Moreover, the Europeans did not intend physically to conquer the Balkans. Influence over the Balkan states would be enough. France and Britain did intend to conquer and rule the Arab world. Any Arab nationalism would be a hindrance to their aims.

The lack of European interest as a cause for the paucity of Arab interest in nationalism can be easily overstated. It is doubtful whether the Arabs would have revolted against the Ottomans even if the British and French had done all they could to foster revolution. Nevertheless, unlike Balkan Christians, any Arabs who thought of revolt knew that they could expect no help.

With the exception of the bedouin forces of the sharif of Mecca, Arab separatism was not much to threaten the Ottomans during World War I. The Arabs largely remained loyal Ottoman subjects, even if for most this meant loyalty first to Islam and then to Islam's political representative, the sultan's government. True nationalism among the Arab masses was to develop as a reaction to British and French conquest and rule. As with the Turks, the true importance of Arabism and nationalist sentiments came after the dissolution of the Empire. Presented with truly foreign rulers, the British and French, the Arabist movement became truly nationalistic. The Arabs demanded, and ultimately obtained, their own states, although they were smaller and divided states that fitted none of the dreams of Arab nationalists.

Dividing Ottoman Asia

There was definitely no internal justification for dividing the Ottoman provinces in Asia. In the Arab provinces, only a small portion of the inhabitants wished for separation. Had they known what awaited them, European control, the Arabs would have been all the more desirous to see the old Empire survive. Of the Muslims of Ottoman Asia, only some of the Kurds and some of the bedouin can be said to have made definite acts of independence, and their desires for tribal independence and marauding rights would have fitted into no modern state.

In Ottoman Asia it was only Christian minorities that developed significant nationalist movements. The majority of Armenians and Greeks of Anatolia probably cared for neither the nationalists nor the Ottomans. They simply wanted to be left alone. However, sizeable numbers of Greeks did support union of western Anatolia with Greece, and sizeable numbers of Armenians supported independence. The problem with their nationalist quest was that there were too few of them: 83 per cent of the population of

Anatolia was Muslim. In no province did the Greek population rise to 20 per cent of the whole. Armenians made up less than 20 per cent of the region of Anatolia that the nationalists claimed as Armenia. Any nationalist state created under such circumstances could only be based on what in later days was to be called *apartheid*.

If the wishes of the majority of the people had been considered, the Ottoman Empire in Asia would never have ended. Ottoman subjects would have thought the termination of the Empire to be a very odd concept indeed. Asked if they wished the Empire to continue or would they prefer smaller, nationalistic states, their response would have been to question the sanity of the inquirer. There had always been an Empire (or so it must have seemed); the world could not change so radically as to end Ottoman rule. But if they could have been convinced to give an opinion, can anyone doubt that the Muslims of the Empire – Turks, settled Arabs, smaller ethnic groups, and perhaps even most of the Kurds and bedouin Arabs – would have voted for the Empire rather than for any government ruled by Europeans or local minorities?

When the Ottoman Empire was divided after World War I the will of the majority was one factor that was always ignored.

5

The Balkan Wars

Macedonia

Macedonia was a desirable prize for any of the Balkan states, and Serbia, Bulgaria and Greece each claimed it, as seen in Chapter 3. Macedonia was poor by most economic measures, but it was strategically located. Its port, Salonica, was the gateway to the region. Whoever ruled Macedonia could be said to be the dominant Balkan power.

Each country attempted through schools, newspapers and cultural organizations to spread their own nationalism among the Macedonian Orthodox Christians. Only the Bulgarians had much success. Most of the region's Christians decided to join the Bulgarian Exarchate, an action which took a two-thirds vote of churches. Some of those choosing the Bulgarian Church undoubtedly were not making a political statement. They may have decided only that they preferred a Slavic liturgy and priests and bishops who were closer to their lives. Yet this was the only public choice of affiliation made by the region's Christians, and it had gone to Bulgaria.

The Bulgarians were presented with large difficulties in turning religious identification into national feeling and absorption of Macedonia into Bulgaria. They were not the largest group in the population. That group was the Muslims, divided ethnically between Turks and Albanians. The Ottoman Empire was also making strides in correcting old injustices that had alienated many in Macedonia. Lands that had been held by absentee Muslim landlords, in which peasants were poor tenants, were being redistributed to peasants. Beginning with the Tanzimat, reforms had increased administrative efficiency. Roads were improved and a rail connection north to the European rail grid constructed, enriching the economy. Macedonia remained a poor place, but it was improving. The demographic and economic situation was not conducive to revolt.

Bulgarian nationalists in and out of Macedonia changed the situation through guerrilla war. The Internal Macedonian Revolutionary

Organization (IMRO) was founded in 1893. Its political intentions have long been debated. Some feel it to have been a Macedonian Slav organization, only tied to Bulgaria for strategic reasons. Others, especially Bulgarians, who did not accept the existence of a separate Macedonian people, defined it as a Bulgarian nationalist organization, but one that was hard to control from Sofia. The organization's slogan, 'Macedonia for the Macedonians', seemed to indicate desire for a separate Macedonia, or at least for autonomy within some form of Balkan confederation. IMRO, however, had extensive contacts with Bulgaria. The other revolutionary association, the External Organization, founded in Sofia in 1895, was dedicated to union of Macedonia and Bulgaria. Whatever their intentions, both groups adopted guerrilla war as their tactic.

IMRO organized within Macedonia, organizing Macedonians for a mass revolt, and began guerrilla attacks in 1897. The External Organization began guerrilla warfare even earlier, in 1895. The two organizations vied for power. They were joined by Greek bands, who opposed both. The main activities of all three were directed at the peasants and townsmen of Macedonia. Those Christians who chose the Bulgarian side could expect attacks from Greek bands. Any who decided to stay with the Greek Patriarchate rather than the Bulgarian Exarchate could expect attacks from the Bulgarians. IMRO and the External Organization demanded loyalty and enforced it by burning, pillage and massacre. All the groups exacted 'contributions' from peasants and merchants. Muslims felt the fury of all three guerrilla organizations. Ottoman officials and soldiers were killed whenever possible.

Starting later than the Bulgarians, the Greek National Society (Ethnike Hetairia) began to organize Greek guerrilla bands in Macedonia in the later 1890s. Unlike IMRO, which often acted on its own and even against directions from the Bulgarian government, the National Society was under the control of the Greek government. Many, perhaps most of the Greeks bands were not native to Macedonia. They were sent from the Greek kingdom.

Like the Greeks, the Serbs organized their guerrilla campaign outside of Macedonia. It was directed from Belgrade and functioned as a branch of the Serbian General Staff. The least successful of the revolutionaries, Serbian bands could count on little local support.

When the guerrilla bands began to attack the Ottoman power structure and each other, the result was near destruction of civil order in Macedonia. What the bands did not destroy was often enough ruined by the Ottoman soldiers who chased the guerrillas and punished their supporters, many of whom had been given no choice but to aid the guerrillas. The state of Macedonia was not anarchy, because anarchy implies a lack of purpose. There was purpose in the civil war in Macedonia, nationalist purpose that punished most those who were intended to become grateful members of the nation.

European intervention in the Macedonian crisis did nothing to help. In 1903, an IMRO-led uprising in Manastır Province seized most of the province (the Ilinden Revolt). The rebels hoped for assistance from Bulgaria and perhaps Great Power intervention. Neither materialized, although large numbers from Bulgaria joined the rebels. The Ottomans eventually put down the uprising with ferocity. One of the activities of the rebels had been attacking Muslim villagers and Ottoman officials, so there was revenge to be considered. The Great Powers blamed the Ottomans for everything, as they usually did. Austria and Russia, supported by the other Powers, forced the Ottomans to accept yet another diminution of their sovereignty in order to calm the Macedonian troubles. The gendarmerie in Macedonia was to be put under a foreign commander and foreign officers, and the Ottoman inspector-general, in charge of Macedonia, was to be watched by two European agents. The Ottoman government was required to pay for the destruction initiated by the rebels. Most damaging of all, the government was made to promise that provincial boundaries would be aligned at a later date to reflect ethnic divisions. This provision caused more bloodshed. Each guerrilla group now acted to try to force out those who supported others. Due to European meddling the situation became worse.

The Tripolitanian War

In all but name, World War I began for the Ottomans in 1912. After 1912, with but a year's respite, the Turks were at war for the next ten years.

Germany and Italy had started late on imperial expansion, when most of the choicest morsels had already been consumed by Britain and France. In North Africa, what remained outside of European control were Morocco, an independent kingdom, and Libya, part of the Ottoman Empire. France was expanding into Morocco from its colony in Algeria. The Germans and Italians wanted it for themselves, but Britain and Russia sided with the French. The Germans stepped down to avoid war. The Italians were given tacit approval by the French, British and Russians to take Libya as a consolation. Thus was the governance of North Africa decided. The Ottomans, who had no place in the dispute, were to pay for the success of European diplomacy.

In 1911 Italy invaded the Ottoman provinces in Libya, not for any clear justification for war but because Libya was the last piece of North Africa without European rulers. The Italians had to take their share before it was all gone, even though Libya had been left until last because it was virtually worthless to any conqueror. The Ottomans knew they could not defend it and did not really try to do so. The Italian fleet was far superior to the few Ottoman ships and Libya was far from the centres of Ottoman power, separated from the Empire by British-controlled Egypt. Instead, volunteer Ottoman officers, members of the CUP, led a successful guerrilla campaign from the desert. Their troops were bedouins of the Sanusiya sect defending their own land. They managed to defeat Italian incursions into the hinterland and keep the invaders to the coast.

The Italians, frustrated that they had not won the easy victory they expected, expanded the war by first bombarding the Dardanelles (April 1912), then seizing the Dodecanese Islands (May 1912) off the southwest coast of Anatolia. The war would have continued without a clean resolution, but the Ottomans sued for peace when a greater threat erupted closer to Istanbul: invasion by the Balkan countries.

The Balkan Wars

The Balkan Wars were a triumph for nationalism. Those who had been part of the Ottoman Empire had now grown strong enough to defeat it collectively. Nationalism as a force for state-building in the Balkans had reached its maturity. It had not, however, left behind the evils that had accompanied its formative years.

Serbia, Montenegro, Greece and Bulgaria agreed that the Ottomans should be expelled from Europe, but they could not agree on the disposition of the Ottoman lands. Each believed that their maximal national aspirations were their due. Unfortunately, much of the land in question, particularly in Macedonia, was seen by Serbia, Greece and Bulgaria as the national patrimony of each. They could only agree that it did not belong to the Balkan Muslims. The Muslims were the largest religious group of Ottoman Europe, making up 51 per cent of the total population, but nationalism ignored such considerations. Unable to agree on division of the spoils, the Allies nevertheless went ahead.

On 8 October 1912, Montenegro declared war on the Ottoman Empire, followed immediately by the others. The Ottomans, their armies divided and most of their troops in Asia, lost quickly. The Serbs defeated them at Kumanova (24–26 October), took Manastır on 18 November, and claimed all of northern Macedonia. The Greeks faced few Ottoman troops. They advanced north and east, taking Salonica on 8 November and holding southern Macedonia.

The worst fighting was left to the Bulgarians. The strongest Ottoman forces were naturally in eastern Thrace, defending Edirne and, most importantly, the road to Istanbul. The Bulgarians defeated the Ottomans at Kırk Kilisse, then at Lüleburgaz (28 October – 3 November), but Edirne held out under siege, not to fall until 26 March 1913. The Ottomans held the Bulgarians on the Çatalca Line, the last defence before Istanbul.

To the Bulgarians, the war had not been fair. They had fielded more troops than Greece and Serbia combined. They had borne the brunt of the battle, but had gained the least. The Bulgarians were incensed that the territories of primarily Bulgarian population were occupied by Serbs, not

Bulgarians. Of course, their sense of majority rule did not extend to the areas they themselves had conquered, which were majority Muslim. The area they viewed as part of their heartland, central Macedonia, whose Christians were overwhelmingly Bulgarian Orthodox, was occupied by the Serbs. Ohrid, the ancient seat of the Bulgarian Orthodox Church, was not held by Bulgarians. The Greeks had taken Macedonia's outlet to the sea, Salonica. For the Bulgarians, the war had been an expensive failure, despite their victories in the field. They could never tolerate this, so they turned on the erstwhile allies, and lost even more territory.

The Bulgarians attacked the Serbs on 16 June 1913, without a declaration of war. Initially, they had some success. They had virtually denuded their other borders of soldiers, however, and both the Romanians to the north and Turks to the south took advantage of this. The Serbs and Greeks recovered and counter-attacked. Bulgaria was soon losing on all fronts. The Turks retook Edirne. The Romanians were within striking distance of Sofia. Bulgaria was forced to capitulate, signing the Treaty of Bucharest with Romania, Serbia, Montenegro and Greece on 28 July, and the Treaty of Constantinople with the Ottoman Empire on 30 September. The Ottomans regained eastern Thrace and Edirne. Bulgaria lost even more of Macedonia to the Greeks and Serbs and the northern Black Sea borderland to the Romanians.

Sufferings of Balkan Muslims

The Balkan conquerors were intent on creating national states. Yet in none of the conquered areas was the majority of the population made up of the conqueror's religious/ethnic group. The populations of the Bulgarian conquest and Serbian conquest were both majority Muslim in 1911, before the wars began. The Greeks were a slight plurality in the area they conquered, but still made up only 45 per cent of the population. This was an intolerable situation for nationalists, but it was easily corrected.

The tactic used to alter the demography of the Balkans was that which had been perfected in the 1877–78 Russo-Turkish War. As Bulgarian, Greek, Serbian and Montenegran armies advanced, they destroyed the Muslim villages in their path. Muslim peasants and town-dwellers were raped and murdered. This, in turn, caused the Muslims in the next villages to flee before the soldiers arrived. Soon an entire people was on the move. Some reached a certain safety in cities such as Manastır and Salonica; many more were not so fortunate. At the end of the war, survivors were not allowed to return. British Vice-Consul Young at Cavalla remarked of this process, 'The track of the invading [Bulgarian] army is marked by 80 miles of ruined villages'.[1] Thus were national majorities created.

The other tactic, murder, obviously worked hand in hand with forced migration. Muslims were killed in great numbers, especially during the first

Balkan War: Turkish prisoners of war were starved to death after the fall of Edirne; massacres of Muslims were commonplace in cities such as Serres, Dedeağaç and Strumnitsa, particularly those regions occupied by Bulgarians; partisan bands, called *komitajis*, killed Muslims on the roads and in the villages.

Finally, and for refugees worst of all, came starvation and disease. Pillaged of their goods, marching to real or imagined safety, Muslim refugees were overcome by hunger and the cold of winter, so many dying that piles of dead were left by the roads. Those who were able to reach refugee camps in Ottoman-controlled territory found typhus, typhoid and cholera.

There was little relief available for the refugees. The only international assistance that was allowed was the transportation – by boat, train and oxcarts – of refugees from the conquered lands. These refugees were the lucky ones. Muslims fleeing from interior regions such as most of Macedonia could not hope to make it to ports or other places of safety. And those who survived often found that their villages had been destroyed or occupied by Greeks, Serbs, Bulgarians or Montenegrins.

The final tragedy of the Balkan Wars came in the autumn of 1913. Albanians in Kosova (now Kosovo) revolted against their Serbian conquerors. The revolt was put down in a most bloody fashion by the Serbian army. Albanian villages were destroyed, their inhabitants killed or forced to flee to Albania. In Albania, which had no resources and no aid from anyone, the refugees succumbed to disease and starvation.

Some 2,315,000 Muslims had lived in the conquered areas of Ottoman Europe; 1,445,000 remained at the end of the wars. The Ottoman Refugee Commission recorded the number of refugees settled in the Empire, 414,000 in total. Of these, most were placed in eastern Thrace and western Anatolia; some were placed as far afield as Syria, a few hundred in eastern Anatolia. From 1921 to 1926 399,000 others came to Turkey. Some 632,000, 27 per cent of the Muslim population of Ottoman Europe, died in the Balkan Wars.

Suffering of Balkan Christians

The suffering of the Balkan Christians was less than that of the Balkan Muslims, but was awful in itself. Greeks, Serbs and Bulgarians did not spare each other when national interests were at stake. Muslims took their revenge on Christians when they could.

Bulgarians suffered the most of the Christian combatants during the Balkan Wars. The experience of Bulgarian refugees from the portion of Macedonia conquered by the Greeks and Serbs was similar to that of the Balkan Muslims – exemplary violence and destruction, followed by wholesale flight. Many of the Bulgars of eastern Thrace, rightly expecting that they would be held accountable for what the Bulgarian army had done to the Turks, fled before the Ottoman army in the second war. Others emigrated after the Treaty of Constantinople ended the conflict and a formal population exchange was initiated.

Bulgarian sources estimated that 14,000–15,000 refugees came to Bulgaria from Macedonia alone. The Bulgarian government estimated that 35,000–40,000 Bulgarians came to Bulgarian territory from all regions during and immediately after the Balkan Wars. It is impossible to verify these figures, but they do not seem to be unreasonable. Unlike Greece, which had abundant Muslim and Bulgarian properties to offer refugees, Bulgaria had won little land, much of it in the mountainous southwest of the country. Of the conquered land, only western Thrace provided some decent land to settle refugees. The Bulgarian refugees were mainly settled there; Turkish and Greek properties were available. The Bulgarian immigrants to western Thrace seem to have fared well until they were forced to move once again in 1920, after the Bulgarians had lost World War I.

Other than deaths in the military, Serbs suffered little mortality in the wars. Regions where Serbs lived in large numbers were not in contention, and very few Serbs ever lived in Bulgaria or Greece. Rather there were new regions now open to Serbian immigration.

Greeks and Greek Orthodox Slavs fled the part of Macedonia occupied by Serbs and Bulgarians; Greece estimated that there were 10,000 such refugees. Greek refugees fled eastern Thrace during the first Balkan War. Many of these returned during and immediately after the second war. They too were later to be evicted. The Greek government claimed that 70,000 Greeks were forced out of western Thrace when it was taken by the Bulgarians. This was a gross exaggeration, however. Comparison between Ottoman statistics and a census taken by the French, who occupied western Thrace after World War I (Chapter 9), indicates the loss of 30,000 between 1911 and 1919, still a great number of refugees and dead.

'Conversion'

Even had they wished to do so, the Serbs could not have rid themselves of the Bulgarian Orthodox population of Macedonia in the way they rid themselves of the Macedonian Muslims. There were very few Serbs in the region. The Bulgarian Orthodox were the only Christians, and their demographic presence was needed. Instead of forced migration, therefore, the Serbian government simply made all the Bulgarian Orthodox into Serbs. They were 'converted' to the Serbian (Greek) Orthodox Church. The administrative structures of Bulgarian Orthodoxy were destroyed.

When the Greeks occupied Macedonia, assertion of Bulgarian or Macedonian Slavic identity was treated as a criminal offence. Those who were wisely silent on questions of nationality simply entered 'Greek' on their identity cards and papers. Bulgarians in Greek Macedonia were later exchanged for Greeks in Bulgaria. The Greek census of 1928 listed only 6 per cent of the population of Greek Macedonia as speaking Macedonian. The Bulgarian Orthodox Church was not listed among religions.

In Serbia and Greece, Bulgarian Orthodox Christians were now officially Serbs or Greeks. Obviously many Macedonians felt themselves to be separate from the Bulgarians, but no one but the most ardent Serbian or Greek nationalists could have believed the Macedonians were Serbs or Greeks. Any national aspirations they might have had were quelled ruthlessly when their land was divided between the Greeks and the Serbs. Administratively, they had ceased to exist.

Coerced change of religion was not simply applied to Christians. As observed by European consuls, there were attempts forcibly to convert Turkish and Albanian Muslims to Christianity during the Balkan Wars, bringing them into the nation of the conqueror through religion. Interestingly, those most subject to forcible conversion were the Bulgarian-speaking Muslims, known as Pomaks. Bulgarians singled them out to be baptized. Those who refused were beaten or killed. The effectiveness of this in changing the self-identification of the 'converts' is doubtful.

The results of conquest

The demographic changes caused by the Balkan Wars were not the product of statistical considerations or analysis of patterns of settlement by religion. They were products of conquest, and conquest seldom considers such niceties as the ethnic make-up of the population. The area won by Bulgaria was not the area where the majority was Bulgarian. The region taken by the Bulgarians was overwhelmingly Muslim in population. Serbia took an area populated by Bulgarian Christians, ethnically either Bulgarian or Macedonian, and Muslims, primarily Albanian. Greece, which with demographic justification should have expanded its territory only slightly to the north, instead claimed the predominantly Muslim regions of eastern Macedonia.

If equity and the desirability of self-determination are considered in the study of history, the Balkan Wars take a high place among illegitimate conflicts. Hundreds of thousands died to advance national ideals that were in no sense just. The wars were not over in the Balkans. World War I was to follow, and justice was to be subverted once again.

6
World War I

World War I brought the most momentous changes since the Turkish nomads conquered the Middle East many centuries before. At war's end, not only had the Ottoman Empire died as a state, but the entire idea of a great Middle Eastern empire had passed. The idea of empire was very old: Sumerians, Babylonians, Romans, Umayyads, Abbasids and Seljuks had cemented empire as the archetype of Middle East rule long before the Ottomans took control. While long periods of divided states and even near anarchy might pass before a great empire asserted dominance, Middle Easterners could always expect, and usually hope for, the next empire. In 1918, that longest of political traditions passed away, probably forever.

The Triumvirate that took control of the Ottoman Empire in 1913 made the military their primary concern. After the Balkan Wars it was obvious that much work needed to be done. The military budget was doubled immediately and steps were taken to modernize the Ottoman military: new capital ships were ordered from British shipyards; an air force was begun; the decision was made to emulate European armies. No better way could be found than to put the Ottoman forces in the hands of the Europeans themselves, who presumably knew what an army and navy should be.

The army, most important of the military services, was to be put in the hands of a German, General Liman von Sanders, who would bring in a contingent of German officers to reform and command. To Enver Paşa, the minister of war, and his supporters, the choice of Germany was obvious. German officers, they felt, were the best in Europe. Germany, moreover, was one European Power that had no, or at least limited, territorial ambitions in the Ottoman Empire. The British, Austrians and Russians had all taken Ottoman land quite recently. The French were known to feel they should have Syria. The Germans, therefore, seemed a logical choice. This logic did not impress the British or French. They made such a diplomatic disturbance in opposing the Ottoman plan that the Ottomans agreed to limit German authority over the army. Von Sanders was appointed only as inspector-general of the First Army, headquartered in Istanbul. Other

Germans were at least nominally under Ottoman officers. No one was fooled. Enver Paşa had never planned to let the Germans command absolutely, certainly not to command him, but German officers in fact began to reorganize and reform the army.

The Germans made a good job of it. While the organizational chart of the army showed few changes, the reality of Ottoman military power increased dramatically. Ancillary corps such as quartermaster corps, military intelligence, and communications rapidly advanced toward twentieth-century practice. Ottoman officers learned the European system of command at first hand. They resented it. The word 'arrogance' was often heard describing their teachers. Nevertheless, all was improved.

The navy, for diplomatic as well as military reasons, was put in the hands of the British. A British naval mission under Admiral Limpus directed reorganization. Older officers were retired to make way for educated younger men. Again, it was the support services, such as dockyards and provisioning, that benefited most.

The French were put in charge of reorganizing the gendarmerie. This paramilitary organization was the backbone of Ottoman control in the provinces. Gendarmes acted as military police in rural areas, but were expected to become regular soldiers in the event of war. They were then essential troops, because they knew well the terrain and local conditions of the districts in which they served. It was in the area of military organization that the gendarmerie most benefited from reform.

The Russians were not asked to help.

The years 1913 and 1914 were times of exceptional government energy. Abdülhamit II had been a builder of railroads, roads and telegraph lines, and the Triumvirate continued in this tradition. Good roads were extended to the east. Railroad construction accelerated, with transportation hubs planned at Kayseri and Sivas. Great effort was dedicated to cutting tunnels through the Taurus mountains to connect the Anatolia and Syrian railroad lines. There was little time before the Great War began, however, and too much needed to be done.

Despite all these improvements, the Ottoman government knew the Empire could not stand alone in war. Russia, the most likely opponent, was too large, its army too strong. The Ottomans needed many years to develop an army up to European standards, not just two years of intensive effort. More time was also needed to build infrastructure: roads to the Russian border were much improved, but there was still no railroad to what would soon become the site of war. The Russians had both roads and a railroad from their heartland to Kars. In violation of their treaty obligations, the Russians had fortified Batum and made it a forward naval base on the Black Sea. They had occupied much of western Iran since 1910, even building a military railroad there, and were in position to turn the Ottoman flank in the east and move into northern Iraq.

World War I began with the assassination in Sarajevo of Archduke

Francis Ferdinand of Austria. Once Austria declared war on Serbia (28 July 1914) and Russia began to mobilize, the system of European alliances brought the continent to war. The Ottomans initially remained neutral.

The Ottoman Empire had no choice but to join the Central Powers in World War I. There were many reasons for the Ottoman decision to side with the Germans, but cold calculation of the chances for the Empire's survival if Russia won the war would have been enough justification for the decision. Russia had whittled away the Empire all through the nineteenth century, taking parts for itself, granting other parts to its friends. The tsars' ambition to claim Istanbul had been well known since at least the reign of Catherine the Great. Their quest for access to the Mediterranean was a national goal. In both the Crimean War and the 1877–78 Russo-Turkish War they had only been stopped by the other Powers from taking much larger territories than they ultimately received. England, which had long supported the independence of the Ottomans, was now Russia's ally. Only Germany seemed capable of stopping the Russian advance.

If the Ottomans had joined the English, French and Russians, or if they had remained neutral, could they have hoped that a triumphant Russia would respect Ottoman territorial integrity? History spoke against that naive belief. For 300 years the Russians had been advancing south at the expense of Muslim states and peoples. In the 1820s, 1860s and 1870s the Ottoman Empire had been forced to accept millions of Muslim refugees forced from their lands by the conquering Russians. Now there was nowhere else for the refugees to go. What else could the Ottomans do but try to stop the pattern?

There were also potential benefits to joining the Germans. The British and French had little to offer the Ottomans. They were friendly with Greece, so returning western Thrace to the Ottomans was unthinkable. Nor would the British ever return Cyprus. And the idea of Russia giving back any of the Ottoman land she had seized in eastern Anatolia was laughable. The Germans, on the other hand, could promise lands occupied by Britain, Greece and Russia. The Germans and Austrians were surely not disinterested Allies. They saw the Ottoman Empire as a fertile ground for economic imperialism. If they triumphed, the Ottomans would have become their economic dependency. That was much better than the only other option, ceasing to exist.

The Ottoman rulers knew all these things, but many opposed entering the war. The reasons were emotional or ideological. Many had been trained to look to the English and French as the exemplars of the sort of liberal society they wished to become. Business connections with the British and cultural connections with the French were strong. These were not, of course, strong justifications for important state decisions, but they were strongly held positions. For many Ottomans, war against Britain and France was unthinkable. After the débâcle of the Balkan Wars, most of the population surely wanted no war at all. Even the cabinet was split. Cemal Paşa, minister of the navy and one of the ruling Triumvirate, favoured the Allies. Had the pro-Allied side engaged in rational explanations, they might have suggested that it would be possible to wait out the war, hoping that the sides so exhausted each other that the Ottomans would be safe. This was not stated, and events overtook the Liberal and pro-Allied side in the government. Enver Paşa had a plan.

Convinced that the Germans could only triumph in the war, always a respecter of Germany, Enver joined the grand vezir, Sait Halim Paşa, in negotiating in secret with the Germans. They had no authorization from the cabinet, but nevertheless signed a treaty of alliance on 2 August 1914. Once announced to the cabinet as a *fait accompli* it was grudgingly accepted. All was secret, however, and opponents still had time to abrogate the treaty. Then the British played into Enver's hands.

As part of military reform, the Ottomans had ordered two capital ships from British shipbuilders. Their construction had been a national obsession, with schoolchildren collecting coins on street corners to pay for the ships. The British, fearful that the ships might be used against them, refused to deliver the completed, and paid for, ships. Ottoman public opinion turned against the British. Soon after, fate intervened to drive the Ottomans into war. Two German warships, the *Goeben* and the *Breslau*, passed into Ottoman waters on 11 August 1914, chased by a British squadron. According to the rules of war, the Ottomans were required to either intern the ships or send them out to fight. Instead, the Ottoman navy gratefully accepted a gift of the two ships. Admiral Souchon, their commander, was made commander of the Ottoman Black Sea Fleet. The German sailors, now members of the Ottoman navy, all donned fezes. The public was overcome with joy: the Germans had given what the British had taken away. The British were not pleased, but did not act.

The Ottoman minister of the navy, much as he liked the British, was a politician who could be swayed by popular opinion and the desire to be on the winning side politically. Enver convinced Cemal Paşa to authorize an attack on Russia that would bring the Ottomans into the war. On 20 October the Ottoman navy bombarded Russian ports and destroyed Russian shipping. Pro-Allied members of the cabinet, who had known nothing of the plan, were furious and called on Enver to apologize and try to avoid war. He did apologize, but did not avoid war. On 2 November Russia declared war on the Ottomans, joined on 5 November by the British and French.

The British and the war

The importance of the Ottoman Empire in World War I is a debated subject. Some feel that the war was to be won or lost in Europe, and that expenditure of men and material in the east was a costly mistake for the British. Others hold that the Suez Canal and the Persian oil fields were of such strategic importance that the Ottoman threat to them had to be eliminated. The Suez Canal was essential to British imperial communication and supply. The British war effort was also to benefit greatly from the importation of Indian soldiers through the Suez Canal; 850,000 of them fought for Britain outside of India. The oil of Persia was even more essential to the British war effort. Just before the war Britain had converted its navy from coal to oil. Southeast Persia was the major and much-needed source of that oil. Given their strategic needs, the British felt they had to fight the Ottomans. Two of the British theatres of war were obvious – Palestine/Syria in defence of the Suez Canal and Iraq in defence of the oil supply from Iran. A third British attack, the invasion of Gallipoli, was undertaken because it seemed to be too good a chance to miss.

Gallipoli

There were two forces behind the British invasion of the Gallipoli peninsula – the needs of the Russians and Winston Churchill. At the end of 1914 the Russians were beleaguered on their western front and as yet unsure of any success against the Ottomans in eastern Anatolia. They looked to their British allies to provide a military diversion against the Turks and hoped for a way to receive the supplies they needed to fight the war. The Ottoman Empire stood in the way of the easiest path to deliver supplies, through the Straits to the Black Sea. Winston Churchill, First Lord of the Admiralty, set out a daring plan. His enthusiasm and force of character triumphed over doubters in the cabinet.

On the map the plan looked simple and reasonable. The Dardanelles, the narrow straits that connected to the Sea of Marmara, Istanbul, the Black Sea and Russia, were felt to be poorly defended. They could be 'forced' by naval action alone. Once British ships passed through the Straits to the Marmara, relatively small contingents of troops could mop up defenders on the shores, moving on to Istanbul. The Ottoman capital was defenceless from the sea. The threat of naval bombardment would be enough to force Ottoman capitulation, driving the Ottomans out of the war. Bulgaria, at the time wavering between neutrality and joining the Central Powers, would remain neutral, perhaps even join the Allies. The Allied presence and commitment would convince the Greeks to join them, as well. The sea route to Russia would be open.

The British felt the Turks would be a vulnerable enemy. Perhaps this attitude can be explained by recent history – the defeat of the Ottomans in the Balkan Wars by countries the British held in no high esteem. A certain element of prejudice and feeling of European superiority also contributed to the British attitude. Most of the Ottoman troops were in eastern Anatolia,

Krakow
GALICIA
Kiev
RUSSIA
AUSTRIA - HUNGARY
Odessa
CASPIAN SEA
ROMANIA
SERBIA
BLACK SEA
BULGARIA
Tiflis
Batum
TRANSCAUCASIA
Baku
ALBANIA
Edirne
Istanbul
Kars
Erivan
Salonica
Ankara
Sivas
EASTERN ANATOLIA
GREECE
GALLIPOLI
Tabriz
Van
İzmir
OTTOMAN EMPIRE
Adana
Mosul

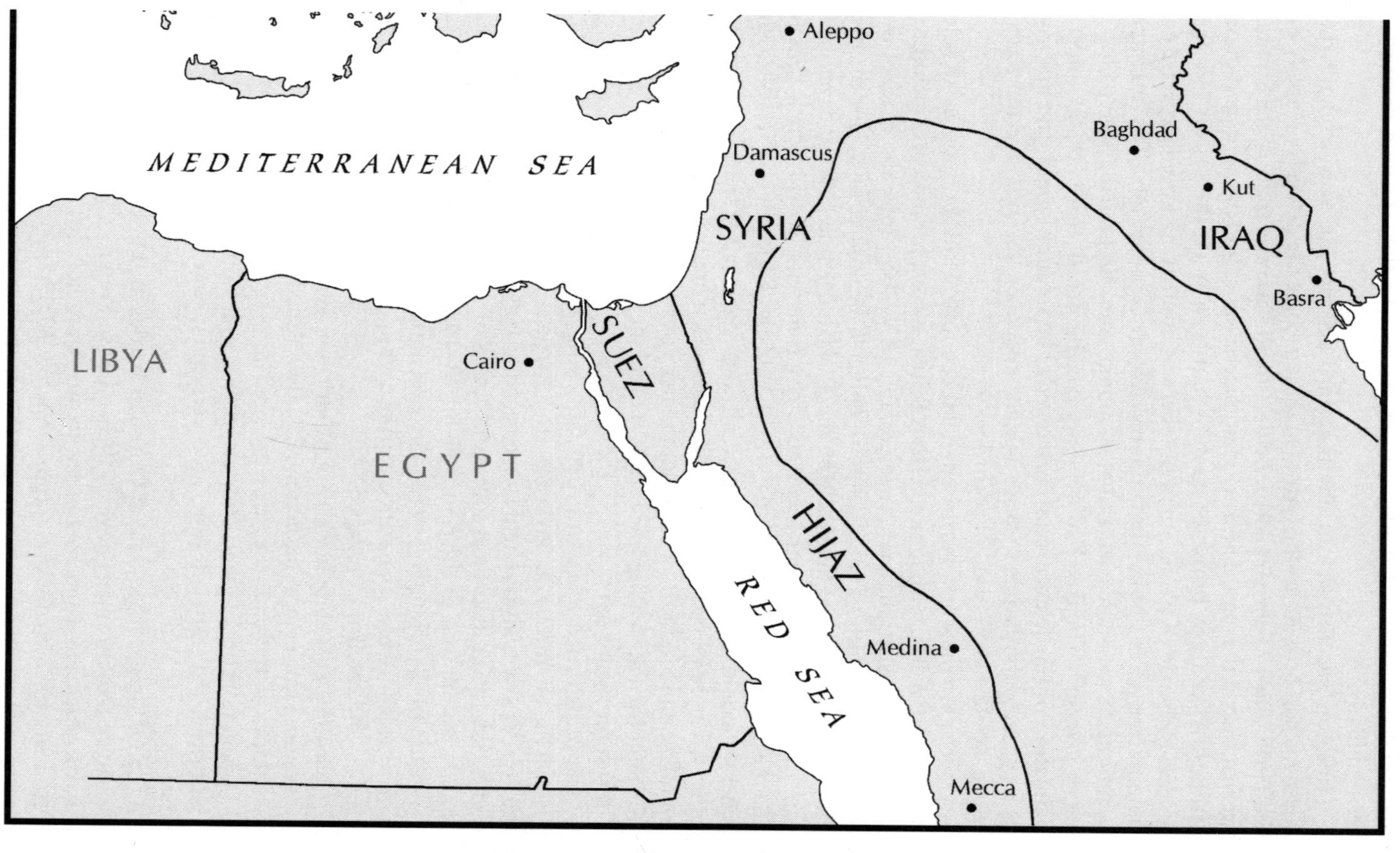

Map 6.1 World War I, theatres of war

Syria and Iraq, and this made a strong defence of the Ottoman heartland seem unlikely.

However, the British did not take into account the new strength the Germans had brought to the Ottoman military, nor the defensive tenacity of the Turks. On 19 February 1915, British squadrons tried to force the Straits, the first step in the plan. The Turks had placed mines and brought up mobile artillery. After three British battleships had been sunk, the British saw the need of a change of plans. Small numbers of infantry had been expected to support the navy. Now the infantry was to do the job. The infantry commitment was increased, and men, animals and supplies marshalled for a major invasion. The cost had gone up, but the British mind-set, the underestimation of the defence, was unchanged. The soldiers would gain an easy victory, seize the beaches, move inland, and open the way for the navy, which would sail to Istanbul according to plan.

Once again the Turks surprised. A French force landed on the Asian side of the Dardanelles, with limited effect. British forces, prominently including soldiers from Australia and New Zealand (ANZAC), took the beaches on the west and south of the Gallipoli peninsula beginning on 25 April, but they could not take the heights from the Turkish defenders. What developed was a caricature of all that was tactically wrong with World War I. British and Turks both dug in, but the Turks held the high ground. The British generals would order their men to advance against the Turkish machine guns. Great bravery led to incredible carnage. Liman von Sanders was in overall command of the Turks, but the hero of the Turkish defence became Mustafa Kemal, whose image in Istanbul newspapers stiffened general Turkish resolve to fight.

The British tried other strategies, attacking on the east of the peninsula, then on the northwest, at Suvla Bay (6–7 August). The slaughter went on, as the invaders were always held to the beaches. Finally, the British capitulated and withdrew. In their most successful action of the campaign British forces abandoned the west of the peninsula on 18–19 December and the tip of the peninsula on 8–9 January 1916. The evacuation was very well organized, with little loss of life. The Turks, fearing a trap, did not come down from the heights, and the British escaped.

Casualties at Gallipoli were, in proportion, similar to those in the great battles in France: approximately 210,000 Allied and 120,000 Ottoman casualties. In the end, the strategic position was exactly as it had been. Ottoman morale had greatly improved. Winston Churchill was out of a job. The British did learn a lesson, however, about how to fight in the Middle East.

The Gallipoli victory ended Ottoman battles in the west, except for the assistance the Ottomans gave to their allies in the great Galicia Campaign (on the Austrian–Russian border in the Ukraine). In August 1916 the Ottomans sent two divisions, approximately 20,000 men, to take part in the Central Powers' victory. At the time the troops could have been much better used in eastern Anatolia, but the Germans and Austrians exacted a price for their support, and Enver Paşa wished to show he was a good ally.

Iraq

Iraq was in all ways a more reasonable site for invasion than was Gallipoli. The British were defending real interests and not advancing fanciful plans. Conquests in Iraq would allow them to defend Iranian oil and perhaps to advance and take the newly discovered oil fields in Kirkuk, north of Baghdad. Holding Iraq would allow them to meet the Russians, who would advance south through eastern Anatolia and Iran. They would also be able to turn the Ottoman flank and threaten Ottoman forces in Syria. All this could be done mainly from India, by sea close to Iraq and a source of men and supplies that would have but limited effect on the needs of the French front. Once again, however, the British underestimated their enemy.

Anticipating the war, the British had sent a brigade of men from India to Bahrain in October 1914. On 6 November they bombarded the port of Fao and landed a division of Indian troops. After minor battles they entered the main city of southern Iraq, Basra, on 22 November.

The most important strategic objectives of the British could have been met by holding southern Iraq with a force sufficient to deter any Ottoman attacks on the oil fields, but the allure of Baghdad was too strong. The Turks began guerrilla actions early in 1915, cutting the south Persia oil pipeline, and this, too, convinced the British to advance from Basra, in order to take Turkish guerrilla bases.

Their numbers now increased to an army corps, the British advanced in April 1915. The main body of Turkish troops did not meet them in open battle. Instead the Turks fought short delaying actions, cut communications lines, and hindered the advance. On 22 November, as they advanced from Aziziye, the British found the Turkish Sixth Army waiting for them at Ctesiphon. Defeated, the British fell back to Kut al-Amara. They were put under siege for 120 days, surrendering on 29 April 1916. Some 2,750 British and 6,500 Indian troops were captured.

As they had at Gallipoli, the British learned the lesson of the Iraq campaign. The Turks would not be defeated easily. What was needed was to concentrate on British advantages. The British could bring more men to the field. They had an immense superiority in all the materials and technology of war. In India they had a vast depot that was, because of sea transport, close to the front. The Ottomans, on the other hand, were overextended on every front. They were deficient in military technology and supply, because their economy was limited. They might be magnificent fighting men, but even heroes need bullets, guns and boots.

Like General Grant in the American Civil War, the British settled down to slow advances, wearing out an enemy that had limited resources. The

British supplied their army by sea, building railroads behind them to carry supplies, and floating gunboats on the Tigris River. They waited to build up a force of five divisions of infantry and two of cavalry. The Ottomans, meanwhile, were forced to withdraw their main force to fight in Anatolia. In February 1917, the British advanced. With very few soldiers on hand, the Ottomans were forced to destroy dikes, blow up bridges, and use hit-and-run attacks, all of them futile. Baghdad fell on 11 March 1917. North of Baghdad, the land of Kurdish and Turcoman tribes, the dangers were greater, so the British moved very slowly indeed. They only took Mosul a week after the war had ended (in contravention of the terms of surrender).

Palestine/Syria

Soon after the beginning of the war, in January 1915, the Ottomans mounted an attack on the Suez Canal. An 80,000-man army marched across the desert. This army was far too small for such an endeavour, but the Ottomans hoped for assistance from the Egyptian populace. This strategy worked in Libya, where a large revolt held the Italians to the coast, but it failed in Egypt. The British had held Egypt for thirty years, politicians were largely, if not necessarily happily, committed to their system, and the Egyptians felt little kinship with the Ottoman Empire. The attack failed. The Ottoman army retreated to the border and prepared defences for an expected counter-attack.

The real outcome of the attack on the Suez Canal was to bring British fears for the safety of the Canal to the fore. It was decided that only an attack on Ottoman positions on the Palestine border would remove the threat. Beyond that, there was little military benefit in British conquest of Palestine. There was, however, another consideration. Conquest of the Holy Land, returning it to Christian rule for the first time since the Crusades, would bolster spirits at home at a time when the western front was bringing little joy to English hearts.

The first British attacks, on Gaza in March 1917, failed. Command was then given to Sir Edmund Allenby, who knew the lessons of Iraq and Gallipoli. He marshalled equipment and men for a slow advance that would play on Ottoman exhaustion and British technological superiority. Transporting supplies across the desert was always a difficulty, so the British built a railroad behind their troops' advance. It provided 2000 tons of goods a day. Water was an even greater problem, especially as the Ottomans destroyed wells in their retreat, so the British built a pipeline, complete with pumping stations, to carry water from Egypt.

On 30 October 1917, Beersheba fell, followed by Gaza on November. In the latter conquest and elsewhere up the Mediterranean coast naval bombardment was a major factor in victory. Allenby took Jerusalem on 9 December.

A change in command helped the Ottomans at this point. Erich von Falkenhayn was replaced by Liman von Sanders. Where von Falkenhayn had depended on German officers, von Sanders brought in Turkish commanders who knew the terrain and the men. They managed to defeat an attempt to take Amman and cut the Hijaz Railway, but it was the last success. The British inexorably moved north. Haifa, Acre and Damascus were taken in September and October. Mustafa Kemal kept the army together, however, and they fell back in good order to Adana. They were preparing to defend Anatolia when the war ended. Mustafa Kemal's great success was to keep the army as a fighting force. It would be needed soon in another war.

East

Ottoman disaster in World War I was guaranteed by Enver Paşa, the Ottoman minister of war. Similar to Winston Churchill in that he was a

Map 6.2 Eastern Anatolia

dreamer of great dreams and planner of grand schemes, Enver believed that bold strokes (*toujour l'audace*) would defeat the Russian enemy, retrieve the Ottoman lands lost to the Russians in 1878, and perhaps even carry Ottoman forces on to unison with their brothers among the Central Asian Turks. Like Churchill's dreams at Gallipoli, Enver's dream killed tens of thousands with only negative results.

The war began in the east on 2 November 1914, with unsuccessful Russian feints across the Ottoman border. The Ottomans tried a small invasion of their own near Batum. Ottoman forces repulsed the Russians; Russian forces repulsed the Ottomans. In retrospect, this was the best result the Ottomans could wish for, since they were beset by internal revolt in the east and unable to mount a credible threat to Russian forces in Transcaucasia.

Armenian revolt

The internal threat was a massive Armenian revolt in eastern Anatolia. The revolt in the mountainous district of Zeytun, ever a stronghold of Armenian independence, erupted even before the war began. The first Armenian rebellions in Zeytun and elsewhere often began in opposition to conscription. The Armenian and Ottoman attitudes showed the low state of Muslim–Armenian relations. Armenian revolutionaries were later to claim that the Ottomans had intended to kill conscripted Armenians, and so the rebels were forced to resist. The Ottomans believed that the Armenian revolts and Armenian unwillingness to serve in the Ottoman army proved that the Armenians were disloyal. Most Armenians, like most Muslims, undoubtedly simply did not wish to be soldiers at all.

Once the Armenians of military age fled the Ottoman draft boards, they had made a political decision and become rebels. There were many waiting to enrol them in the greater rebellion of Armenian revolutionaries. Armenian politicians, some even elected to the Ottoman parliament, most only representing their parties of revolutionaries, organized large-scale rebellion. Between 4000 and 6000 went across the border to train in Russian territory in Kağızman. Another 6,000 formed in İğdır into a small army. These Anatolian Armenians were trained and armed, and many were sent back across the border. They were joined by others who had stayed behind in Anatolia. The Ottomans estimated that 30,000 had formed into guerrilla and partisan bands in Sivas Province alone, probably an exaggeration, but there was a great number of rebels nevertheless. When war began, these bands revolted all across the Ottoman east, acting as agents of the Russians in the hope that the Russians would ultimately favour Armenian independence. All the history of the Russians should have indicated to them that this was impossible, but the Russians were nevertheless their only hope. In the mythology of Armenian nationalism, Russia as a 'Christian Power' was necessarily better than the Muslim Ottomans.

For some time before they took action, Armenian rebels in Van had moved men and weapons into the city. Van was a strategically important transportation link between Anatolia, Iraq, Iran and Russia, and was the largest city in the far southeast. The revolutionaries began to seize the city during the night of 13 April 1915. The Ottomans brought up what troops were available, including units from the front, but were unable to dislodge the rebels. The Armenians held the city until they could be relieved by the Russians. The Russians sent a force led by a brigade of Cossacks, but primarily made up of approximately 4000 Armenian volunteers, mainly from the Caucasus, and Armenian guerrilla bands from the Caucasus and Anatolia. By the middle of May they had defeated the few Ottoman troops in their way. They relieved Van on 31 May, and moved south of Lake Van, threatening Bitlis. By the end of July, however, the Ottomans had brought up strong forces that drove the Russians and Armenians from Van and the surrounding area. The Russians were forced to abandon Van on 4 August. The entire Armenian population between Van and the border accompanied them on their retreat.

The Ottomans were unable to advance far and were only able to control part of the Lake Van area, the western and southern shores of Lake Van and Van itself. The Ottomans reoccupied what remained of the city of Van. The situation remained stagnant throughout the remainder of 1915.

The occupation of Van was the most successful, and most prominent, of the Armenian actions, but it was only one of many Armenian actions. Before the war, in anticipation of what was to come, Armenian revolutionaries, supplied by the Russians, had secreted vast caches of weapons, even including military uniforms, all over the east. The Ottomans were only able to uncover a small percentage of the caches. The Armenian rebels, functioning both in small guerrilla bands and in units large enough to seize cities, became a major military threat to the Ottoman east. Kara Hisar was taken by the rebels, but the Armenians were ultimately expelled. In Urfa, Armenians armed with Russian machine guns held the city until regular army units could be brought against them (and thus, of course, not sent to the Russian front). Other cities such as Reşadiye and Gevaş were attacked unsuccessfully. The Armenians of Bitlis, like those of Van, rose and took the city until the Russians advanced. As in Van, the Muslims in the city were killed in the streets. At Musa Dağı, near Antakya, 5000 Armenian rebels resisted Ottoman troops until they could be rescued by a French warship. All over the east, Armenian rebels attacked Ottoman officials and Muslim civilians, leading to a mass exodus of villagers seeking places of safety.

Armenian bands targeted all that was necessary to the Ottoman war effort. Local officials, especially army recruiters, were assassinated, government buildings burned, gendarmerie stations reduced, isolated defence posts attacked, etc. The east dissolved into near anarchy as Armenian bands attacked Kurdish villages, and Kurds, themselves an armed force, in turn attacked Armenian villages. Nestorians (or Assyrians), a smaller Christian group in the south of Van Province, joined in the attack on the Muslims, themselves being attacked by Kurdish tribesmen. The roads were safe only for large detachments of armed men, but both Muslim and Armenian peasants and city-dwellers needed to flee the fighting, and were then attacked on the roads.

By themselves, the rebels would have been isolated and destroyed by Ottoman forces, but they were not alone. The Armenians acted in concert with the Russians. They were 'shock troops' for the Russian advance and a guerrilla force harrying the Ottomans behind the lines. The worst tactical damage was done by cutting communications line and diverting troops and supplies from the front.

Unfortunately for the Ottomans, the Armenian revolt coincided with and followed upon Enver Paşa's disastrous invasion of Russia. The need to keep divisions from the front to battle the Armenians should in itself have precluded a major offensive. Insofar as it ever applies to military actions, common sense should have told Ottoman generals that their proper position in the east was defensive. Presented with an enemy, Russia, that had a much larger army and better lines of communication and transportation, the Ottoman army should have stayed in defensive positions, sallying forth only when victory over small units was assured. Under the cautious general Ahmet İzzet Paşa that is exactly what was done. A small Russian force was defeated at the beginning of November, but İzzet was not willing to commit to an offensive strategy. He knew the army's limitations.

For Enver Paşa, planning in far-off Istanbul, defence was anathema. Sure that the Russians were fully committed against the Austrians and Germans in Europe, Enver dreamed of a swift coup that would open the Caucasus to the Ottomans. Losses in the 1877–78 war would be avenged. Brother Turks in Azerbaijan would be united with the Turks in Anatolia. Because Enver dreamed no small dreams, even unison with the Turks of Central Asia seemed possible. He ordered the invasion of Russia. İzzet Paşa resigned. Enver took personal command. What followed was one of the worst losses of any army in modern warfare.

On 21 December, the Ottoman Third Army crossed the border. The worst enemy was the winter. Officers who knew the region well had advised Enver that a winter campaign was perhaps possible, but only with proper clothing and special winter equipment, neither of which was available. This did not deter Enver. Most soldiers did not even have greatcoats or warm boots. Food was scarce; soldiers had only rations of bread. A heavy snow had fallen on 19 December, and a blizzard followed on the 24th. When the Turks awoke from infrequent rests the ground was always littered with men who had frozen to death. In this state they met Russian troops who were well dug in and provided with superior artillery. The Turkish Third Army, comprised of veterans who were the sole effective defenders of the Ottoman east, was destroyed. Of its 75,000 men, only 15,000 survived. Enver returned to Istanbul, never again to lead an Ottoman army.

The Russians did not precipitously follow up the Ottoman defeat. They slowly built their forces until, in 1916, a reinforced Russian army of approximately 130,000 infantry and 35,000 cavalry attacked the Ottoman east. With few troops to defend the region, the Ottomans rapidly lost on a wide front. Erzurum and Muş both fell to them on 16 February. Bitlis and Rize were lost early in March, Trabzon in April, Bayburt and Erzincan in July. More than a million Muslims became refugees.

The Ottoman disaster in the east seemed complete. All of the easily defensible ground in eastern Anatolia was lost. The way west was open. A 1917 campaign would probably have cut off Ottoman armies in Iraq and Syria and perhaps advanced even to Istanbul, but the Ottomans were saved by the Russian Revolution.

Early in 1917, Russian troops in Anatolia, as on other fronts, began to walk home. By the end of 1917 the Russian army that had successfully invaded Anatolia no longer existed. What remained were officers, Armenians, and few others. The Russian officers may have remained out of duty or an understandable lack of desire to return home. The Armenians saw their chance to create an Armenian state, but they could not hold the large amount of territory they claimed in Anatolia.

The Ottomans attacked in the east in 1918. Vehip Paşa led the Ottoman Third Army into territory conquered by the Russians, now held by the Armenians, in February. By the end of March, they had regained all they had lost since 1914. By the end of April, Ottoman forces had retaken all that had been lost in the 1877–78 war. They even marched across Transcaucasia to Baku to aid the Azerbaijan Turks who were beleaguered by Armenian nationalists and communists. However, it was all to no avail. On 30 October 1918, the Ottoman government signed the Armistice of Mudros. It had lost the war. The Ottoman army in the east retreated to approximately the 1914 border, awaiting developments but largely intact. The survival of this army was to play an important part in future events.

The result of the war, the Russian invasion, and the Armenian revolt was an intercommunal war, a war of extermination, in the Ottoman east. In a real sense, the war had begun more than a hundred years before with the Russian invasion of Transcaucasia. Armenians had joined the Russian side and fought alongside them when the Russians advanced in Transcaucasia and Anatolia. Muslims had allied themselves with the Ottomans. The upshot had been a great population exchange of Muslims and Armenians. Muslims had fled or been forced out of Erivan Province and other regions of Transcaucasia, as had the Circassians, Abhazians and others from the eastern Caucasus. Anatolian Armenians, in turn, had fled when the European Powers had forced the Russians to give up part of their conquests in 1829, 1856 and 1878. Further intercommunal wars between Muslims and Armenians had occurred in Azerbaijan during the Russian Revolution of 1905. Although the majority of the Muslims and Armenians surely wished only to be left alone, they were forced into the conflict. By the time World War I erupted, both Muslims and Armenians feared for their survival if the 'other side' was victorious.

The first actions of the Armenian rebellion cemented the fears of both sides. In Van, the rebels who seized the city burned the Muslim quarter and killed the Muslims who fell into their hands. Kurdish villagers in the Van region were killed in great numbers. In one case, thousands of Kurds were driven into a great natural bowl in Zeve, outside of Van, and killed by Armenian troops, using rifles and machine guns, shooting from the surrounding cliffs. The villagers who escaped were hunted down on the roads as they fled. When the Russians relieved Van, Cossacks joined the Armenians in pillage and murder.

The Kurds killed by the Armenians had friends. Kurds in Van and elsewhere avenged the slaughter of defenceless Muslims by slaughtering equally defenceless Armenians. Other Kurds simply took to their old habit of raiding whenever government power was weak. Unless they could escape to safety with the Russians, Armenian villagers were killed.

In the east, the die was cast. Imperialism and nationalism had created a state in which both Muslims and Armenians knew that they had the choice of killing or being killed. The only other option was flight. When the Armenians and Russians triumphed in 1915, Muslims who could do so escaped to the Ottoman forces. When the Ottomans drove back the Russians, the Armenians fled and Muslims returned. Then, in 1916, when the Russians and Armenians returned it was Muslim refugees who were once again on the roads.

The fate of many of the millions of Muslim and Christian refugees in 1915–16 was starvation and disease. Entire populations were on the move with few places to go. The Armenians who accompanied the Russians to Russian Armenia starved there. The Muslims who accompanied the Ottoman forces in retreat starved in Anatolia. Those who were able to return briefly to their homes had little time and no supplies to plant crops, so they starved at home. Disease – cholera, typhus, typhoid – accompanied starvation, as it always did in wartime.

The Ottoman government matched the expulsion of the Muslims of the east with deportation of most the Armenians who remained in Ottoman-controlled areas. On 26 May 1915, the government gave orders to relocate Armenians from potential war zones and the proximity of important installations. The Armenian population in each province was to be diluted so that no more than 10 per cent of the population would be Armenian. The intent, a common one in governments fighting guerrilla wars, was to deprive the rebels of the support they needed to carry on their battles. Armenians were to be settled in Greater Syria, far away from the Armenian rebellion and from regions where they might aid invaders.

The Ottoman intentions in ordering the resettlement of the Armenians have been debated with ferocity ever since 1915. The only actual Ottoman documents on the deportation show a soliticiousness for the welfare of the deportees – instructions on properly selling property, defending columns of Armenians from marauders, caring for health and sanitation, and other measures for their welfare. In reality, such good intentions were seldom carried out. The welfare of the Armenians was left in the hands of local officials whose troops were occupied in fighting Russians and Armenian bands. In some cases the Armenians were to be protected by those who had seen the depredations of other Armenians on Muslims. This was not a recipe for a successful mass movement of peoples. Some officials exacted revenge on Armenians. Kurdish tribes attacked Armenian columns for both revenge and plunder. Even the officials who wanted to protect the Armenians had few soldiers and police to act as guards. As with the Muslims attacked by Armenians, the innocent suffered: Armenian rebels were in the field, fighting the Ottomans and killing innocent Muslims. Muslims, especially tribesmen, killed innocent Armenians on the march to Syria.

It is also true that actual deportations exceeded the original directives. Armenians were deported from provinces in which they were already less than 10 per cent of the population. Some of these were in coastal provinces where invasion, given the experience of Gallipoli, was justifiably feared. However, Armenians were also deported from interior provinces in which there was no immediate danger. Some local officials, particularly on the Black Sea and in Mamuretülaziz (Harput), supervised the murders of large numbers of Armenians. The Ottoman authorities tried 1400 for such crimes against Armenians, executing many, but a large number undoubtedly escaped legal judgement. As in the Armenian murder of Muslims, hatred bred by past history and recent events undoubtedly led to great inhumanity.

In the end, approximately 225,000 Armenians survived to arrive in the Ottoman Arab provinces and Egypt. Most of these had been deported; some had fled in advance of armies. (By 1920, 400,000 others were refugees in the USSR, 50,000 in Iran, and the remainder mainly in North America and Europe, making a total of 811,000 surviving Armenian refugees.) In military terms, the deportation was a success. Deprived of the support of local Armenians, the Armenian rebellion died out in the east, but the cost was great.

Both Muslims and Armenians were to suffer great losses again at the end of World War I. The Russian Revolution led to the effective dissolution of the Russian army in eastern Anatolia. Some Russian officers remained, but the army in occupation was now made up of Armenians. At first these were nominally troops of a short-lived Transcaucasian Federation of Georgia, Armenia and Azerbaijan, then of the independent Armenian Republic. The Russians had planned to integrate the territory into the Russian Empire after the war and so made an attempt at ensuring civil order in 1916. The Armenians who succeeded them took up the war against the Muslims once again. Murder, kidnapping, destruction, and all the horrors that had been seen in southeast Anatolia now broke out in the northeast. The lucky among the Muslims fled to the mountains.

The Armenian occupation did not last long. When Ottoman forces attacked in 1918 the Armenians were quickly defeated. The Armenians were well equipped with Russian weapons, but ill trained. They were no match for seasoned Ottoman forces. They began to retreat precipitously. Probably assuming that they would never return, the Armenian forces destroyed all they could, killing the Muslims who fell into their hands. Ottoman troops who entered Erzincan found that the population had been slaughtered. Turks had been brought into the city from surrounding villages and killed there, as well. More than 1000 houses had been destroyed and bodies filled the streets. Similar sights were to greet the Ottoman soldiers as they entered other cities such as Tercan and Erzurum and throughout the countryside. After such experiences, Ottoman soldiers killed those Armenians who were unable to flee.

The Ottoman army advanced to the 1914 border and beyond to the 1876 border, but the war was over. They retreated to await the development of the peace.

Allied plans for the peace

During the war the Allies made many promises to enlist support for their cause. As will be seen in Chapter 7, the promises were easily broken once they had won. There were promises they meant to keep, though. These were promises to certain Balkan nations and to themselves.

It would have been impossible for the Allies not to reward Serbia in any peace settlement. The Serbs had fought gallantly against the Austrians and Bulgarians before defeat. This had made them the focus of a tremendous propaganda effort. Their sufferings were described, then magnified, until they had become the image of an oppressed people in Britain, France and the United States. Serbian actions had started the war, but this was forgotten. Serbia would be rewarded, just as Bulgaria and the Ottoman Empire would be punished.

The allegiance of Greece had been in question until the end of the war. Ruled by a pro-German king, Greece had remained neutral through most of the war. In what was essentially an act of war, French and British forces had invaded northern Greece, finally forcing a change in government that brought Greece into the war. There was much residual affection for Greece in Western countries. Greece too would be rewarded.

The Armenians would be left with broken promises.

It was from the Ottoman Empire that the Allies themselves would take their share of the spoils of war.

7

The peace conferences

Seen from the future, the deliberations of the peace conferences were an absurd mixture of uninformed idealism, hypocritical greed, and Western European hubris. This judgement is easier to make now than at the time, but is nonetheless true.

The division of conquered land by congresses of the European Powers was an old tradition. In 1648, European diplomats gathered at Westphalia to end the Wars of Religion. Later, smaller gatherings decided the ruling house of Spain, the ownership of American colonies, the end of the American Revolution, and the division of Poland. The Congress of Vienna decided the borders and many of the governments of Europe after the Napoleonic Wars. The Congress of Paris ended the Crimean War. The Congress of Berlin divided the Balkans.

The aim of these congresses was the straightforward division of territory. Diplomatic debates at the congresses dealt with power politics and, especially in the Congress of Vienna, the retention of privilege of ruling classes and dominant countries. At its heart, the Paris Peace Conference that ended World War I was the same. The main consideration of the victorious Allies (the Entente) was what they would win from the deliberations, what new territories they would occupy. But two factors were added to the agenda of the Paris Peace Conference.

The first factor was revenge. During the war, Allied propaganda had painted the Allies' adversaries as black indeed. Babies on bayonets, massacres of civilians, attacks on priests and nuns – all the panoply of propaganda had been used to show the people of the Allied countries that they were fighting not just another war for land or economic advantage, but a Holy War against evil. In fact, it is doubtful if either side in the war had been more evil than the other. No one's hands were clean. The Allies had won, however, and their populations now demanded revenge for what they had been told were the events of the war. Even without the question of war guilt, Allied civilians and politicians wanted someone to pay for the privations their people had suffered in the war. This thirst for revenge was a factor not much seen in the earlier European congresses. The Congress of Vienna had been lenient with France, and the Congress of Paris had been lenient with Russia. Germany, Austria and the Ottoman Empire were not to experience such leniency.

The other factor was a new democratic morality, an ideology that attempted to forestall future wars by drawing up a just peace and granting freedom, civil rights and political self-determination to peoples. These considerations were brought to the table by Woodrow Wilson, president of the United States, an idealist who had brought his people into the war by promising that American ideals would cleanse the old political habits of Europe, 'to make the world safe for democracy'.

Wilson's morality had a clear effect on the deliberations of the peace conference. In the contest between self-interest, revenge and morality, however, morality took a distant third place. Wilson did affect the public image of the conference's decisions, though not their substance. Lip-service was duly paid to his principles. This meant that the conference awarded no new colonies to the conquerors. Instead they were to be given League of Nations 'mandates' over new possessions:

> To those colonies and territories which as a consequence of the late war may have ceased to be under the sovereignty of the States which formerly governed them and which are inhabited by peoples not yet ready to stand by themselves under the strenuous conditions of the modern world, there should be applied the principle that the well-being and development of such peoples form a sacred trust to civilization and that securities for the performance of this trust should be embodied in this Covenant.
>
> The best method for giving practical effect to this principle is that the tutelage of such peoples should be entrusted to advanced nations who by reason of their resources, their experience or their geographical position can best undertake this responsibility, and who are willing to accept it, and that the tutelage should be exercised by them as Mandatories on behalf of the League.[1]

Other than the need to file yearly reports with the League of Nations, the practical differences between a mandate and a colony were few. The legal principle at work in the mandates was very interesting: first the territory was conquered, then the conquerors decided who should rule it. It was styled a mandate and theoretically given to the League of Nations, who then delivered it to the 'mandatory', i.e. the country that the conquerors had already decided would receive it. One would have thought that a sincere mandate would have been given to an 'advanced' but disinterested nation that could properly carry out the 'sacred trust of civilization', perhaps the Swiss.

Wartime promises

During World War I the Allied (Entente) Powers had made promises whenever necessary and to whoever might believe them. Some they meant to keep, some they did not. During the war, they hoped that those who had been promised land and concessions would not compare notes, because the same land had been promised to more than one potential ally.

Italy had been nominally the ally of Germany and Austria before the war. This did not affect her decisions once war broke out. She negotiated with both the Allies and the Central Powers to get the best deal. The Allies were able to offer more. In the Treaty of London (26 April 1915)[2] and the Agreement of Saint Jean de Maurienne (18 August 1917), Italy was promised Austrian territory on Italy's northeast border, islands off the Dalmatian coast, increase of its territories in Africa, part of the Albanian coast (Sasano and Vlore), and part of southern Anatolia (Antalya). Italy would also be allowed to keep the Dodecanese Islands (off southwestern Anatolia) that she had promised to return to the Ottoman Empire.

In March 1915, Britain and France promised the straits region – the Bosporus, the Dardanelles, the Sea of Marmara, the city of Istanbul, and the surrounding region – to Russia in the so-called Constantinople Agreement of 4 March–10 April 1915.

To gain the support of the sharif of Mecca, the leading Ottoman notable in Arabia, the British promised him an extensive Arab kingdom if he would revolt. In correspondence with the sharif from July 1915 to March 1916, Sir Henry McMahon, the British High Commissioner in Egypt, speaking for the government, delineated the proposed kingdom as including Ottoman Arabia and Syria, with the exception of an area roughly corresponding to today's Lebanon. An unspecified special arrangement was to hold in Iraq. The Anglo-French Declaration of 7 November 1918 promised to aid in the construction of Middle Eastern governments that 'derived their authority from the initiative and free choice of the indigenous populations'.

In order to attract Jewish support, the British also promised part of Ottoman Syria to the Zionist organization. The promise was contained in the indefinite words of the famous Balfour Declaration (2 November 1917):

> His Majesty's Government view with favour the establishment in Palestine of a National Home for the Jewish People, and will use their best endeavours to facilitate the achievement of this object, it being clearly understood that nothing shall be done which may prejudice the civil and religious rights of existing non-Jewish communities in Palestine, or the rights and political status enjoyed by Jews in any other country.

'National home' was not a term definable in international law. The inherent conflict between promising preference to Jewish settlement and not prejudicing the rights of others was not considered in the statement. When the Arabs discovered the Balfour Declaration, however, the British promised in the Hogarth Message of January 1918 that any Jewish settlement in Palestine must be 'compatible with the freedom of the existing population both economic and political'. The Hogarth Message also stated that:

> The Entente Powers are determined that the Arab Race shall be given full opportunity of once again forming a nation in the world. This can only be achieved by the Arabs themselves uniting, and Great Britain and her Allies will pursue a policy with this ultimate unity in view.

The statement was not diplomatic obfuscation; it was an outright lie. The British and French had already decided what would be done with the Middle East. They had promised it to themselves. They would divide the Ottoman Empire to be ruled by the victorious Entente powers. The Sykes–Picot Agreement (23 April–16 October 1916) was the one promise that the Allies meant to keep, the promise to themselves. It stipulated:

- Russia was to gain the Straits and all of eastern Anatolia.
- Italy was to take southwestern and much of southern Anatolia, with a 'zone of influence' to the north of its territory.
- France was given coastal Syria, the remainder of southern Anatolia, and much of central Anatolia.
- Britain took southern and central Iraq and Kuwait.
- An Arab kingdom was granted the Hijaz in Arabia (most of which was desert), as well as central Syria and northern Iraq. The latter two were to be held under 'French influence' and 'British influence' respectively.
- Palestine was to be an 'International Zone', under European control.
- The Turks were to be left with a rump state in north and north-central Anatolia.

Despite their vocal commitment to the Armenian cause, no provision was made for the Armenians; the Russians would not stand for that. The various peoples and religious groups to be effected by European conquest were to be given the same amount of self-determination allowed to other colonial subjects: none.

The British had promised Palestine as a Jewish home, even though under the Sykes–Picot agreement the British would not control Palestine and so could hardly promise it. The British later attempted to say they had meant to exclude Palestine from their commitment to Sharif Husayn, but the language of their commitment leaves no doubt that they promised it to him. They had also neglected to mention that his kingdom, whatever that might entail, would largely be under British and French 'influence'. When the war was won and Italian support no longer needed, the British and French were to renege on much of what they promised Italy in Anatolia, as well.

The participants

The Paris (Versailles) Peace Conference and subsidiary peace conferences were governed by a Supreme Council which governed the conferences, decided agendas, and made all final decisions. The members of the Supreme Council were Great Britain, France, Italy, the United States and Japan. In practice, decisions concerning the Middle East were made by Britain and France, with Italian input present but often ignored. Japan was not a real part of decisions on matters outside of Asia. The United States delegation was highly visible and a great favourite of the press, but woefully incompetent in affecting decisions. Smaller nations, even those who had been allied with the victors in the war, approached the conferences as supplicants.

Great Britain

It is a charitable understatement to say that David Lloyd George, the British prime minister, was not well-educated in international affairs. He was a man of opinions, and on Middle Eastern and Balkan affairs he made up his mind without personal knowledge of the area or recourse to his own experts. He could see no good in Turks and nothing but good in Greeks, so he kept foolish promises to the Greeks, even when British interests were severely compromised. Less concerned about Armenians or Arabs, he felt no scruple in abandoning both when practical politics demanded. Lloyd George was precisely the wrong man for the times.

The primary interest of the British was preservation of the British Empire. By the inexorable logic of imperialism this meant the expansion of the Empire. The enemy was no longer Germany or Russia. Each had been humbled, by war and revolution respectively. That left France, an ally for the time, but alliances changed. France unquestionably planned a colonial empire in the Middle East, which might someday threaten the land route to India, the sea route through the Suez Canal, and the British oil fields in Iraq and Iran. A strong Italian presence in the eastern Mediterranean might also be a threat. Either French or Italian power in the Mediterranean also might compete with British commercial interests. The answer was to ensure that new French possessions in the Middle East were countered by new British possessions. The Italians would be neutralized by enlarging and strengthening Greece until it provided regional competition for the Italians.

France

The French could not be accused of idealism, unless it was the ideal of spreading French civilization across the globe. Not for them the nationalist sentimentality of the Fourteen Points. Their primary aims at the peace conference concerned the containment of Germany, the acquisition of land on the German border (Alsace-Lorraine, the Saar), and obtaining huge reparations from Germany. The overwhelmingly felt need for action against Germany meant that the French could be manipulated. To retain the support of others for their main objectives, the French were forced to concede on matters such as the occupation of western Thrace and western Anatolia by the Greeks. They also were not able to realize their maximal goals in the Arab world.

In the Middle East, the French wanted clear title to coastal Syria, which they had coveted for generations. France had long been the pre-eminent European power in the Ottoman Syrian provinces. Her trade had been active there since the sixteenth century, but France's most important tie was emotional and religious. France was the 'Protector of Latin Christians' of the Ottoman Empire. She had long-standing relationships with the uniate Christians of Syria, particularly the Maronites (Chapter 10). French companies had built more in Syria than any other Ottoman concessionary. On the Mediterranean coast of the Arab world, including British-occupied Egypt, the intelligentsia looked on France as the first nation of Europe and font of European culture. That culture was spread in the region by French missionaries. To the French, those centuries of cultural and economic contact defined a French special interest in Syria.

Premier Georges Clemenceau, who led the French delegation at the conference, was not particularly interested in the Middle East. He was nevertheless forced to advance the French interests in the region. The French parliament and French public opinion had made it clear to Clemenceau that he was expected to secure Syria for the French. Yet France could not simply demand the region allotted to it in the Sykes–Picot Agreement. British agreement was needed to impose a punitive peace on Germany. The British army controlled Syria. Therefore, the French were constrained to support Britain and to defer to them in decisions on the Middle East and Balkans. In practice, this was to mean the French would abandon some claims (Palestine, northern Iraq) and construct the terms of their occupation of Syria according to British overall plans for occupation of the Middle East. Britain would get the oil fields and the best strategic position. France would get northern Syria, the present-day countries of Syria and Lebanon.

Syria was to become the focus of all French interest in the Middle East. The French were to prove willing to fight for control of it, and even to ally themselves with the Turks in order to retain it.

The United States

Alone among the victors, Americans had no territorial aims in the Middle East or Balkans. Why then were Americans involved at all in the disposition of war spoils in the region? Ideals. For four generations American missionaries sent by the American Board of Commissioners for Foreign Missions had been spreading the Gospel and educating the Christians of the Ottoman Empire. They had come to the Ottoman Empire at first to convert Muslims, Jews and Orthodox Christians, but when the Muslims, Jews and Orthodox refused to consider conversion to Protestant Christianity, the missionaries turned to the Armenians, the only Middle Eastern group ever to convert to Protestantism in any number. Even among the Armenians, though, conversions were relatively few. The missionaries began to turn to education as their role, especially education of Armenians. The Armenians were thus their protégés and their reason for existence.

During the war the missionary establishment and its supporters had organized a massive aid campaign for Armenians and other Ottoman Christians. In order to gain support for this good purpose the missionary establishment had carried on a campaign of vilification against the Turks: Turkish crimes were magnified, Armenian crimes unmentioned. The campaign brought in more money than had ever before been collected by a charity in the United States ($116 million), so it was most effective. The image left behind in the minds of Americans was of blood-thirsty Turks attacking innocent Armenians. This distortion does not seem to have bothered the missionaries, who undoubtedly believed it to be mainly true. It had the effect of focusing the energy of the American public on the Middle East, where it expected the United States to do something for the Christians.

Woodrow Wilson, president of the United States, has entered history as a somewhat naive idealist, a character who could have been created by Henry James, the simple, honest American taken in by the wily and sophisticated Europeans. On 8 January 1918 he presented his Fourteen Points as the moral framework for a just peace. People all over Europe and the Middle East, including many in the Ottoman dominions, took one of his points very seriously – there should be self-determination of peoples within state boundaries drawn along national lines.

What is often neglected in the study of Wilson is that what seems to be unflinching idealism can often be the pig-headedness of a man who is blind to his own prejudice. Much has been written of Wilson's racial prejudice. This prejudice extended well beyond African-Americans. He never saw self-determination as applying to colonial peoples. As far as the Middle East and Balkans were concerned, Wilson steadfastly refused to apply his principle of self-determination to Muslims. He was in thrall to American missionaries and a firm believer in Christian triumphalism. To Wilson, self-determination in the Middle East and Balkans meant independent rule by Christian peoples, and only that. The United States, he believed, must be willing to make sacrifices to bring about this ideal. This would include taking on a quasi-colonial role in the Middle East.

The forces arrayed in America against Wilson and against any American part in the affairs of Europe shared all of Wilson's feelings about the Middle

East and the Balkans except one. They thought the United States should have nothing to do with the region. A deep dislike of European politics and diplomacy had abated only briefly for the war. Now it had returned with full force, making Wilson's idealistic sound and fury mean nothing. The US Senate frustrated Wilson's plans for the Middle East, as they did his plans elsewhere.

The Italians

Italy's primary concern at the peace conferences lay in regions close to her: Austrian property to the northeast of Italy and on the Aegean littoral. The Treaties of St Germain (1919) and Rapallo (1920) gave Italy most of what she wanted in that region, mainly at the expense of the new Yugoslavia, which, however, retained Dalmatia. Secondarily, Italy wished to expand her power into the eastern Mediterranean. The Dodecanese Islands, occupied by Italy since 1912, and southwestern Anatolia had been promised to Italy by Britain and France in order to bring Italy into the war on their side.

Italy had a problem at the peace conference: her power, whether military or economic, was the most negligible of all the major victorious nations, with a concomitant weakness of influence. Britain, much more powerful in every way, did not want a strengthened Italy as a competitor in the eastern Mediterranean. Italy was to gain her main war aim – territory taken from Austria-Hungary – and was to keep the Dodecanese Islands. She was to gain nothing in Anatolia and her power in the eastern Mediterranean was to remain weak.

The Ottoman Empire

The Ottomans were ill-served at the peace conference. Their delegation was led by Damat[3] Ferit Paşa, the grand vezir (described in Chapter 8). An unelected representative of the sultan with a limited constituency, Ferit Paşa did everything wrong. He adopted a policy of 'admitting' all the claims, some true, most false, made by the Allies against the Ottomans. These he blamed completely on the previous government. He personally loathed the Committee of Union and Progress and was most willing to blacken its name. His position was that now that the old government had been disbanded and a responsible government, his own, had been put in place, the Allies should treat the Ottomans gently: Anatolia, including Mosul (northern Iraq today), should be left to the Ottomans; the sultan should name the governors of the Arab provinces, which would be granted much autonomy; the Ottomans would themselves negotiate a border with the Armenians; no European mandates should be given for any part of the Middle East.

This was not what the Allies had expected to hear. They were first incredulous, then brought to laughter, and finally angry. Most of what Ferit Paşa was requesting was, in fact, simply an application of the spirit of Wilson's Fourteen Points to the Ottoman Empire. The British responded for the Allied Powers, letting the Ottomans know what was thought of them:

> Yet in all these changes [in Ottoman rule] there is no case to be found, either in Europe or Asia or Africa, in which the establishment of Ottoman rule in any country has not been followed by the diminution of it material prosperity, and a fall in its level of culture; nor is there any case to be found in which the withdrawal of Ottoman rule has not been followed by a growth in material prosperity and a rise in the level of culture. Neither among the Christians of Europe, nor among the Moslems of Syria, Arabia and Africa has the Ottoman Turk done other than destroy what he has conquered; never has he shown himself able to develop in peace what he has won by war. Not in this direction do his talents lie.[4]

The statement went on to announce that it was the duty of the Allies to dismember the Empire. Of the British official comments, this was the most temperate. In another, Lord Curzon spoke of the need 'to cut this canker which has poisoned the life of Europe' and described Istanbul as 'the hot bed of every sort of eastern vice'.[5] Things had not gone well for Ferit Paşa. It was obvious what the Ottomans could expect from their conquerors. Ferit Paşa had admitted to crimes his people did not commit and blackened the name of the Turks, all to no avail. There is no need to consider any further the Ottoman delegation at the peace conference. They were never a real part of its deliberations.

Armenia

Armenian claims at the peace conference were extensive. Two Armenian delegations – one from the new Armenian Republic and the other from overseas Armenians – demanded most of eastern Anatolia, parts of central and northern Anatolia, and Cilicia, the region around the city of Adana, which was to be given to Armenia as its outlet to the Mediterranean.

The British and French were victims of their own wartime propaganda. In alliance with the American missionary establishment, the British propaganda office had built a picture of 'starving Armenia' that played on emotions at home and abroad to mobilize animosity toward the Ottomans. Only the Serbs had been given similar treatment. The Armenians were portrayed both as unarmed innocents who had been slaughtered by 'The Unspeakable Turk' and as a plucky people who had fought for the Allies.

Such contradictions were allowed in propaganda. The Armenian delegations declared that it was now time to reward the Armenians for their suffering and loyalty to the Allied cause.

The final disposition of the Armenian question was made, or rather avoided, at the San Remo Conference, a continuation of the deliberations of the Supreme Council, which began on 18 April 1920.

The French were little concerned for the Armenians. They had other matters to deal with, and the Armenians were demanding territory claimed by the French in the Sykes–Picot Agreement. The British bore the brunt of the decision. They would have been glad to award the Armenians as much as possible, had there not been insurmountable problems. Though the British delegation at the conference willingly used and publicized false population statistics presented by the Greeks and Armenians, the Foreign and War Offices knew the demographic situation in Anatolia. (When the British government sent their agents to the Ottoman Empire they gave them tables from Ottoman population registers, because those, they told the agents, were the best picture of the population.) The statistics showed that before the war Armenians had been only 17 per cent of the region they claimed. They had surely not increased their proportion of the population during the war. No Armenian state could endure under such circumstances unless it was supported, they estimated, by 100,000 foreign troops. The troops would have to remain in place for generations.

None of the European Allies was willing to send 100,000 troops to occupy eastern Anatolia. It was doubtful if the public in Britain, France or Italy would support the sending of any troops to eastern Anatolia on a long-term basis. The solution was first to tell the Armenians that they would have to accept a smaller region, probably the region awarded to the Russians in the Sykes–Picot Agreement. It was agreed that President Wilson would make a final determination of the borders. The British further attempted to wash their hands of the Armenian claims by suggesting that America accept a mandate for Armenia. President Wilson and his aide-de-camp, Col. House, had indicated previously that suggestion of an American mandate over Armenia would be viewed favourably in the United States. He was wrong. Despite lobbying from the White House and anguished pleas from the missionary establishment, the isolationists in the Senate wanted no part of an action that was all expense and no benefit.

Frustrated in the attempt to push their Armenian troubles off on the Americans, the Allies fell back on hypocrisy. Whereas previously they had pleaded to the Americans that the Armenians could not survive without American military intervention, they now declared that Armenia could stand on its own and control all the territory awarded it. The only assistance needed would be supplies and some European officers. The Armenian Republic accepted this, probably out of fear that not even the supplies and officers would be forthcoming had they not done so. President Wilson agreed to draw up the borders of Armenia. He delivered a completely unrealistic map, one that ignored all demographic, political and power realities, in November 1920, shortly before the final defeat of the Armenians by the Turks and the Bolsheviks (Chapter 8).

Even those, such as this author, who feel that a large Armenian state would have been an unjust imposition of minority rule, must judge the Allied treatment of the Armenians as craven. Idealistic support of the Armenian cause, no matter how wrong-headed, was proclaimed. Armenians were encouraged to resist their enemies, rather than try to come to accommodation with them, because the Europeans and Americans would soon give the Armenians all they wanted. Then it was, 'Sorry, too expensive for us. You're on your own. All the best.'

Greece

Judged by its contribution to the Allied war effort, Greece was owed little by the victors. King Constantine I (ruled 1913–17, 1920–24) took the Greek throne in 1913. He was a German himself, a cousin of Kaiser Wilhelm II of Germany, and loyal to his roots. Had it been possible, he would have entered the war on Germany's side. But the sympathies of the prime minister, Eleftherios Venizelos, were with the Entente. With the Ottomans on the side of the Germans, it was the Allies who could offer Greece the region it coveted in western Anatolia. Political stalemate kept the Greeks from taking any side. Venizelos's government was forced to resign in 1915, then brought back to power in the subsequent elections. The stalemate continued until broken by the Allies.

In September and October 1915, against the wishes of the Greek government, Allied forces landed in Salonica. Their intention, never carried out, was to aid the Serbs. What was in fact an invasion of her territory and an act of war provoked a domestic crisis in Greece. Venizelos again resigned, but this time went to Salonica and formed a new government, protected by the Allies, who recognized it as the legitimate government of Greece. An Allied fleet finally sailed to Piraeus, the port of Athens, threatened the royal government, and forced the king to abdicate on 12 June 1917. Venizelos now ruled Greece. The Greek army joined a much larger Allied force in attacking Bulgaria in September 1918. Greece thus came to the conference table as a somewhat tardy ally of the Entente.

Greece was blessed with a most able diplomat as prime minister. Prime minister Venizelos was a great salesman who convinced the Allies that Greece could greatly expand her territory in the Aegean region with a minimum of problems for either the Greeks or the Allies. The Allied heads of state believed him, even when their own experts disagreed. Wishful thinking was a part of the Allied belief; they wanted to believe that their troubles in the region would be settled by the Greeks, without expense or effort from their own tired countries. It took Venizelos to paint a picture

Map 7.1 Western Anatolia and the Balkans

they could believe, though. By the time the Allies realized they had erred, another war had erupted, this time between the Greeks and the Turks.

Greek demands at the peace conferences were based on history, fabricated population statistics, and the deep affection for everything Greek of men such as Lloyd George. Greece claimed southern Albania, all of Thrace, all of the Aegean Islands (including the Dodecanese, occupied by and promised to Italy), a large part of southwestern Anatolia, and even Cyprus (a British colony). All these had at one time or another been under some form of Greek rule, but only Cyprus and the other islands had Greek majorities. In fact, Greeks had been a distinct minority for half a millennium in most of the regions they claimed. Venizelos avoided this problem by presenting the peace conference with his own statistics, ostensibly drawn up by the Greek Patriarchate, but actually commissioned from one Professor

Soteriades, who was paid to falsify the data. It was a mark of Venizelos's charm that Lloyd George refused to believe the statistics used by his own War Office and Foreign Office, which showed sizeable Muslim majorities in southern Albania, eastern Thrace and southwestern Anatolia. Lloyd George instead used the Greek statistics as justification for satisfying the Greek demands.

Italy was an obstacle to Greek desires. She had been promised the Dodecanese and southwestern Anatolia as a condition of her joining the war. The Sykes–Picot Agreement specifically reserved those regions for Italy. The United States delegation opposed most of the Greek claims, because the Greek statistics were false. The British War Office also opposed the Greek plans on the sensible grounds that Greeks were a minority, no matter what Venizelos's statistics stated. The Foreign Office concurred, more diplomatically. The British India Office opposed the Greek plans out of fear that public opinion among Indian Muslims would be adversely affected if majority Muslim lands were given to the Greeks. It all made no difference. President Wilson wished the Greeks to succeed, so he overrode his experts. Lloyd George supported the Greeks and ordered British delegates to do likewise. The British were also affected by a Greek announcement that the Venizelos government would fall if it did not gain its goals. The British were counting on him as a friend to steer Greek foreign policy in their favour. As stated above, the British planned to rely on a friendly Greece to cement their interests in the eastern Mediterranean. Britain therefore offered Greece almost complete support at the peace conference. Only Cyprus was off-limits; giving up British land would have been going too far.

The British and Americans, supported by the French, agreed in May 1919 that the Greek forces would be sent to occupy 'the Sanjak of Smyrna' – İzmir and its surrounding district – in advance of any treaty with the Ottoman Empire. This was a violation of the armistice agreement with the Ottomans. The justification was given that massacres of the Greek population were taking place. This was completely false. The British knew from reports of agents on the spot that the Ottomans were keeping good order. The real reason was desire to please the Greeks and forestall any Italian effort to enforce the promises made to Italy by landing Greek troops.

On 15 May, the Greeks were landed at İzmir. They met no opposition, as the Ottoman government had decided to give in to the Allies in every particular. Massacres of Turkish civilians and officials began on the first day. They continued as the Greeks expanded their control, moving far beyond the region allotted them by the peace conference (Chapter 8).

In a rare admission that there might have been problems with their plans, the British were constrained by the French and Italians to investigate Greek actions in Anatolia. The Italians obviously had their own interests, and the French were beginning to feel that complete alienation of the Turks might not serve their own interest in the Middle East. (The French were later to adopt a pro-Turkish position.) The British government was hearing probing questions in parliament on Greek actions. A Commission of Inquiry was sent to Anatolia. It reported on 8 November 1919 to the Supreme Council of the peace conference. The report stated that there had been no massacres of Greeks, and so the Greek occupation was unjustified, and that the occupied area was largely Muslim in population. Blame for disturbances and massacres was placed on the Greeks. It recommended that Greek troops be replaced by an inter-Allied contingent. The Supreme Council accepted the Commission's report, but the British kept it from publication. Instead of reacting to the report by restricting Greek actions, the British renewed their support of the Greeks. Perhaps this was fear of admitting a grave error, perhaps it was simply the overwhelming affection for Venizelos and the Greeks that had already been shown by Lloyd George and Wilson in particular. Whatever the reason, the British were to support the advance of Greek troops throughout western Anatolia and Thrace. As will be seen in Chapter 8, this led to disaster for the Greeks and horror for the people of Anatolia.

The Treaty of Sèvres

The result of all the months of conference deliberations on the fate of the Middle East was the Treaty of Sèvres, signed on 10 August 1920. The Treaty of Sèvres was never enforced. Its provisions were obviated by the armed refusal of the Turks to accept them. Nevertheless, the provisions of the treaty are an instructive lesson in European hubris. They explain why the Turks had no choice but to resist the imperialism of the Allies and the nationalism of the Greeks and Armenians (Chapter 8). Had they not done so, they would almost surely have ceased to exist.

- İzmir and the surrounding region were put under Greek administration, with the proviso that a plebiscite would be held in five years to decide if the region should be annexed by the Greek kingdom. Greece also received eastern Thrace up to a few miles of Istanbul (the Çatalca Line).
- The Ottoman Empire would accept the decision of President Wilson on the border between it and Armenia, would demilitarize border areas if Wilson so decided, and would grant Armenia access to the sea.
- Syria and Iraq ('Mesopotamia') were 'provisionally recognized as independent states subject to the rendering of administrative advice and assistance by a Mandatory until such time as they are able to stand alone'. (Britain was to take Palestine and Iraq, France to take what became Syria and Lebanon.)
- The Balfour Declaration, creating a Jewish Home in Palestine, was written into the treaty.

- The sharif of Mecca was given a 'free and independent State' in the Hijaz (west and northwest Arabia) only.
- Italy gained the Dodecanese Islands and was recognized as having a 'special interest' in southern Anatolia (the Antalya and Konya regions).
- A French 'special interest' in Cilicia (the Adana, Antep, Urfa and Mardin regions) was recognized.
- The Anatolian Railway, the Mersin–Tarsus–Adana Railway, and the portions of the Baghdad Railway in Ottoman territory 'shall be worked by a company whose capital will be subscribed by British, French and Italian financial groups'.
- The coal mines in Zonguldak (northwestern Anatolia) were conceded to the Italian government.
- Ottoman land forces were reduced to 50,000 men, most of whom would be gendarmes. There was to be no regular army. The navy was similarly restricted. All Ottoman forces would be effectively under the control of Allied officers.
- The Capitulations were restored. An Allied Commission would supervise and manage the collection of the Ottoman debt, as before. It would also oversee the state budget, taxes, loans, etc., in effect controlling Ottoman finances.

What territory remained to the Ottomans in the Treaty of Sèvres was approximately what had been foreseen in the Sykes–Picot Agreement – northwest and northcentral Anatolia. The one concession was Ottoman retention of Istanbul. This would probably have proven to be temporary: Greek soldiers were to be within cannon range of the city. The Ottomans were forbidden to keep warships on the city's coastline. They were not allowed an army to defend the city or anywhere else in their small state.

What remained of the Ottoman Empire was to be independent only in name. It was to be unable to defend itself, and its finances, transportation system and police force were to be in the hands of foreigners. Many more Turks would have been outside its borders than within, were it not for the fact that so many of the Turks of southwestern Anatolia were being forced out of the area of Greek occupation. Given the precedent of the Balkan Wars, more forced migration could be expected.

None of the vengeful peace treaties that followed World War I was as brutal as that visited on the Ottomans. The government of Ferit Paşa signed it, and have been branded traitors ever since for their actions. The Turks did not accept it. For them the significance of the Treaty of Sèvres was the reinforcement of their will to resist their conquerors. The treaty showed in stark terms what awaited them if they failed.

8

The Turkish War of Independence

On 30 October 1918 the Ottoman Empire signed the Armistice of Mudros with the Allied Powers. The details of the armistice were sketched in briefly, leaving much to interpretation. What was agreed was the disarmament of the Ottomans, in return for which the Allies would make only minimal changes in the Ottoman state and unoccupied lands until a final decision on their disposition was made by treaty. Most of these provisions were quickly broken by the Allies.

In Istanbul, the government of the Committee of Union and Progress was ejected. Talât and Cemal were later to be assassinated by Armenians, and Enver was to die while fighting the Bolsheviks in Central Asia. The new sultan, Mehmet VI (ruled 1918–22), was an implacable enemy of the CUP. He had chafed at his subordinate position to the CUP in the last year of the war and blamed the CUP for the troubles that had befallen the Empire. In fact, the survival of independence in the Middle East was of much less importance to him than the survival of the Ottoman dynasty. The sultan chose Damat Mehmet Ferit Paşa to head a new government. He and his followers were not chosen for their dedication to Turkish independence. In its past incarnations his party, misnamed the Liberals, had proven that its primary loyalties were to its own power. Hatred of the CUP and their own survival were the main aims of the sultan and his government. Ferit Paşa drew his cabinet and officials from old enemies of the CUP government.

Ferit Paşa and his government put their trust in a mistaken belief that the Allies would remain true to their wartime promises. They seemed to believe that the Fourteen Points of Woodrow Wilson, which directed that majorities would have their own states, applied to Turks. Resigned to the loss of provinces that did not have ethnic Turkish majorities, they assumed that a smaller Ottoman state in Anatolia and perhaps eastern Thrace would be created, a state that they would rule. To this end, the government cooperated with the Allies, playing into Allied prejudices. As seen in Chapter 7, they portrayed themselves as the 'good Turks' who had opposed the war. All the problems of the war had been the fault of the CUP. Ferit Paşa 'admitted' all sorts of crimes of the past government, most of which had never happened. The government even held kangaroo courts in which officials and generals of the past government, usually tried *in absentia* and thus unrepresented, were convicted of crimes real and imagined. Ottoman officials and military officers were ordered to cooperate with the Allies in all cases, even when Allied orders were plainly in contravention of the armistice agreement. Ferit Paşa went to the Versailles Peace Conference, where he grovelled. None of it did any good. Mercy was not part of the Allied project at the Versailles Peace Conference. The Allies had other plans. On 13 November 1918, Allied troops took the city of Istanbul and put it under martial law. From that point, not even the quisling government of Ferit Paşa was independent.

The Treaty of Sèvres (10 August 1920) left the Ottoman Empire with north-central and northwestern Anatolia, a region that excluded more of the Turkish population than it included. Istanbul was left to the pocket empire, but the Allies were to remain in control there for an indefinite period. In any case, the territory allotted to the Turks could not be defended by the 50,000-man army stipulated by the treaty, so it could be expected that even this land would not be long held against their enemies. The treaty did not make an award to the Armenian Republic. Instead the American president, Woodrow Wilson, was to decide the Armenian borders. It was expected that he would give the Republic all of northeastern and much of eastern Anatolia, which he subsequently did. Greece, which had not fought against the Ottomans in the war, was given İzmir and its surrounding territory, which had been 75 per cent Turkish before World War I. Italy and France shared southern Anatolia. In short, despite pious pronouncements on the 'sovereignty of peoples' and the need for states that reflected ethnic boundaries, the Allies completely ignored the demographic realities in Anatolia.

The Treaty of Sèvres was dead even as it was signed. Military events overtook and obviated its clauses. The Turks had begun to fight back.

Before they fled Istanbul, the leaders of the CUP had already begun preparations for a national resistance to the plans of the Allies. The CUP was in a good position for this. It had an extensive political network all across Anatolia and eastern Thrace, as well as a secret organization (the Teşkilât-i Mahsusa) that was well versed in clandestine activities. Caches of arms and supplies were hidden and organizers sent out to prepare the resistance. Although Ferit Paşa's Liberals forced all prominent CUP members and sympathizers from the government and the bureaucracy, they could not root out lesser officials in the time they had. These officials were to prove important to the resistance, acting as spies, transferring materials to the resistance, and thwarting the intentions of the government and the Allies.

The Ottoman military and the bureaucracy, faced with the power of the Allies and with a government that was proving itself to be subservient to the conquerors, did what government officials always have done in such difficult situations: they procrastinated. According to the terms of the armistice, Allied 'control officers', mainly British army officers, were to oversee the decommissioning of the Ottoman army. Weapons were to be turned in to the Allies and armies disbanded. But as the Allied officers fanned out across Anatolia they found a confusing situation. Armies could not be immediately disbanded because of the threat of unrest in local areas. Depots of weapons were mysteriously empty. When weapons had been collected, guards seemed willing to turn their backs as these weapons then disappeared. Large numbers of disaffected military officers were mysteriously spirited to safety in Anatolia before they could be arrested in Istanbul. Allied complaints to the government were met with anxious hand-wringing by senior officials and assurances by junior officials that something would be done.

The Ottoman army itself had withdrawn from areas of confrontation in the east and south of Anatolia. Its place was taken by forces of the Armenian Republic, once again claiming lands they had briefly held until evicted by the Ottomans in 1918. In Cilicia (the region whose main city is Adana), French soldiers took a large part of Anatolia as the northern districts of their new colony in Syria. Italians landed to the west of the French to claim their own portion of the south (Antalya, Konya).

In both the east and the south Turks were beleaguered by opponents confident of victory. But it was the occupation of İzmir that finally spurred the Turks to organized resistance.

Animosity between the Greeks and Turks was a consequence of the Balkan Wars. Before or during the world war the Ottoman government did not engage in a policy of deportation of Anatolian Greeks to match the deportation of the Balkan Muslims, but the Committee of Union and Progress did give the Anatolian Greeks cause to fear. The CUP organized a boycott of Greek business and a policy of intimidation against Greeks in the Ottoman Empire. In smaller cities and the countryside houses were burnt, livestock was stolen, and there were murders. Anatolian Greeks naturally feared that Turks would take revenge on them for actions of the Greek kingdom. It did not help their fears that Turkish refugees from the Balkans were naturally settled in the western Anatolian provinces closest to their old homes. Those were also the provinces with the largest Greek populations. Perhaps 20,000 Greeks left western Anatolia as a result, settling mainly in the Greek islands off the coast. (Another 80,000 may have left eastern Thrace during the Balkan Wars.) Their houses were taken by the Turkish refugees from the Balkans. During World War I an unknown number of Greeks were deported to the interior of Anatolia as potential partisans to the Allies who attempted to invade at Gallipoli. Most of these groups of refugees and deportees seem to have survived the war, but they held animosities to match the rancour of the Turkish refugees.

Western Anatolia had been spared warfare, but the population had suffered heavily during World War I. The war had drained off food, farm animals, and men, many of whom did not return. Nearly a million refugees from the Balkans and eastern Anatolia had come to the region, adding to misery from starvation and disease. During the war many of these refugees had been housed in the farms and dwellings of Greeks, and of a number of Armenians, who had earlier fled to Greece. Now they returned, aided by and watched over by the victorious Allies, leaving the Muslim refugees once again homeless. Unlike the Christians, they were not allowed to return to their homes. The Balkan states would not admit them, and eastern Anatolia was still a war zone.

The Turkish War of Independence was fomented by the Allies. At war's end they were presented with a supine population and a subservient government. The Turks were sick of war. Many political leaders had always opposed the CUP and held friendly feelings toward the British and French. Americans, who espoused self-determination and the ethical treatment of conquered peoples, were especially looked to for principled decisions and behaviour. Had the Allies kept to the terms of the Mudros Armistice and their own avowed principles of self-determination of peoples, a defeated Turkish people would have been hard pressed not to accept defeat. The Allies did not do so. Meeting in Versailles, they had set a policy of division of Anatolia without regard to population or ethnicity. The American ideals were obviously not to be applied to non-Europeans. The agents of the Allies in the Aegean region were to be the Greeks. The Turks had seen in the Balkan Wars what they could expect from them.

The Allies at Versailles never had exact plans for the disposition of western Anatolia, other than a vague notion that land should be given to the Greeks. They never gave any real consideration to the will of the people or to the demographic make-up of the population. Before the war, Greeks had made up only 14 per cent of the population of western Anatolia;[1] Muslims, most of them Turks, constituted 80 per cent. The only way for the Greeks to rule the territory was to evict the Muslims, a necessity which the Allies ignored but the Greeks understood very well.

Greece had played a small part in the world war: Greek troops took part in the final battles against Bulgaria in the Balkans, which lasted little more than one week. Though it had been of limited assistance in the war, Greece was favoured by the Allies. In part this was the result of cold calculation. A moderately powerful Greece friendly to the Allies, especially the British, would be a valuable ally in the eastern Mediterranean. Both Britain and France feared that if Greece did not take southwestern Anatolia, Italy would do so, and neither wanted a more powerful Italy in the eastern Mediterranean. The main reason for Allied support for Greece, though, was emotional. Greece had always held the affections of the British and French, more from memories of ancient Greece and Byzantium and as a bastion of Christianity than from modern history. Greece was well served by Venizelos as its ambassador. He was an able diplomat and tactician who made friends among the powerful at the conference at Versailles: 'The charm and genius of M. Venizelos obtained for Greece concessions which a man of less supreme diplomatic ability could scarcely have secured'.[2] The Allies were convinced that Greek rule would be beneficial to all. Greek treatment of the Turks in the Balkan Wars and before was ignored. Indeed, British prime minister Lloyd George, Greece's main friend at the conference, was no student of Balkan history and probably had no real idea of the events of past years. The Allies decided to award territory in Thrace and Anatolia to Greece.

The ostensible justification for the Allied invasion of Anatolia was Article VII of the Armistice signed between the Allies and the Ottoman Empire. This stated that 'the Allies have the right to occupy any strategic points in the event of any situation arising which threatens the security of the Allies'. There was in fact no situation that threatened Allied security until the Greeks created such a situation by their occupation. And not even a Foreign Office lawyer could bend the meaning of that armistice clause to include occupation of Ottoman territory by the Greeks alone, rather than by the Allies as a group. The governor of the İzmir Province, upon hearing that the occupation would take place and fearing the worst, asked that Allied troops, not Greeks, be used, or at least that the Greeks be accompanied by Allied troops. The British commander of the operation refused.

At first, the Versailles Conference had decided that the Greeks were to occupy only the 'District of Smyrna', the city of İzmir and its hinterland. Prime minister Venizelos had loftier plans. On 15 May 1919, a Greek army landed at İzmir, watched over by British ships. Enrolling local Greeks in their forces, the Greeks quickly moved to the boundaries of their conquest. A brief check by disorganized Turkish forces was quickly overcome. By July 1920 the Greeks had occupied all of the Aegean coast and inland areas. Each time they advanced the Allies ignored past orders and forgave their violation of the terms of their grant. Rather than rebuking the Greeks, the British enlarged their conquest. British forces moved from Istanbul, took the İzmit peninsula, and presented it to the Greeks.

More than a million Turkish refugees fled the advancing Greeks. They had good reason to flee: slaughter of Turkish civilians had begun on the day the Greeks landed. Turkish shops and factories were looted of all their goods. More than 700 Turks were killed. A longtime British resident of İzmir, Donald Whittall, reported what he had seen:

> From there [the custom-house] up to the Kramer Palace Hotel I was the unwilling witness of the massacre of some thirty unarmed men, who were being marched with hands up. This butchery was committed by Greek soldiers entirely.

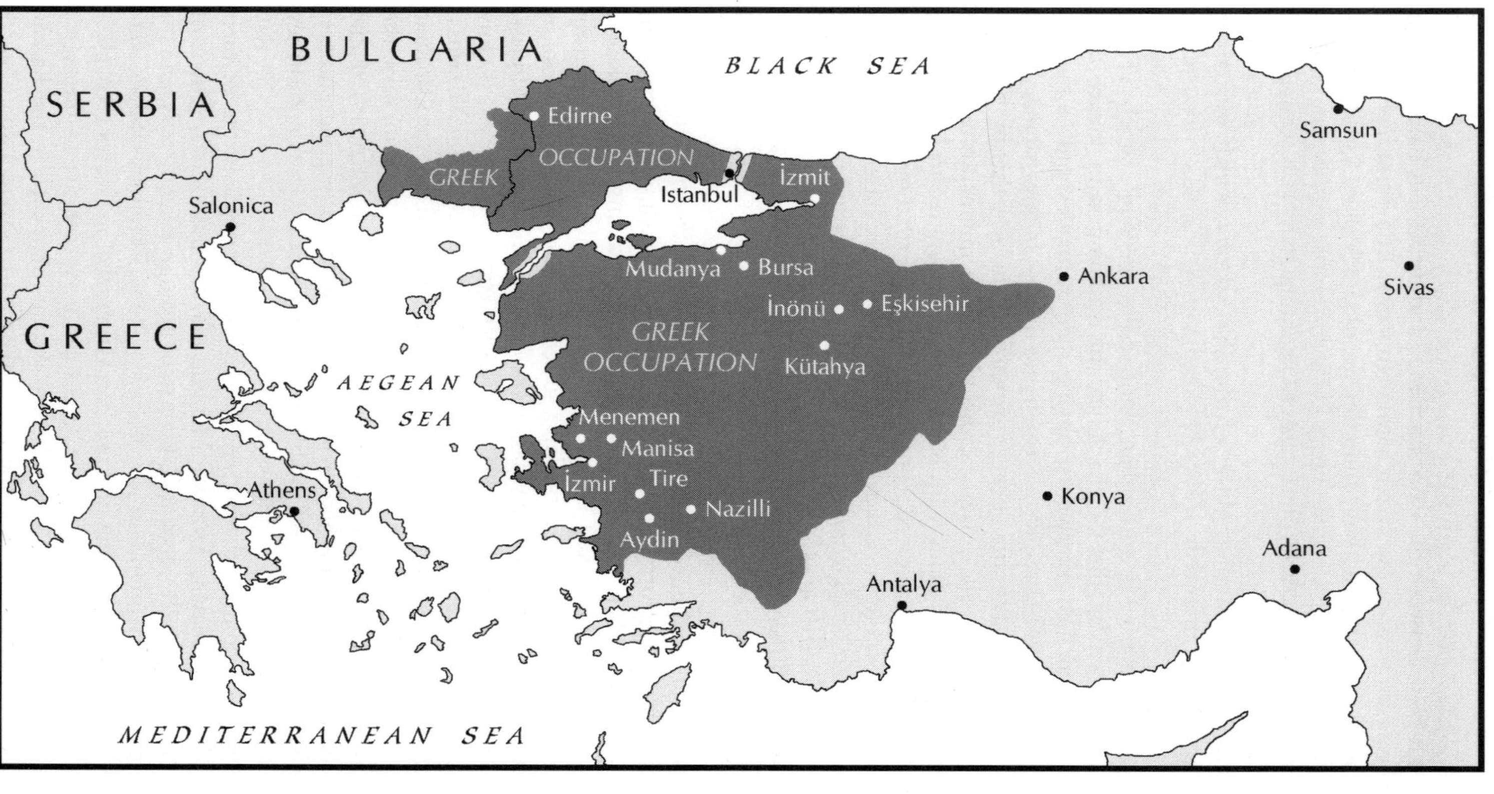

Map 8.1 The war in the west

> At a point between the Corn Exchange and the Orient Bank I saw six being shot out of one batch within ten yards. At a point higher up I saw five others succumbing under the fire of Greek rifles. Close to the landing place of the Cordelio boats I saw a lot more shot down. Near Kramer I witnessed three more cases of shooting . . .[3]

The American commanding officer of the USS *Arizona*, which was taking part in the action, reported:

> Old men, unarmed, and other unoffending civilian Turks were knocked down by the Greeks, killed by stabbing with knives or bayonets, and then afterwards, having their valuables and clothing stripped off their bodies, were thrown into the sea. In one instance, the man was again shot after being thrown into the sea, this by Greek soldiers. Many of the prisoners, including high military officers, as they were marched along with hands up were permitted to be beaten by the rabble who followed. Specific instances are cited by these same eyewitnesses where Turkish soldiers and sailors were bayoneted from behind by their Greek guards, while the rabble rifled their pockets and then threw their bodies into the sea. Many of the worst instances of inhuman treatment of the Turks were while they were under arrest and on the open sea front at noonday.[4]

The destruction continued in the region surrounding the city, and villages were sacked and destroyed. The British control officer who investigated the situation reported: 'The Greeks in the country round Smyrna have looted the arms-depots, have sacked Turkish villages, and hunted down Muslims'.[5] Ottoman soldiers in İzmir particularly suffered. Many were beaten, many murdered, as were prominent civilians who were viewed as agents of the old order – government officials, newspaper editors, etc.

Greek actions in İzmir were so flagrant that even the Allies took notice. An Allied Commission of Inquiry sent to the city reported that the Ottoman government had kept proper order in the city until the invasion, at which point civil order broke down completely. The Commission reported that Greek soldiers and civilians had then set up a campaign of beatings, murder and theft. The Commission set the blame squarely on the Greek authorities. The Allies suppressed the Commission's report.

The mayhem continued wherever the Greeks occupied. In the cities of Aydın, Tire, Menemen, Kasaba, Manisa, Nazilli and others, Ottoman gendarmes (police) were disarmed, their guns given to local Greeks, and the towns pillaged, with attendant murders of civilians. Ottoman officials were singled out for imprisonment and murder. Organized massacres took place in cities and all over the countryside. Greek civilians were given Greek army weapons and organized as armed bands. As had happened in the Balkan Wars, local residents who took the side of the invaders were used as 'shock troops' to speed the advance of the Greeks and cause the local Turks to flee from the occupied zone. The plan was extremely effective. As the Greeks advanced, Turks fled. Many parts of the Aegean region became devoid of Turks.

Not only Muslims, but Jews as well suffered from the Greek invasion. This repeated the pattern of the Balkan Wars and earlier wars in the Balkans, in which Jews were viewed as allies of the Turks. A certain amount of anti-Semitic prejudice also was surely present. The feeling against Jews might be better described as a general dislike of non-Christians. In Anatolia, more than half the Jews in the Greek zone of occupation were either killed or exiled.

The Greeks moved to the far north of western Anatolia, to areas within sight of Allied-occupied Istanbul, after the British gave them the İzmit Province. There they were in full view of Allied and other European observers. Nevertheless, confident of Allied support, their depredations continued. By this time it was obvious that their actions were part of a deliberate plan to expel the Turks of the region until the only remaining population was Greek. The British officer sent to investigate events in the İzmit region, General Franks, and the American High Commissioner in Istanbul, Admiral Bristol, both reported to their governments that the Greek government was involved in a systematic destruction of the Turks, which Bristol described as a 'prearranged plan'.

All the Greek actions against Turks were reported by 'control officers' of the Allies, mainly British soldiers and diplomats, who had been sent to observe the situation and disarm the Ottoman soldiery, as stipulated by the Mudros Armistice. The British knew exactly what was happening, but they did nothing and suppressed the reports. Too much was invested in the Greek occupation for the Allies to admit that it had been a disaster. The Turks knew, however, and it became obvious that they could not trust the Allies either to protect them or to keep to the terms of the Armistice. The Greek invasion instead stiffened their resolve to resist.

Refugees

The British estimated that by the end of September 1919, four months after the first Greek actions, there were already 177,000 Turkish refugees in the Aydın Province (whose capital was İzmir). One year later the numbers had increased to almost 500,000, and many more were to become refugees in late 1920. To the numbers of refugees in Anatolia must be added refugees from Greek-occupied eastern Thrace. The Ottomans estimated their numbers at 30,000 in the Istanbul region, making 200,000 with the refugees still there from the Balkan Wars. In all, approximately 1.2 million were refugees from the Greek invasion.

Many of the Turkish refugees had fled a number of times – fleeing the

İzmir district for nearby areas not yet conquered, then forced to flee again when the Greeks advanced. A large number of these were initially refugees from the Balkans, refugees once again. They were thrust on fellow Turks and on a government that had little to give them. General Harrington, the British commander in Istanbul, remarked that he did not see how the refugees could exist on what they were being fed, a bowl of soup every two days and some bread.

A number of Turks remained in the conquered territories. They either could not escape the fast-moving Greek advance or hoped that all would be well when the fighting ended. To them, 'administrative measures' were applied. High taxes were levelled and crops confiscated. Villagers were drafted into forced labour for the conquerors. Use of Ottoman currency was forbidden, and Ottoman notes could only be exchanged at an artificially low and ruinous rate of exchange, bankrupting businessmen and villagers alike. Travel by Turks was curtailed, except for those who were leaving the Greek-occupied zone; for them travel was facilitated.

Greeks did not escape the effects of the Greek invasion. Driven from their villages, Turks often formed themselves into armed bands, hiding from Greek troops and exacting revenge wherever they could. These bands descended on Greek villages, killing and looting in their turn. Such events were relatively few in the initial stages of the invasion, because there was little chance for them. The numbers of Greek refugees increased greatly when the Greeks ultimately lost the war.

The Turkish opposition

The invasion of Anatolia by the Greeks, and corresponding occupations of the east by the Armenians and south by the French, galvanized and unified the Turks in a way that had never been possible before. Now the Turks could see a practical reason for unity. Outsiders caused them to draw together. They were being vilified as Turks by the Europeans. Turks were being expelled from their homes and often massacred because they were identified as Turks. Islamic identification was by no means forgotten, but it coalesced with Turkish identification now that the Arabs were no longer in the picture. Greeks, Bulgarians and others might have adopted nationalism because of its benefits. Turks were driven to it by their enemies.

Turkish resistance to the Greeks began immediately upon the Greek invasion. It was at first weak and ineffective. Sometimes assisted by CUP organizers, villagers organized self-defence units and raided Greek soldiers and civilians. As more land was taken by the Greeks, resistance increased and disparate units cooperated in 'Societies for the Defence of the Rights of Turks'. The old political organization of the CUP was a factor of unification and communication between the different groups and supporters in Istanbul.

The great need, however, was for trained soldiers to lead the fight. Here the fact that Ottoman armies in the south and east had retired in good order and remained as organized units made the difference. When the army and gendarmerie switched their loyalties from the government to the people a real defence became possible. The first indication that the troops would not submit to the dismemberment of Anatolia came in the city of Aydın on 30 June 1919, when Ottoman soldiers acted on their own authority to retake the city briefly and save Turks there from massacre. Regardless of their orders, the military found it impossible to stand by and watch the destruction of the Turkish population. All over Anatolia, officers began to refuse to deliver their weapons to Allied control officers or to disband their units. Weapons that had been collected mysteriously disappeared from armouries. Sympathetic bureaucrats in Istanbul arranged for ammunition to be misdirected to the very armouries the Allies least wanted to receive deliveries.

Although Ferit Paşa never intended it, the Istanbul government provided leadership for the Resistance. Mustafa Kemal, hero of Gallipoli and one of the few officers who had defeated the Russians in battle in the east, had moved his army intact from Syria to southern Anatolia. He travelled to Istanbul, where he was given a pivotal assignment as inspector-general of Ottoman forces in north and northeastern Anatolia, with authority over civilian and military affairs. The intention of the government in making the appointment has never been understood or explained. Mustafa Kemal had not been a friend of Enver Paşa. This may have convinced the government that he would welcome their anti-CUP policy. Some have held that members of the government who secretly opposed the Allies appointed Mustafa Kemal, knowing that he would never accept the occupation of Anatolia. Whichever is true, Mustafa Kemal landed at Samsun and immediately began to organize what was later to be called the Turkish Nationalist Organization. Realizing its mistake, the Istanbul government recalled him, and even put a price on his head, but it was too late.

Mustafa Kemal proved to be as able a negotiator and conciliator as he was a general. Bringing together in common cause the politicians, religious leaders, merchants, landowners and military men of Anatolia was in itself a signal accomplishment; leading them to an agreement on purpose and action was a near miracle. Yet Kemal managed to draw together the leaders of Anatolia at two congresses at Erzurum (July and August 1919) and Sivas (4–11 September 1919). The Sivas Congress passed resolutions to be known later as the National Pact. These demanded that the integrity of all the regions inhabited by Turks be maintained, and that the Turks be politically independent within them. Liberty and equality under the law were to be guaranteed for all, but no special privileges would be extended to minorities. Those resisting the Greeks and Armenians were to be accepted as legitimate defence forces.

For a time it appeared that even the Istanbul government might be brought into the nationalist fold. The British showed a lack of sense unexpected in successful conquerors bent on achieving their own purposes, and allowed elections to the Ottoman parliament. The new parliament met on 12 January 1920 and passed the National Pact as the law of the land on 18 February. The British were furious, probably as much at themselves for having allowed this expression of democracy as they were at the Turks. They dissolved the parliament, arrested 150 pro-Nationalist officials, and made it obvious to the Turks that the Istanbul government was longer its own master.

Many members of the parliament escaped to Mustafa Kemal's headquarters at Ankara. They joined with military officers, civilian and religious leaders, and leaders of the Anatolian resistance movements in a new parliament, the Grand National Assembly. Mustafa Kemal was elected its president. The Assembly, not without bickering, created a unified military command under İsmet Paşa and set about organizing war with the Greeks.

Cilicia

The Allies who won World War I were not much interested in possessing Anatolia themselves. They knew its ethnic and religious divisions and its history of increasing intercommunal violence, and wanted none of them. Reading the diplomatic documents of the time, it is obvious that they considered Istanbul to be the only truly desirable property in Anatolia and eastern Thrace. Possessing Istanbul would be trouble, but the natural riches that came from trade and the fine strategic position would make it worthwhile. Not so eastern and central Anatolia.

South-central Anatolia, called Cilicia since Ancient times, was an acceptable possession for the Europeans because it was geographically close to Syria, awarded to French rule after the war. On the map Cilicia does seem to be a part of Syria, hemmed in by mountains and major rivers. In fact, it was a typically polyglot Ottoman region. The vast majority of the inhabitants, 83 per cent, were Muslims, but they were ethnically Turks, Arabs and Kurds and religiously divided into the Sunni Orthodox and groups, such as the Alevi and Yezidis, considered heterodox by the majority. Armenians made up two-thirds of the Christian population, but there were also Greek Orthodox, Syriac, Jacobite, Chaldean and Protestant Christians. The Armenians were themselves divided into Gregorian, Protestant and Catholic (uniate) sects.

While the region was too far from the Russian border for Armenian insurrection to have been a success, the Armenians had tried rebellion in 1915. Muslims remembered their losses from Armenian attacks on villages and cities. Armenians, most of them now refugees in Syria, remembered the horrors of deportation. Both groups remembered the region's Armenian–Muslim conflicts of the 1890s and 1909, although their memories of who was at fault were considerably different. Expecting that Armenians and Turks would live together in peace after such a history was a typically European conceit: if only Frenchmen showed these people how to live properly, all would be well. It was not to be.

The French occupation of Cilicia soon after the end of the war was a violation of the Mudros Armistice, which only allowed the Allies to occupy the Taurus railroad tunnel system and 'to occupy any strategic points in event of a situation arising which threatens the security of the Allies'. There was no danger to Allied security, at least not until the French violated the terms of the Armistice, and no conceivable threat could have been enough to justify the occupation of entire provinces. But the Allies were never overly fastidious in keeping promises made to Middle Easterners.

The Ottoman army had kept to the terms of the Armistice, which required it to move out of Cilicia. It marched west to Pozantı, on the road to Konya, and waited. The French were not able to replace Ottoman authority with their own. They had few men in the region. They wished, however, to exert their control as soon as possible. They therefore sent in members of the Armenian Legion, approximately 5000 Armenian soldiers and officers who had enlisted specifically 'to fight Turks' (and only that), later augmented by French colonial troops. In effect, Armenian revolutionary groups, the same groups that had shared massacres and reprisals with the Muslims earlier, were now the police. They were violently anti-Muslim, even fighting with French Muslim troops from Algeria.

Attacks on Muslims began as soon as the Armenians took up their assignments. Villagers fled to the mountains as the Armenians attacked. Murders, rapes, and all the now familiar atrocities were common wherever the Armenian Legion occupied. The British, who were still in overall command of the territories they had taken from the Ottomans, refused to allow the Armenian Legion to continue its actions. The French themselves recognized what was transpiring: the French General Hamelin, speaking of Turkish complaints against the Armenians, described them as 'complaints, unfortunately most often well-founded, against all sorts of [Armenian] excesses against the population (robbery, armed attacks, pillaging, murders)'.[6] Following Armenian riots in İskederun, riots that attacked French interests as well as Muslims, the French realized the damage that was being done to their future rule. They disbanded the Armenian Legion. Legionnaires then deserted, organized into bands, and redoubled their attacks on Turks. The French, without French troops to call on, continued to use Armenian auxiliary units, even distributing seized Turkish guns to local Armenians. The attacks on Muslims continued.

As attacks on Muslims increased, tens of thousands of Armenians were coming to Cilicia by sea and land. Some were returning to their homes, others arriving as a first step toward moving to other regions, once these were safe and accessible. They often took the homes of Muslims who had fled the Armenian Legion, just as earlier Muslim refugees from the attacks of Armenians and Russians in the east had been housed in the houses of deported Armenians. In 1919 property rights had become a military matter. Armenians claimed possession for a while, but they were to be dispossessed once again.

Had the French not depended on Armenians and supported the Armenian cause in Cilicia, or had they at least controlled the Armenians who acted in their name, they might have held the region, or at least held it much longer. Instead, the French created their own opposition by allowing the Armenian attacks on Turkish civilians, leaving the Turks with no alternative but to fight. It would have been obvious to the Turks of Cilicia how short their future would have been under French/Armenian rule. As in western Anatolia, the Turks organized in response to the foreign invasion. Each Armenian action drove more Turks to the mountains and the partisan bands that were forming there.

In March 1920 the Turks of Cilicia began their active resistance. In the far east of the French zone of occupation, Armenian and Turkish bands had battled since the initial occupation. The Turks finally took Maraş, the main city of the region, from the French. Maraş itself was destroyed by French artillery and burning by retreating Armenians. The French and Armenians, including most of the Armenian population of the region, suffered from starvation and Turkish attacks as they retreated the great distance to the coast. They, in turn, destroyed all the Turkish villages in their path.

Conflict continued between the Armenians and Turks of Cilicia, with the Turks, under the command of the Turkish Nationalists, gradually taking control of all but the coastal cities. Armenians fled to Adana, Mersin, and French-controlled regions to the south.

The French eventually showed political realism in Cilicia, although to the Armenians their action was cowardice and betrayal. General Gourad, the French commander, disavowed the Armenians and complained that it was their actions that had, in fact, betrayed the French. Whoever was responsible, the French decided that their national interest lay in Syria, not Cilicia. As will be seen in Chapter 10, they were thoroughly enmeshed in one imperialist enterprise and did not feel they could spare French troops for a second. The experiment with the use of colonial and Armenian troops to extend French power had not worked. They therefore made friends with the Turks.

On 21 October 1921, the French signed a treaty with the Ankara government. In it they agreed to abandon their claims in Anatolia and to recognize the terms of the Turkish National Pact. This broke the united front of the Allies. British support for Greece remained strong, but Britain could not count on France for support. Peace with France also freed Turkish troops to move from Cilicia for the fight against the Greeks in the west.

The French abandoned their position in Anatolia in December 1921. They evacuated Cilicia, taking with them 30,000 Armenians. The remainder of the Armenian population soon followed.

Turkish victory in the east

In eastern Anatolia and Transcaucasia the century-long conflict between Armenians and Muslims drew to a close in the War of Turkish Independence.

At the end of World War I the Ottoman troops who had defeated the Armenian Republic were withdrawn to the west. Far away from the centres of Allied power, they were able to keep their weapons and organizational structure. Allied control officers made little headway in disarming them. The greatest problem was desertion of troops who had fought for years and wanted nothing but home. As in western Anatolia, Allied actions had their effect on these troops. It seemed very likely that there would be no home to return to. Even Kurdish tribal forces in the northeast, who had been ambivalent in their support of the Ottoman war effort, could see that they were presented with the need for action. For them, as for the Turks of the east, the problem was once again the Armenians.

When the Ottomans retreated, their place was taken by Armenians, who once again returned to most of the areas they had been driven from in 1918. The British also intervened, holding the region of Kars–Ardahan, which had been part of the Russian Empire after 1878, with a small force. The British had no wish to remain in eastern Anatolia. It was far removed from what they viewed as their sphere of interest. They tried to convince the Italians, then the Americans, to take control of the region as a 'mandate', and carry out the impossible task of keeping the Armenians and Muslims from carrying on their conflict. But neither the Italians nor the Americans would be fooled. The British, therefore, handed Kars over to the Armenian Republic and evacuated.

Other than small groups in cities and mountainous redoubts, there were few Armenians left outside of the zone of Armenian occupation. They had fled or died during the war. This was not always true for Muslims in the territories occupied by the Armenians. In the old Russian territories in northeast Anatolia many of the Muslims had remained through the war, outside the conflict. Muslims also had returned to the old Ottoman territories with the victory of Ottoman forces at the end of the war. Both groups of Muslims were now under control of the Armenians, and the conflict continued. Outside of the Armenian Republic proper (the old Russian province of Erivan), where the majority of the Muslims had fled or been killed, Armenians controlled the cities, the large towns, and easily defended rural areas on the plains. Kurdish fighters and Muslim refugees controlled the mountains of the northeast and parts of the countryside.

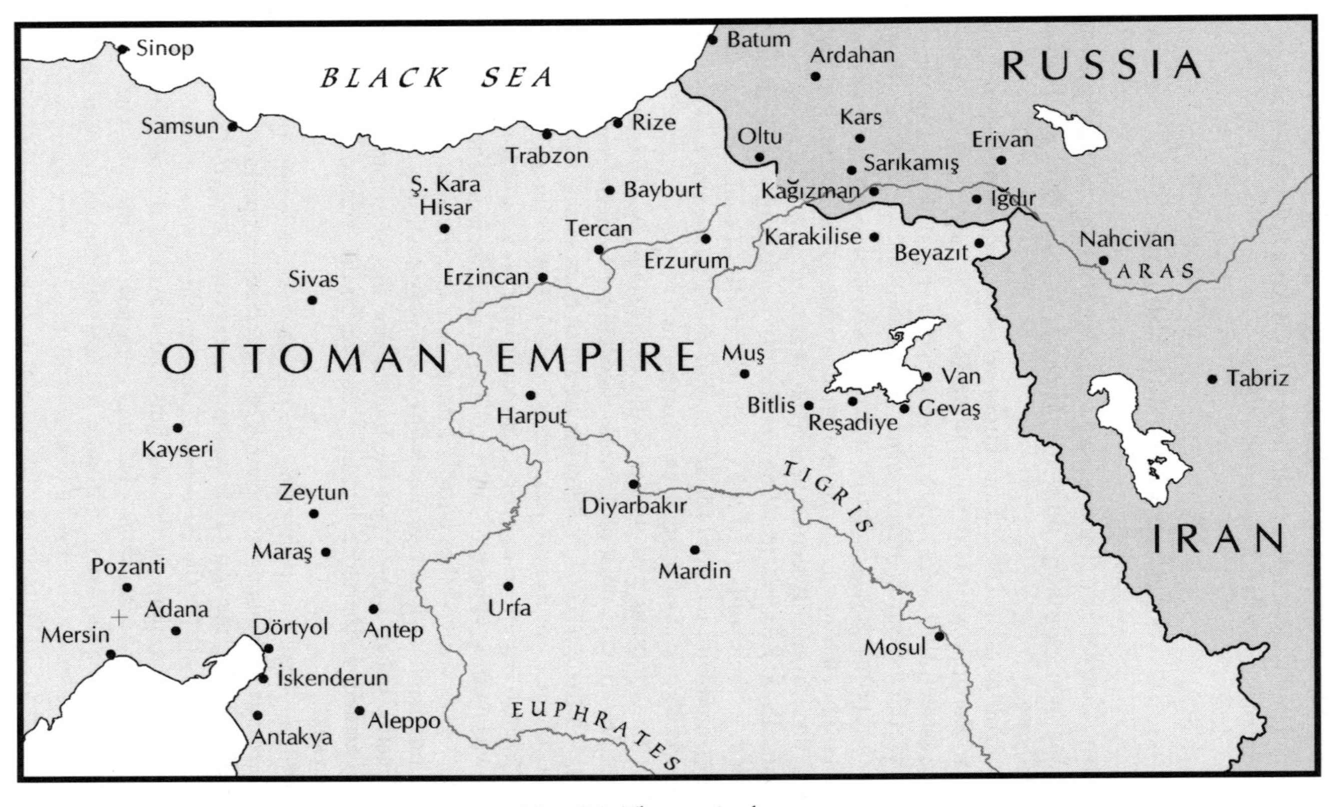

Map 8.2 The war in the east

The fate of Muslims who fell into Armenian hands was too similar to much of what has been described earlier to need description here. Massacre and forced migration were once again the order of the day. As they had before, Muslims were forced to flee Armenian territories. Hundreds of villages which had escaped earlier destruction, mainly in the Kars region and Nahcıvan, were now destroyed. Refugees were once again on the roads. Even the British, confirmed allies of the Armenian Republic, formally complained to the Armenian government of the actions against the Muslims. One of the few European observers on the scene, the control officer Colonel Rawlinson, reported:

> I had received further very definite information of horrors that had been committed by the Armenian soldiery in Kars Plain, and as I had been able to judge of their want of discipline by their treatment of my own detached parties, I had wired to Tiflis from Zivin that 'in the interests of humanity the Armenians should not be left in independent command of the Moslem population, as, their troops being without discipline and not being under effective control, atrocities were constantly being committed, for which we [the British, who gave Kars to the Armenians] should with justice eventually be held to be morally responsible'.[7]

Nearly 250,000 Muslims from the Kars district became refugees, as did untold numbers from other regions of Armenian occupation, at least 400,000 refugees in all.

The Armenians were actually in an impossible situation. In numbers, they were a small country, never in modern times a majority outside of Armenia proper. Left to their own devices, they would eventually be defeated. Their hope was in the Allies, who had made extravagant promises of a Greater Armenia. Allied armies would be needed to bring this to pass, and no armies were forthcoming. Except for supplies and some military equipment, the Armenians were left on their own. They were faced with enemies on all sides: Georgia to the west, Azerbaijan to the east, Nationalist Turkey to the south. To the north, the Bolsheviks had triumphed in the Russian Civil War. They intended to return as much of the Russian Empire as possible to their rule, and the Armenian Republic had been carved from the Russian Empire. With hindsight it can be seen that the Armenians should have withdrawn to Armenia and prepared defences against the Bolsheviks. This was not politically or emotionally possible. The Republic was committed to Greater Armenia and hoping for Allied assistance.

The Turks in the east were mobilized under the command of Kâzim Karabekir, a veteran of the Ottoman war in the east. Much as Mustafa Kemal did in the west, Karabekir mobilized the Turks of the east and melded them to his army. The Grand National Assembly, despite great need in the west, allowed Karabekir to keep his troops. In October 1920, moved to action by reports of massacres of Muslims, Karabekir moved on the Armenians and swiftly defeated them. Kars was taken on 30 October and the 1877 borders were re-established. Once again, it was the turn of the Armenians to become refugees. As the Turks attacked, all Armenians who could escape did so. Those who were left behind suffered the same fate so recently visited on their Muslim adversaries. The Armenian presence in Anatolia was no more. In Armenia itself few Muslims remained, as did few Armenians in Anatolia and Azerbaijan. The great and bloody population exchange between the Muslims and the Armenians was complete.

The Armenian Republic sued for peace. In the Treaty of Alexandropol of 3 December 1920 the Armenians acquiesced to the new borders and gave up claim to eastern Anatolia. The Republic was soon invaded by the Bolsheviks, who accepted the terms of the treaty. Karabekir's troops were now free to move west and join in the struggle against the Greeks.

Mortality in the east

As is true for all the sectors of the Independence War, it is impossible to estimate the numbers of dead in eastern Anatolia and Transcaucasia with complete accuracy. Migration clouds the picture. The estimates are fairly reliable, however, and presented with such inhuman slaughter a few percentage points make little difference. Mortality was naturally worst in the regions where Armenians and Muslims fought their intercommunal war. Table 8.1 shows Muslim deaths in the entire period of the world war and the Independence War. The statistics are not strictly of mortality but rather of population loss, the original number of inhabitants minus the number of survivors. Actual mortality, which cannot be statistically calculated, was greater, because the unknown numbers of children born in those ten years should be added to the equation, were it possible to do so.

Table 8.1 Muslim mortality in Ottoman eastern Anatolian provinces, 1912–1922

Province	Population loss	Percentage lost
Van	194,167	62
Bitlis	169,248	42
Erzurum	248,695	31
Diyarbakır	158,043	26
Mamuretülaziz	89,310	16
Sivas	186,413	15

Source: Justin McCarthy, *Muslims and Minorities*, New York, New York University Press, 1983.

Muslim mortality can be stated by province, because the Muslims ultimately retained control of the east. Numbers of surviving Muslims after the wars can be subtracted from Muslims numbers before the wars. The same cannot be done for the Armenians, who were gone from their homes in the end. Statistics can only be given for the mortality of all the Armenians of Anatolia. These show amazing suffering. Nearly 600,000 (40 per cent) of the Armenians of Anatolia were lost in World War I and the Independence War. The proportions of Muslim and Armenian dead in the east were not much different, equally horrible results of a general inhumanity.

Turkish victory in the west

During 1920, in Ankara Mustafa Kemal struggled to keep his disparate coalition together while the new army trained, collected supplies and ammunition, and became a cohesive force.

The Greeks decided to end any threat from the Turks by attacking before the Turkish forces could fully develop their strength. Twice, in January and March/April 1921, the Greeks advanced toward Eskişehir, but both times they were held at İnönü by İsmet Paşa's defence. Events were beginning to favour the Turkish side. Men and material streamed in and concluded a successful campaign in the east. On 16 March 1921, the Turkish Nationalists signed a treaty with the Soviets which brought arms and money in what the Soviets viewed as common cause against the Allies.

The Greeks realized correctly that they had to act soon and with great force. All was put into a summer campaign in 1921. The Turks retreated before it until Greek forces had arrived near Ankara and their guns could be heard in the capital. Many in the Grand National Assembly had feared Mustafa Kemal's power and tried to restrict his authority. Now, in fear of final defeat, the Assembly named him commander-in-chief and gave him total authority. From 13 August to 13 September Greeks and Turks battled at the Sakarya River. The Greeks finally broke and retreated. Exhausted, the Turks were unable to follow up the Greek retreat, but the Greek defeat broke the common front of the Allies. The French signed a treaty in Ankara in which they agreed to leave Cilicia and recognized the Nationalist government. In effect, the British were alone in their support of the Greeks.

In August 1922 the Turks advanced and quickly defeated the Greeks all over western Anatolia. By the middle of September all resistance was over. The Turks entered İzmir on 9 September 1922.

On 13 September a fire broke out in İzmir that destroyed much of the city. While the Greeks and others have long claimed that the fire was deliberately set by orders of the Turkish Command, such an idea is ridiculous. Is there anything else in the history of the Turks in the Independence War to indicate such irrationality? Was Mustafa Kemal the sort of man to destroy his most productive city just as he had conquered it, the only reason being dislike for its previous inhabitants? This does not just stretch credulity, it ties it in knots.

Within the 1914 borders only the British in the Dardanelles zone and Istanbul and the Greeks in eastern Thrace remained. The Nationalists began to move troops to attack. The French refused to cooperate with the British in defence, but London might have stood alone. Common sense prevailed, largely because the British commander, General Harrington, Mustafa Kemal and İsmet Paşa, the Turkish commander at the Dardanelles, kept cool heads. The British prevailed on the Greeks grudgingly to evacuate eastern Thrace. An armistice was signed between the British and the Nationalists at Mudanya on 3 October 1922. The British occupation force left Istanbul on 2 October 1923, after the signing of the Treaty of Lausanne.

Mortality in the west

More than 1.2 million Muslims of western Anatolia had not survived the wars. In all, nearly 3 million Turks and other Muslims of Anatolia had died in the Balkan Wars, World War I and the War of Independence.

Table 8.2 Muslim mortality in Ottoman western Anatolian provinces, 1912–1922

Ottoman province	Percentage lost
Aydın	19
Hüdavendigâr	10
İzmit	4
Ankara	8
Konya	27

Source: Justin McCarthy, *Muslims and Minorities*, New York, New York University Press, 1983.

As was true for the figures given above for eastern Anatolian mortality, the figures in Table 8.2 are actually of population loss in the period – the population in 1922 subtracted from the population in 1912. They do not include the refugees from the Balkan Wars. If these were added to the 1912 figures, the real mortality would be seen to be even greater. Migration considerably clouds the mortality picture. The provinces of western Anatolia were the most fertile in Anatolia. After the war, many Turks migrated to western Anatolia partly to take the place of the dead. This explains, for example, the seeming high mortality in Konya Province, from which Turks migrated.

Greek mortality cannot be given by province. Of the Anatolian Greeks, not including the Istanbul region, 313,000 did not survive the wars: 25 per cent of the Greek population had been lost. This figure includes Greeks who died when forcibly moved from northern Anatolia (the Pontus region) when the Nationalists feared Allied invasion there, as well as deaths among Greek refugees at war's end.

The Treaty of Lausanne

The British had not lost all their hopes of bringing the Turks to heel. At the Conference of Lausanne, called to negotiate a new treaty with the Turks, the British first attempted to recognize both the Istanbul and the Ankara governments as representatives of the Turks, with a seat at the table for each. The Nationalists refused, claiming that they were the sole representatives of the Turkish people. The Nationalists had advantages: the French and Italians had already decided to curry favour with the new Turkish government, and the Turks knew that the British had found military action against them to be politically impossible. The British public was sick of war and could see little profit in fighting yet another battle in the Near East. The Turks, therefore, could demand much, as long as they did not touch the new order that the British and French were creating in the Arab world.

The advantage of the British was that much of Turkey had been destroyed in the wars. The Turks needed an end to conflict and normal relations with Europe to lick their wounds and build their economy. On matters that did not touch the heart of Turkish independence, therefore, İsmet Paşa, the Turkish representative, accepted Allied wishes. He easily accepted British and French colonial rule in Palestine, Syria and Iraq. Even Mosul Province, which the Turks viewed as part of Anatolia, and thus theirs, was not allowed to be a sticking point. Both sides agreed to let the Council of the League of Nations decide the point. (It later gave Mosul to Iraq.) The Straits were neutralized, control only returning to the Turks in 1936. Although İsmet would surely have loved to negate the old Ottoman debt, a great weight on the new state, he accepted a proportional division of the debt among the successor states of the Empire.

On matters of independence, the Turks would not move. The Capitulations and all the rules that had allowed foreigners to have their own legal systems in the Ottoman Empire, their own post offices, and other extraterritorial rights, were ended. Foreigners and minorities were to be governed by the same sets of laws and have the same rights as the Turks. Social and religious institutions of Christians were specifically allowed, but not separate political institutions. The new Turkey was to be a state like other states, in charge of its own politics and laws.

The Treaty of Lausanne sealed the expulsion of populations in the Balkans with a final population exchange. Greeks had lived in Anatolia for millennia, and Turks had lived in what now was Greece for more than 500 years, but both Greece and Turkey recognized that Greeks and Turks could live together no longer. The hatreds of war had destroyed the tolerance that had marked the Ottoman Empire. Most of the Turks of Greece, in fact, had been expelled after 1878, especially in the Balkan Wars. Most Anatolian Greeks had fled in 1922. At Lausanne, Greece and Turkey agreed to relocate most of the Muslims and Greeks who had remained in the other's country. Only the Greeks of Istanbul and the Turks of western Thrace were excluded (Chapters 9 and 11).

After the Independence War, most of the Greeks and Armenians of Anatolia were gone, as were most of the Turks of Greece and Armenia. Not only the Ottoman Empire had died in the wars. Ottoman society, with its multiplicity of ethnic groups and religions, had died as well.

9

The Balkans after the wars

The Balkans after World War I were very different from how they had been before the Balkan Wars. Whole populations had been moved from their ancestral homes. Some had moved voluntarily to be with their ethnic group as borders shifted. Others had been moved in forced population exchanges agreed by the governments of Bulgaria, Greece and Turkey. Many had been forced out at gunpoint. National states had been created out of the mosaic of the Ottoman Balkans. The ethnically mixed populations of the Ottoman Balkans would never have fitted the unitary ideology of nationalism; therefore they had to be moved.

Some could not be moved. Defeated in war with the Turks, the Greeks were forced to allow the Turks of western Thrace to remain there. In exchange, the Greeks of Istanbul were also allowed to remain. The Albanians were simply too many to be moved. They were instead divided among Albania, Greece and Yugoslavia. (Yugoslavia might have been more accurately called Greater Serbia, but was instead named 'The Kingdom of the Serbs, Croats and Slovenes' on 1 December 1918. The appellation gives an idea of the position of Macedonians, Bosnians and Albanians in the state.) Macedonians were also divided among three states. Each for its own reason, Greece and Bulgaria did not admit that Macedonians existed. To the Serbs Macedonia was now southern Serbia. Macedonia was not to re-emerge until 1945, when it was recognized as one of the constituent republics of Communist Yugoslavia.

While it is not easy to find the data to compare the economic state of the successor states in the Middle East, some comparisons can be made. Despite wartime losses, the make-up of the population of the Arab states remained largely the same as before World War I. In Turkey, the situation of at least the Muslim population before and after the wars can be compared, with allowance for immigration. Boundaries in Turkey and the new Arab countries were close enough to the old boundaries of Ottoman provinces to allow comparisons. None of this was true for the regions taken from the Ottoman Empire in the Balkan Wars. Borders were not neatly drawn and

Map 9.1 The Balkans in 1923

post-war statistics do not differentiate the economies of new territories from old. Trade patterns and economies had changed so radically that such comparisons would make little sense.

In what had been Ottoman Europe entire populations had changed, sometimes more than once. Bulgarian refugees, for example, had moved into western Thrace in 1913, then were moved out again after World War I, to be replaced by Greeks from Greece and Anatolia. Many of the Muslims had left in 1912–13. In Macedonia, the people who had been listed in Ottoman statistics as Greek Orthodox and Bulgarian Orthodox were now listed in the census as 'Orthodox'. This makes it impossible to compare the status of the groups before and after the wars. With the changes in population came changes in the types of schools, as well as in the people who attended schools. Trade patterns changed, but the statistics do not tell us if those trading with Belgrade in 1925 were Serbs who moved into Macedonia or perhaps Macedonians or Bulgarians who altered their trading patterns.

Some analyses can be made, but they are often tentative estimates. The statistics in Table 9.1 indicate that Muslims were not the only migrants after the Balkan Wars. Serbs, Greeks and Bulgars each migrated from areas conquered by the others. The table does not include much of the migration during and after World War I, however, so another factor must have been at work. Obviously there was a good deal of rapid conversion among the Balkan Christians. Bulgarians in both Greece and Serbia were prevailed upon to change their affiliations. None of these conversions were the result of theological debate. In fact, theology did not enter into the changes. All three groups were Orthodox. They had the same basic theology. What separated them were liturgical language and ecclesiastical authority. These problems were managed by denying the use of any but the desired liturgical language and changing bishops. A small but important constituent of the refugee migration was made up of Bulgarian priests and bishops fleeing Serbian and Greek conquests.

Table 9.1 Populations of areas conquered by Greece, Bulgaria and Serbia in the Balkan Wars (thousands)

	Greece			Bulgaria			Serbia		
	1911	1923	Change (%)	1911	1920	Change (%)	1911	1921	Change (%)
Muslim	746	124	–83	328	179	–45	1,241	566	–54
Greek	797	1,774	+131	29	0	–100	286	949	+232
Bulgarian	145	0	–100	205	193	–6	782	0	–100
Jewish	75	66	–13	1	1	–23	9	6	–38
Other	8	7	–11	19	1	–95	22	18	–17
Total	1,770	1,971	+11	582	373	–36	2,341	1,540	–34

Source: Justin McCarthy, 'The Population of Ottoman Europe Before and After the Fall of the Empire', in Heath W. Lowry and Ralph S. Hattox (eds), *Proceedings of the Third Conference on the Social and Economic History of Turkey*, Istanbul, 1990, pp. 275–98.

Notes:
Western Thrace is under the Bulgaria column.
'Greek' in 1923 Greece is Greek Orthodox; some Greek migrants from Anatolia and eastern Thrace are included in this figure.
'Greek' in 1921 Serbia is Serbian Orthodox.
There may be some undercounting of Albanians in Greece and Serbia.

Comparison of the plans for various countries in the secret Allied agreements is an interesting study. As seen in Chapter 7, the Allies planned to dismember the Ottoman Empire completely, with no regard for religious or ethnic identity of the population or self-determination. The Balkan countries, with the exception of Albania, were to fare much better. Bulgaria was to lose its territory in western Thrace, and with it Bulgaria's outlet to the Aegean Sea, along with a few small parcels of land on the Yugoslav border. The loss was economically significant for Bulgaria and disastrous for the Bulgarians of western Thrace. Nevertheless, Bulgaria lost only 10 per cent of its pre-war territory. Greece, which had done little in the war, was to be enlarged enormously, gaining land both in the Balkans and in Asia Minor. Serbia was to take territory from Bulgaria, Austria and Albania. At best, the Ottomans and Albanians were to have small rump states encompassing only small proportions of their population. It is not coincidental that these two were primarily Muslim countries.

Albania and the Albanians

The Albanians came late to nationalism. They were perhaps the last large European population to think of themselves as a nation. Most Albanians, especially the estimated 70 per cent who were Muslims, probably would have been content to remain in the Ottoman Empire, with the proviso that Ottoman rule remain light. In particular, the Albanians had no wish to pay taxes. This naturally caused conflict with the centralizing tendencies of the reforming Empire. In 1878, Albanians had gathered in a congress in the city of Prizren to oppose the division of Albanian lands by the Powers, with no success. Those who wished a strong union within the Ottoman Empire dominated the Albanian movement and won the votes at the congress, but there were those who campaigned for autonomy and resisted the Ottomans. They were defeated by the Ottoman army, supported by other Albanians, in 1881. Even those who wanted to hold off the Empire had wanted some degree of autonomy, not independence.

Albanians were finally dragged into nationalism and separatism by the chaos that surrounded them in the Balkans. They had the misfortune to live in the Macedonian provinces that were claimed by Greeks, Serbs, Bulgarians and Macedonians. One of the few areas of agreement among the Christian guerrilla bands was that Muslims had no place in the states they planned, so the Albanians were attacked by all. They suffered particularly in the Ilinden Uprising of 1903 in Macedonia. By no means were all Albanians innocent victims. They had for centuries been engaged in battles with non-Albanians, particularly Serbs in Kosova. Raids on innocent villagers had been common. With the coming of European intervention in the Balkans and the creation of independent Christian states, the sides were increasingly unequal. The Ottoman Empire was proving unable to defend the Albanians, so they began to organize for their own defence.

Efforts at Albanian unity naturally brought them into conflict with the Ottoman state. Albanian leaders wanted the Ottomans to sanction the creation of a somewhat autonomous Albania, which was to include a large amount of territory – from the Serbian border in the north to the Aegean Sea. Many schemes included the city of Salonica in the Albanian land. The naivety of such proposals indicates the lack of sophistication of their proponents. It was not only the Ottoman government that would deny them their wishes; all of the Powers of Europe would do so, as well.

The CUP government actively pursued the centralizing policies of earlier governments in Albania, and attempted to collect taxes where they had never been collected before and even to conscript Albanian males. At the same time, troubles continued in Macedonia. Bulgaria had declared its independence and Austria-Hungary had annexed Bosnia in 1908. This did not increase Albanian confidence in the Ottoman ability to protect them. A revolt in 1910 was put down by Ottoman forces with great difficulty, and revolt broke out again when Italy attacked the Empire. The leaders of Albania had decided that they would fare better on their own. Albanian leaders attempted to keep to a policy of neutrality in the first Balkan War, although Albanian volunteers and conscripts fought in the Ottoman army. The Albanian separatists were mistaken in believing the dissociation with the Ottoman Empire would protect them. What awaited them was disaster. Neutrality was a failure, since none of the belligerents accepted it. Serbia and Montenegro had designs on Albanian land. The Albanians were neither sufficiently politically united nor sufficiently militarily prepared to face the onslaught of the Balkan Wars. Albanians suffered the brunt of Serbian and Montenegran attacks on Muslims. As reported by European observers, Serbs engaged in large-scale massacres of Albanians in all the Albanian areas Serbia invaded. Albanians in Kosova and Macedonia were the Serbs' main targets. Montenegro invaded Albania proper (i.e. within today's borders). Not satisfied with killing those who could not escape them, the Montenegrins cut down the trees and destroyed the houses on their line of march so that refugees would have nothing to return to. What was at work in Albania was more than cold-blooded political calculation. Generations of raids and small-scale massacres between Albanians on the one side and Serbs and Montenegrins on the other had left a legacy of hatred that led to mass murder.

Large sections of Albania were laid waste in the Balkan Wars. This was especially true in the east and north of present-day Albania. Greece had taken the southern section of the region where Albanians had been the majority, and Serbia had taken the western section. What remained was approximately half the land that an accurate ethnic division would have created.

The Greeks, Serbs and Montenegrins had planned to divide all of Albania among themselves. The European Powers had other plans. They were not concerned with Albanian self-determination, but Austria and Italy had no desire to see a strong Serbia with a port on the Adriatic Sea. Albania might prove to be a bulwark against Serbian expansion. Russia supported the Serbs and Montenegrins, but was not yet ready to go to war for them. Russia therefore agreed reluctantly to the creation of an Albanian state. The Albanians themselves, meanwhile, had organized under Albanian leaders, but this was unacceptable to the Powers. A European Commission of Control was named to run the country. Conflict between Italy and Austria limited its effectiveness. Albania was to have a European king, William of Wied, a young German. Its gendarmerie was put under the control of Dutch officers. Nothing was done about the starving Albanians dispossessed by the war or the approximately 60,000 refugees crowded into Albania.

The Albanian peasants revolted in 1914, directing their fury against their own landlords and, especially, the Control Commission and the European-imposed government of the king. William abdicated, a king for six months only. The Europeans became occupied with World War I. The ensuing condition in Albania has been described as anarchy, although it might better be characterized as rule by traditional local authorities.

Each of Albania's neighbours took advantage of the outbreak of war to claim a portion of the country: Greece took the south (Korçe), Montenegro the northwest (Shkoder), and Italy the west central coast (Vlore). Serbia, usually described as a victim in World War I, began the war by itself seizing the central region of Albania (Tirana). After Austria defeated Serbia it for a while took Serbia's place in Albania. All of this left little under Albanian control, but conflicts among its conquerors were to save Albanian independence. In the Treaty of London (1915) the Allies had given western Albania to Italy as part of its price for entering the war on the Allied side. Greece and Serbia agreed to divide the country in 1919, the Greeks to keep the south, Italy to take the east centre and hold a protectorate (in fact a colony) over the rest. Great Britain objected that Serbia (later Yugoslavia), not Italy, should be given the north. Agreement proved to be impossible, which worked to the advantage of the Albanians. They were ultimately allowed to rule their own country, at least the part of it that had become independent in 1913. In fact, Albania was to come increasingly under the sway of Mussolini's Italy, where it remained until Italy seized complete control in 1939.

Bulgaria

Few countries have been as unlucky in their choices as Bulgaria. Dissatisfied with its conquests in the Balkan Wars, Bulgaria attacked its erstwhile Allies and lost part of what it had gained. Allied with the Germans in World War I, it lost even more. It was to repeat the same mistake in World War II.

The Bulgarian people lost much in World War I. At the end of the war the Bulgarian economy was in ruins, with agricultural production at half its pre-war level and 200,000 refugees taking a toll of state and private resources. In the Treaty of Neuilly of 27 November 1919 Bulgaria was forced to pay an indemnity of 2.25 billion gold francs ($450 million), which it could never pay, and send tens of thousands of farm animals to its erstwhile enemies. Western Thrace was ceded to the Allies to assign it as they saw fit. With western Thrace went Bulgaria's only opening to the Aegean and the Mediterranean beyond. More important to the Bulgarian people, the Bulgarians of Thrace were first harassed, then evicted by treaty from their lands. More refugees came to Bulgaria from territories in western Bulgaria, taken by Yugoslavia.

Although Bulgaria was guaranteed a commercial outlet to the Aegean in the treaty, Greece never allowed Bulgaria to have a commercial corridor across Thrace that would be under Bulgarian control. As Bulgaria would accept no less, Bulgaria never achieved her outlet.

Guerrilla war in Macedonia had not ended with the armistice. Bulgarian bands still crossed into Macedonia to attack Serbian installations. For the Bulgarian Macedonians, the Serbians had replaced the Ottomans as the focus of national animosity. The bands were not able to do much damage to Serbia (now a part of Yugoslavia), but they upset Bulgarian politics. Members of IMRO killed the reforming prime minister Stamboliski in 1922 and generally disrupted political life in Bulgaria.

Western Thrace

The Bulgarian government protested both before and after the signing of the Treaty of Neuilly that the principles of self-determination should be applied to both eastern and western Thrace. Bulgaria was not in a position to object for long. Her army had been demobilized and was limited to 20,000 men by treaty. Allied Commissions of Control oversaw her army, navy and air force. Another Inter-Allied Commission, established to make sure reparations were paid, exercised effective control of her state economy.

At war's end, Thrace was occupied by the French. French administration seems to have been well received by the Bulgarians and Turks in western Thrace. Turks and Bulgarians were particularly satisfied. The French did not wish to leave. It is unclear if they hoped to retain Thrace themselves, but they were strongly opposed to occupation by the Greeks. The French had organized a census when they first occupied western Thrace (Table 9.2).

Table 9.2 Population of western Thrace according to the French census

Community	Population
Turks	74,730
Pomaks	11,848
Bulgarians	54,092
Greeks	56,114
Jews	2,985
Armenians	1,880
Others	3,041
Total	204,690

While surely an undercount, no group seems to have been more undercounted than another. It indicated, as had the Ottoman census before the Balkan Wars, that Greece had no demographic claim on the region.

The Bulgarians had expected, or at least hoped, that all Thrace, eastern and western, would be governed by an inter-Allied administration. The Bulgarian prime minister, Alexander Stamboliski, stated:

> We have consented to give up Thrace to the Entente Powers and to America and we have declared many times that we are prepared to give autonomous Thrace our full support. We can scarcely express our satisfaction at the fair regime which the French authorities have introduced into Thrace. As a result of this regime the whole province is quiet and the whole population is busy working. To replace the French authorities by Greek troops would arouse the greatest resentment not only amongst ourselves but amongst the Turkish and Bulgarian population in Thrace who constitute a considerable majority. Why disturb a real peace which has been obtained at a cost of so much effort?[1]

The Bulgarians and the Muslims of western Thrace, by no means friends in the past, seem to have united in opposition to the Greek occupation. They complained to the Allied Powers, only to find deaf ears. The greatest cause for resentment among the Bulgarians remaining in western Thrace was religious. Forcible conversions to Greek Orthodoxy took place and a number who refused were imprisoned, according to British reports. (The same condition was present in eastern Thrace, also occupied by Greece.) Forced changes in traditional trade patterns were also resented. Export of grain to Istanbul was forbidden, for example, even though Istanbul was under Allied occupation. Armed opposition was slight, however. Refugees had formed armed bands, but they made no headway against the occupying Greek army.

A majority of the Bulgarians in Thrace left just before the end of French administration, obviously fearing for their safety under Greek rule. Allied observers estimated 40,000, a slight exaggeration, had left. The refugees included nearly all of those who had come to western Thrace during and after the Balkan Wars. Those who remained were Bulgarians who had long been residents of the region. They had farms and businesses and were loathe to leave them. This made no difference. Under the terms of a 'voluntary' exchange of populations between Bulgaria and Greece, all the Bulgarians of western Thrace eventually left for Bulgaria. The Greek census of 1928 recorded no Bulgarians in western Thrace.

Population and refugees in Bulgaria

Bulgaria lost heavily in the Treaty of Neuilly (27 November 1919). Some 2600 sq. km went to Serbia and 8700 sq. km to Greece. The loss to Greece was the more significant, not only due to its greater size. Bulgaria was forced to cede all of western Thrace to Greece, which lost Bulgaria its only outlet on the Aegean Sea and forced its commerce to pass through the Straits before reaching the Mediterranean.

Bulgaria was forced to accept a large number of refugees, although not as many as either Greece or Turkey. After the wars, nearly 5 per cent of the population of Bulgaria was made up of refugees.

Table 9.3 Refugees in Bulgaria in 1928

Origin	Number
Asia Minor	7,139
Western Thrace	29,814
Eastern Thrace	57,292
Greek Macedonia	46,878
Serbian Macedonia	3,214
Dobruja	11,698
Western regions	6,741
Total	162,779

Source: Georges T. Danaillow, *Les effets de la guerre en Bulgarie*, Paris, Dotation Carnegie, 1932, p. 146.

The refugees listed in Table 9.3 were those who had survived until 1928. They may be a slight undercount, but the statistics appear to be otherwise reliable. Some 40 per cent of them were refugees from the time of the Balkan Wars. Considering the time that had passed and the high mortality of refugees, the original number of refugees must have been in excess of 200,000. Note that in the table the refugees have usually identified themselves by their original homes. Many of the refugees who went to western Thrace from eastern Thrace in 1913 then from western Thrace to Bulgaria in 1920 are identified as coming from eastern Thrace, their home in 1911. The Bulgarian census of 1926 listed 213,000 Bulgars as having been born in Macedonia, Thrace, the sections of western Bulgaria taken by Yugoslavia after the war, and Turkey. Not all of these, however, would have been refugees.

The Mixed Commission that oversaw the Greek–Bulgarian population exchange from November 1922 stated that 30,000 Greeks left Bulgaria for

Greece in the 1920s, joining 16,000 who had left during the wars, and 92,000 Bulgarians had left Greece, 39,000 of them before the Commission began its work. These were figures for the number who registered with the Commission and availed themselves of its services in transferring and selling property. Those who had died before November 1922 or did not have reason to register were not included.

Turkish statistics give a very imprecise picture of the migration of Bulgarian refugees from eastern Thrace in 1913, because the population was counted before the Balkan Wars and not again until 1927. Some 72,000 Bulgarian Christians had lived in 1913 in the part of Europe retained by the Ottomans (Istanbul not included). Less than 1000 remained in 1927.

It is impossible to calculate how many Bulgarians died from 1912 to 1922 in what had been Ottoman Europe. The Bulgarian population from before the wars in the regions taken by Greece and Yugoslavia is known, but that after the wars is not. The Greek and Serbian governments did not admit that Bulgarians existed, registering them simply as Orthodox. (The Yugoslavian census listed neither Bulgarian Orthodox nor Bulgarian-speakers, although the latter may have been included under the small number listed as 'other'.) Therefore, no count of the Bulgarians who survived the war can be made. Guessing from the number of refugees in Bulgaria in 1920 and the known diminution of the Bulgarian population in Bulgaria itself between the 1910 and 1920 Bulgarian censuses, it is likely that at least 5 per cent of the Bulgarian population of Ottoman Europe died in the Balkan Wars, World War I, and the Bulgarian exodus from western Thrace.

What can be said with certainty is that the Bulgarian population recovered fairly rapidly from wartime losses. By the mid-1920s it was increasing at a faster rate than it had before the wars.

Yugoslavia

During World War I, Serbian Macedonia was occupied by Bulgaria. With the occupation came a brief resurgence of Bulgarian education, religion, and ethnic identification. Then, when Bulgaria lost the war, schools were closed once again and churches 'converted' again to the Serbian branch of Greek Orthodoxy. Attacks by Macedonian/Bulgarian partisan bands damaged civil order in Macedonia until prime minister Alexander Stamboliski of Bulgaria signed the Treaty of Niš. The two countries agreed to patrol the borders and keep the partisans out of Macedonia. This was effective, but resulted in Stamboliski's assassination by the IMRO partisans soon after.

From that point, Bulgarians in Serbian Macedonia disappeared. Tens of thousands had migrated to Bulgaria. The remainder took on protective colouring, worshipping at Serbian churches and fitting insofar as possible into the new polity.

The disbanding of everything Bulgarian in Macedonia had an adverse effect on the region's education. The Bulgarians had operated an extensive system of schools (Chapter 3). Prior to the world war, Bulgaria had the best educational tradition in the Balkans. Bulgaria's per capita expense on education was more than twice that of Serbia and a third higher than that of Greece. Approximately 12 per cent of the populations of Bulgaria and Greece were in school, as opposed to only 5 per cent in Serbia. Once Serbia conquered the region, the Bulgarian schools were closed. The Ottoman state school system, never very strong in Macedonia, was largely disbanded during and after the Balkan Wars. Viewed as representatives of the Ottoman state, teachers and education officials had suffered high mortality. Those teachers who could do so migrated. Serbian replacement schools only slowly developed to take their place. The 1921 Yugoslavian census found that 84 per cent of the Macedonians over twelve years of age were illiterate.

In all areas of economic development Macedonia took last place in Yugoslavia. Of course, much of this underdevelopment was due to the troubles that the region had passed through: property had been destroyed in the Balkan Wars and World War I; much of the middle class of Macedonia had been Bulgarians, many of whom had fled. But Macedonia was also last in consideration for the government and private investment. In 1918, Macedonia and Kosova had only 3 dinars per person in investment capital in industry per capita, compared to 192 in Slovenia, 113 in Croatia, and 107 in Serbia. Just before World War II, Slovenia had more than twenty times the per capita industrial production of Macedonia; Serbian industrial production per capita was more than five times that of Macedonia.

Greece

Greek nationalism, the so-called Great Idea of creating a Greece on all sides of the Aegean, in western Anatolia, and in Istanbul, foundered in the Anatolian War. As seen in Chapter 8, Turkish success in war ended the Greek presence in Anatolia and eastern Thrace. Greece was left with a monumental refugee problem. Western relief agencies and governments helped a great deal, but refugee starvation was ever a danger. More than starvation lurked. The Anatolian Greeks, who had once been the richest community in the Ottoman Empire, were now dispossessed, destitute, and anxious for revenge. Like the refugees in Turkey, they offered the potential for further years of pointless war. As in Turkey, a statesman controlled their rage and got on with the business of forging a new country.

Eleftherios Venizelos would not at first be thought to have been a moderate nationalist. He had been instrumental in joining Ottoman Crete with Greece, a union that resulted in the expulsion of the island's Turks. An able advocate of Greek interests at the post-war peace conference, he had been the initial architect of Greek expansion into Anatolia and Thrace. Yet when he took office as Greek prime minister in 1927 Venizelos realized that irredentism could only do damage. He signed a pact with Turkey's Atatürk in 1930 guaranteeing Greek–Turkish borders. Despite various bouts of animosity, the borders have remained. Greeks and Turks had proved unable to live together, but they could live in peace.

The Greco-Turkish population exchange

Without quite stating it, Greece and Turkey decided at the Congress of Lausanne that Greeks and Turks could no longer live together. Hatred had become too deep. After extensive negotiations, a forced exchange of populations was written into the terms of the treaty. The exchange was to cover the Turks and Greeks who had left the territories of the other since 18 October 1912, the beginning of the Balkan Wars. Most of those covered by the exchange had already emigrated, but inclusion was, in theory, to allow them to sell property. Some special provision was also made for sale of properties of those who had left earlier than 1912. The only exclusions were to be the Greeks of Istanbul, seat of the Greek Orthodox Patriarchate, and the Turks of western Thrace, the only compact group of Turks left in Greece. A mixed commission of four Greeks, four Turks, and three members chosen by the League of Nations was to oversee the exchange and sale of property.

The exchange formally began on 1 May 1924, although many were exchanged earlier. From 1923 to 1926 190,000 Greeks were sent to Greece and 356,000 Turks to Turkey. Property of the Greeks and Turks who migrated after the Balkan Wars was liquidated fairly equitably. That of the Turkish migrants of the Balkan Wars period was seldom recompensed.

The exact number of refugees who migrated from Turkey (i.e. the area that was to become the Turkish Republic) and elsewhere to Greece is higher than indicated in Table 9.4, because a number of the original Greek refugees from Anatolia would have died before 1928. Nevertheless, these figures are the only ones available that result from an actual count of the refugee numbers. (Pure estimates from the time vary widely. Some estimates list more refugees than there were Anatolian Greeks.)

Greece was forced to accept 1.2 million refugees in a country whose population was only 6.2 million in 1928. Many of them were refugees from the Greek débâcle in Anatolia who arrived with virtually nothing. The Greeks could use the houses and properties of the 600,000 Muslims and 100,000 Bulgarians who had died or emigrated during and after the wars, but this was scarcely enough for resettlement of the Greek immigrants. In addition, many of these properties had decayed or were in areas unsuitable for mass settlement. Some refugees, such as those who spoke Turkish as their mother tongue, could not simply be planted on farms, given seed, and left to their own devices. Swamps had to be drained, lands

Table 9.4 Refugees in Greece in 1928

Origin	Number
Asia Minor[a]	627,000
Eastern Thrace	257,000
Pontus[b]	182,000
Constantinople	38,000
Sub-total	*1,104,000*
Bulgaria	49,000
Russia	59,000
Other countries	10,000
Total	1,222,000

Source: Greek census of 1928.

Notes:
[a] Western and central Anatolia.
[b] Northern Anatolia.

redistributed, and other agrarian measures taken before farming could be undertaken.

Most of the refugees at least initially went to cities, especially to Athens/Piraeus and Salonica. Houses had to be built and trades found. The refugees were, as a group, more skilled in crafts, trade and commerce than the mainland Greeks, so they could become active in the economy if provided with the proper tools. Some had managed to bring large amounts of money with them, and these could hire others in new enterprises, which they did. The problems were nevertheless daunting.

Greece succeeded in settling the refugees through great national will and assistance from the outside. The League of Nations began to provide assistance to the Greeks in 1922, including administrative assistance paid by the League. Great Britain provided an initial donation of £50,000, matched by £100,000 from other countries. American relief organizations fed more than 500,000 a day. The Bank of England loaned £1 million in 1923 for refugee work, then another £1 million in 1924. The League of Nations arranged a loan of £10 million in 1924. In 1928 another loan of £6 million was taken from European and American banks and the American government granted a loan of £2.5 million. While the first loan was at normal rates, the others were at advantageous rates, the American government loan at 4 per cent.

Greece was undoubtedly aided by the fact that it had suffered less than any other Balkan country during the Balkan Wars and World War I. Greece had been on the winning side of all the conflicts. She had never been invaded, so her industrial and agricultural infrastructure was intact.

Macedonians

Macedonians in Greece were denied most expressions of ethnic existence, much less nationalism. Table 9.1 indicates the 'non-existence' of Macedonians in southern Macedonia. In Ottoman statistics (1911 in the table) most Macedonians were listed as Bulgarian, because they were members of the Bulgarian Orthodox Church. They did not disappear by 1923. The Greek government simply refused to admit they were there. Administratively, they had become Greeks. In fact, most of those who identified as Macedonian seem to have remained, whereas most of those who identified as Bulgarians left. Many died in the Balkan Wars.

The Muslims of Greek Macedonia and the region immediately to the north of 1911 Greece did not change their religion. More than 80 per cent of them had either died or been forced out to Albania and Turkey during and after the Balkan Wars.

10

Mandates in the Arab provinces

The division of the Arab world by the European conquerors was a disaster that continues to our day. Much as they had in Africa, the European colonialists created theoretical states on maps, regardless of economic and social realities, then enforced their creation. Ethnic groups were divided, traditional trade routes severed, and, ultimately most damaging of all, cadres of local politicians with little loyalty to the greater good of the Arabs were created. The Arab world created by the Europeans is the divided Arab world of today.

The Arab state

If the Ottoman Empire were to be dissolved, the obvious alternative to it would have been an Arab state. Those who wish books to get right to the point will object that such a thing was never possible; the European Powers would never have allowed an Arab state to be created. In evaluating what actually occurred, however, it helps to think of what might have been.

A state that included the Ottoman Arab provinces would have been less linguistically and ethnically varied than the Ottoman Empire. It would have been large enough, though, to have some power in the world. It would have perforce concentrated on regional issues, which would have been national issues. Would it have become a 'nation-state'? Almost surely. Arab nationalism was a small phenomenon in the period immediately after World War I. Nationalists would have to build it, as their counterparts in the Balkans had done. It would not have been hard, for the prerequisites of nationalism were already present. The concept of 'nation' is created in the minds of its believers, and so there are no definitive criteria for the concept. Common language, history, customs, and often a dominant religion are the building blocks of nationalism. The Arabs had all these. Nationalism also grows in the fertile soil of hatred, usually hatred of foreign oppression, and this was about to be provided by the British and French. Uniting all of what had been the Ottoman Arab world would have been possible. What stood in the way of an Arab state was not internal barriers. External forces kept the Arabs apart.

Successful states are usually integrated economically, with transportation and communications ties between various regions bringing the nation's people together. Greater Syria – the region that was to become Syria, Lebanon, Palestine and Trans-Jordan under the mandates – fitted the criteria for nationhood particularly well: language was the same basic dialect of Arabic; Sunni Islam was the religion of the vast majority, and other religions and sects were too small and too divided religiously and politically to create a separate nation; railroads and roads, while not of the highest standard, nevertheless tied the Greater Syrian region together, as did a common coastal trade; cities and economies of the interior (Damascus, Aleppo, Jerusalem) were dependent on port cities of the coast (Haifa, Beirut). Most important, the inhabitants were used to thinking of themselves as part of a larger entity, the Ottoman Empire; only some Christian and Jewish minorities, such as the Maronites in Lebanon and Zionists in Palestine, favoured the creation of smaller states.

Iraq might have been included successfully in a greater Arab state. Iraq's population was significantly different from that of Syria – approximately half Shia Muslim by religion, with a large Kurdish minority. However, Sunni Muslims were politically dominant. The Iraqi mercantile and landowner classes were well accustomed to belonging to a larger entity and favoured it. They would have probably preferred to remain in the old Empire, if it had been on offer. The Shias and Kurds would perhaps not have favoured belonging to a larger state, but they would not have disliked it any more than belonging to a Sunni Arab dominated Iraq, which was what they received. Iraq was unquestionably economically integrated with Syria, primarily through the transit trade, and had been for centuries, a factor supporting consolidation.

Iraq had never been a real political, cultural or economic unity in modern times. The Ottomans had recognized this by dividing what was later to become modern Iraq into three very different provinces: Mosul in the north, with its Kurdish majority; Baghdad, with most of the Arab Sunnis, in the centre; and Basra, largely Shia, in the south. There was no justification in joining the three regions together into one state except for the need for larger states to protect the inhabitants' interests and integrate economies. Those interests would have been better served by integrating into an even larger state.

Egypt would not have fitted so well into a Middle Eastern Arab state. Except for very brief periods of central control, Egypt had been in practice independent from the Ottoman Empire for centuries and had developed its own institutions. Under the forty years of British occupation, Egypt had moved even farther from the Ottoman system. Culture and even language were in many ways quite different from those of the Syrian or Iraqi Arabs. Including Egypt in an Arab state would have strained the assumptions of modern nationalism, so there would have been some reason to exclude it.

The potential benefits of a greater Arab state need little delineation: economic integration and duty-free internal trade, economies of scale in everything from building universities to outfitting armies, regional conflicts handled by police rather than international conflicts handled by armies, eventually a much more equitable distribution of oil wealth, and many other benefits. The benefits are so great that it is impossible to see any reason to divide the region except the armed might and determination of the European conquerors. Of course, in an age of imperialism, that was sufficient reason. Europeans would never allow the Arabs to create their own state.

The effects of World War I

The population of the Arab provinces of the Ottoman Empire suffered greatly during World War I. In Ottoman Palestine, the region that was to become the British Palestine mandate, for example, the population decreased by 6 per cent from 1914 to 1918, losses from death and migration. Lebanon may have suffered even higher mortality. The causes of the decline were not all war-related: famine in Lebanon and locust attacks in Palestine were caused by nature, not man. The fact that food stocks were low and relief supplies hard to find was the fault of the war, however, and this exacerbated the loss due to famine or locust infestation. Trees had been cut down for fuel and animals taken for military use. Allied blockade had ended trade and destroyed industries. Only by comparison to the losses in Anatolia are the Arab population losses less impressive, but it should be considered that the Ottoman Arab provinces suffered worse mortality than any European country in World War I except Russia. (Anatolian loss was much worse than that of Russia.)

The major difference between Anatolia and the Arab provinces was the effect of the war on the future economy. The richest regions of Anatolia were largely destroyed in the wars, but the productive power of society in the Arab provinces was little diminished by the war. World War I had limited structural effect on the Arab provinces. The Ottomans had fought their battles against the British outside of cities, mainly in the desert, and they never organized the sort of urban warfare that was to disfigure cities such as Beirut in later years. The British army found conquered cities intact; and though the populace did not universally welcome them, neither did they organize uprisings against their conquerors – that is, not until they learned of the Allies' real plans for them.

Arab plans, European plans

At the end of World War I, the Arabs had reason to expect great changes. Allied wartime promises had been taken seriously by Arab leaders, who mistakenly believed what they had been told. The British had promised to allow the creation of an Arab state. While not all believed that all the old Ottoman Arab provinces would be united, it was assumed that at least all of Greater Syria would be united, with only coastal Lebanon perhaps excluded. The French and British as late as November 1918 had publicly promised to end divisions in Syria. Damascus was its obvious capital. On 1 October 1918, the amir Faysal, son of the sharif of Mecca, the leader of the bedouin revolt against the Ottomans, led his Arab contingents into the city in advance of the British army. Elections took place in May 1919 for a National Syrian Congress, and on 19 December the Arabs formed a national government at Damascus. Faysal accepted the title of king on 7 March 1920. Faysal's bedouin warriors and local ex-soldiers became the small army of the new Arab kingdom.

The Arabs were naive. While World War I was being fought the Allies had already begun to divide the Ottoman Empire, at least on paper. Their intentions were set forth in secret agreements such as the Sykes–Picot Agreement, described in Chapter 7. The Ottoman Arab provinces were to be divided between the British and the French, some areas to be controlled by them, some to be under their 'influence'. It was always and unquestionably the Allied intention to take these lands for themselves. Once they had defeated the Ottomans, the Europeans violated the promises to the sharif and claimed even greater control of the Middle East than they previously had planned. Meeting in Versailles and San Remo, the Allied victors divided the Arab Middle East between the French and the British. The British and French definitively agreed to divide the Arab world between them in September 1919. In the Treaty of San Remo of April 1920 there was no further mention of 'spheres of influence'. Outside of Arabia, which the Europeans neither wanted nor felt they could rule, all was to be divided between the French and the British. The French received the northern section of Ottoman Syria (later Lebanon and Syria). The British claimed southern Syria (later Palestine and Trans-Jordan) and Iraq (the Ottoman provinces of Basra, Baghdad and Mosul).

The planned mechanism for colonial rule in the Arab Middle East was the mandate of the League of Nations. In theory, the British and French did not take over the Arab region by or for themselves. They were administering it for the League of Nations, their sole intention to help the people of the mandates. In the glory days of imperialism, Europeans had felt no need to justify their conquests, other than perhaps a reference to the need to convert the natives to Christianity. Having fought a war 'to make the world safe for democracy' and needing to at least appear concerned for the welfare of

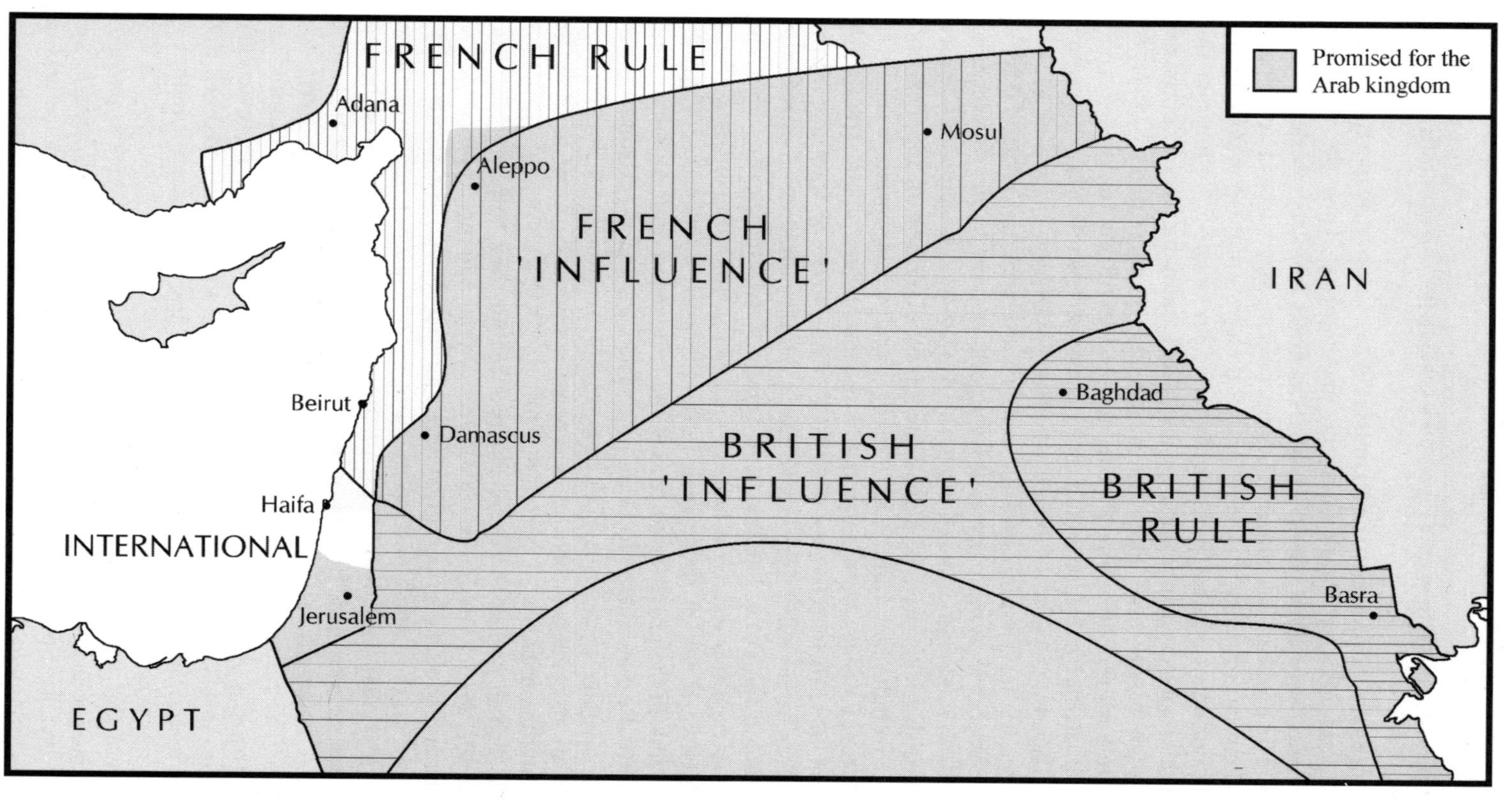

Map 10.1 The Sykes–Picot Agreement and promises to the Arabs

subject peoples, the Europeans invented a scheme for colonies that were not colonies.

The primary purpose of the mandates was to advance the economic, political and military interests of the mandatories. Thus the mandate governments were often aimed at different goals from the needs of their citizens. The problem was inherent in imperialism. States would never have undertaken the conquest of foreign lands if there was nothing in it for them. This did not mean that colonial powers could not and did not improve the lives of their subjects. If nothing else, a satisfied and more well-off populace was known to be more likely to accept its government, less likely to cooperate with the government's enemies, and less likely to demand independence. Richer subjects would be a better market for home country goods. Therefore, while the benefit to the populace of the mandates was never primary, it was surely possible and even desirable to the mandatories.

The British had good reasons, at least good reasons by the standards of imperialism, to take their mandates in the Arab world. As stated in Chapter 7, the British felt the need to defend the Suez Canal, their oil supplies, and the route to India by air and sea. Control of Iraq was necessary because of oil. All other considerations paled before the need of petroleum. The British navy and the British economy were fuelled by the oil of Iraq and south-eastern Iran, and so Britain felt it needed a military presence to protect the oil fields and the ports. Palestine and Jordan were strategically important because of their relation to the Suez Canal and the oil of Iraq and Iran. With good highways, which the British built, the ports of Palestine were an efficient link in the provision of troops and supplies to Iraq. An oil pipeline was eventually constructed to bring oil to Palestine and the Mediterranean (as well as one through Syria/Lebanon). Most prominent in strategic considerations, Palestine held by an enemy would be a threat to both the canal and the oilfields.

If the British had concrete self-interest behind their rule, how can one explain the French desire to rule Syria? Syria had no appreciable oil deposits, and could never be a great outlet for French industry. Strategically, the only thing the French had to defend in Syria was what they brought to Syria – their own system and French nationals. The primary reason behind the French interest in Syria can only be classified as psychological. France had been culturally and economically involved with coastal Syria for centuries. The Maronite Christians of Lebanon had long been 'adopted' as French protégés. As in many of the French conquests in Africa, there was the matter of the advancement of French civilization to be considered. To this must be added, in the calculus of imperialism, the real French fear that if they did not take Syria the British would.

None of this demonstrates that there were not actual benefits, particularly economic benefits, for the French in Syria, only that it is hard to see how the benefits outweighed the costs. The main benefit to France was in trade, because in her mandates, with some encouragement, France quickly became the country from which goods were imported. Balancing this were the costs of the French army, which was needed to keep the mandate citizens in check.

Occupation

The salient point in understanding the history of the European mandates in the Middle East is that the Europeans were not wanted. This had not been true, or at least was true to a much lesser extent, of the Ottomans. During World War I, the only Arabs to attack the Empire had been the bedouin, who never accepted any outside authority except under force. (They cannot be called rebels, because most of the bedouin had never accepted the authority of the sultan.) As an Islamic Empire, the Ottoman state laid claim to a loyalty that transcended ethnic differences. As rulers who had been in place for 400 years, the Ottomans fitted expectations of who should rule – caliphs and sultans. There were stirrings of Arab nationalist movements during the final decades of Ottoman rule in Syria, but these never rose to the level of even minor armed revolt. Not so the movements against French and British occupation.

The Armistice of Mudros (30 October 1918) found the British in control of all the main cities of Syria and all but Mosul in Iraq. Mosul was taken soon after. The British then extended their control to secondary cities and rural areas. Militarily, all of the Arab provinces were theirs, but they had made promises. The promises to themselves, to the French, and to the Jews in Palestine were largely kept.

A small French contingent had occupied part of the Syrian coast at the end of the war, anxious at least to have a presence in the region the British had conquered. The contingent was fortified until it numbered 90,000 men, an occupying army. In July the French issued an ultimatum, demanding that Faysal accept French control of Syria, as ordered by the British and French agreement at San Remo. The ultimatum stipulated the Arab army be reduced, that those who opposed the French be punished, that the French be allowed to garrison soldiers where they wished, and that later French actions be accepted, even though these were not defined. Faced with the French army, Faysal proved unable and unwilling to fight for his kingdom. He capitulated. The populace in Damascus promptly revolted. Although the Damascus riots were quelled by the Arab government, the French army used them as an excuse to advance, with considerable loss of life on their line of march. Faysal reported to the British that the French had destroyed villages with aeroplanes and artillery, leaving 20,000 homeless. The French defeated Arab forces easily at Maysalun (24 July 1920) and entered Damascus, ultimately taking control of the region allotted to them at San Remo (today's Syria and Lebanon, plus what is today the Turkish province of Hatay or Alexandretta).

Damascus never warmed to its conquerors. When a revolt broke out in Jebel Druze against the French in 1925, the city welcomed the rebels. To defeat the rebellion the French bombarded the city, the capital of their mandate, inflicting the sort of damage Damascus had escaped in the war. They were to bombard again in 1926 and in 1945.

The British fared only slightly better than the French in winning acceptance for their governments. In May 1920, the British were attacked in the Mosul region. In June, a great revolt in southern Iraq nearly ended British control of Iraq and cost Britain more than 1500 men to put down. In Palestine, the focal point of Arab discontent was Zionist immigration and settlement. No responsible Arab group in Palestine, religious or secular, ever accepted the mandate or Jewish immigration. Attacks on Jewish settlements began in the 1920s and broke out in widespread Arab–Jewish violence in 1929 and full rebellion against the British in 1936.

Divide and rule

In the face of opposition by the majority, both the French in Syria and the British in Palestine attempted to divide the political forces in their mandates, according to the principle of *divisi et impera*. Soon after gaining their mandate over Palestine, the British divided it in two in 1921 and formally made it two separate states in 1923. Palestine proper remained under British control. The territory across the Jordan was given to one of the sons of Sharif Husayn, Abdullah, as described below. Trans-Jordan, as the new kingdom was called, was partly independent, but military affairs and some other governmental functions remained in British hands.

The British mandate in Palestine initially showed obvious favouritism to the Zionist Jews. The creation of a National Home for the Jews was written into the terms of the Palestine mandate, whereas Arabs were not even mentioned specifically in the official 'constitution' of the mandate, the basic law decreed by the League of Nations. Arabs were referred to as 'non-Jewish communities' and 'natives'. A Jewish Agency was created in the basic law 'for the purpose of advising and cooperating with the Administration' on matters touching Jews and 'to assist and take part in the development of the country'. The Zionist Agency was recognized as that Jewish Agency. The basic law also stated definite economic preference: 'The Administration may arrange with the Jewish Agency mentioned in article 4 [the Zionist Organization] to construct or operate, upon fair and equitable terms, any public works, services and utilities, and to develop any of the natural resources of the country, insofar as these matters are not directly undertaken by the Administration'.[1] In economic matters, as in other matters, Arabs were unmentioned.

The Arabs in Palestine were in an impossible position. The British demanded that the Arab Executive, a body made up of leaders of the various Arab organizations, must accept the mandate if it was to take a place in advising the government similar to that taken by the Jewish Executive. No Arab organization could do this, because the mandate included the Balfour Declaration. To accept that would be to accept Zionism in Palestine, and no Arab organization could do that and represent the will of the Palestinian Arabs. For this reason and because of general opposition to the colonial government, Arabs refused to participate in a legislative council offered by the British in 1922. That left religious organizations as the only legal representatives of the Arabs. These were by nature divisive, because the Palestinians were divided into Muslims and various Christian sects. The political situation was thus not simply divided between Jews and Arabs. The Arabs were divided against themselves, their divisions encouraged by the British.

In Iraq, the British at first depended on Kurdish and Assyrian levies to support their rule. The Assyrians were Nestorian Christians who had fled from southeastern Anatolia when their wartime revolt against the Ottomans failed. Kurds were traditionally in an antagonistic relationship with the settled Arab population. Reaching 7500 men, this auxiliary army was much hated by the Muslim Iraqis. While the British were in control, the fledgling Iraqi army was only a secondary force, weaker than the Assyrian levies. When Iraq became independent, however, the Assyrians were massacred in their villages in revenge for the past, leading to wholesale emigration of Assyrians. One-third of the Assyrian population fled to Syria.

Almost immediately after their occupation of Syria the French began to dismember it. The most lasting of the divisions was the creation of Lebanon. This was an artificial state which had never existed previously. In late Ottoman times Europeans had forced the Ottoman government to accept an autonomous district of Mount Lebanon, ruled by a Christian governor. That district was almost entirely Maronite Christian in composition. The French more than doubled its area and named the creation Lebanon, signalling their intentions as to who would be the dominant element in the new state, the Maronites. The Maronites, a Christian group that had accepted papal authority, had been close to the French during Ottoman times. From the first, the French relied on the Maronite minority as aides in their occupation. Indeed, the Maronites were the only group who can be said to have welcomed the French and initially cooperated with them.

The French attempted to further divide Syria, with considerably less success than they had in Lebanon. In 1920 and 1921, the French divided Syria into 'states'. The states were Damascus, Aleppo, an 'Alawite state' with its capital at Latakia, a 'Druze state' with a capital at Suwayda, and Iskandarun (İskenderun, Alexandretta). The states of the Alawites and the Druze were attempts to divide Syria confessionally as well as politically. Both the Alawites and the Druze were religious groups considered heretical by Sunni Muslims. As practical administrative divisions, however, these divisions did not work, and the French were forced to alter them in 1925. In

Map 10.2 Syria

theory, they retained the Alawite and Druze states and combined the others into a Syrian state. In administrative fact, the French mandate was divided into two states – Lebanon and Syria.

Dependence upon and stress upon religious differences was a feature of all the mandates in the Arab world. In a political atmosphere in which the majority opposed their rule, developing ties with minority groups was an obvious step for the mandatories. By stressing divisions among the populace and favouring some support, they would both keep local forces from uniting against them and gain at least some groups upon which they could depend. The mandatories were successful in exacerbating long-standing divisions among the Arabs. In the end, the Europeans' policy failed in perpetuating European rule, but it did have great effect in perpetuating divisions that served as the basis of future conflict.

The creation of separatism

The division of the Ottoman Arab provinces created what were to become self-sustaining states. Nationalism in the new states, as opposed to Arab nationalism, was fostered by the political environment of the mandates. Syrians opposed to the French fought different battles from those of Palestinians opposed to the British. Local concerns arose that were more pressing than pan-Arab interests. In Lebanon and Palestine, Maronite Christian and Jewish populations developed into constituencies for their respective smaller states, Lebanon and Palestine/Israel. Both would have been politically swallowed by the large numbers of Muslims in a greater Arab state. In Iraq a state was artificially created. With each division developed a separate cadre of politicians.

The family of the sharif, having failed to gain an Arab kingdom, became the first to give up the Arab state and accept division of the Arabs. When the French deposed his brother Faysal, the amir Abdullah rode to the salvation of the Arab kingdom. Responding to pleas from Syrian Arabs, in 1920 Abdullah moved with a force of perhaps 1000 men from the Hijaz into what today is Jordan. He intended to march into Syria to oppose the French, which would have been a difficult undertaking. In the interests of peace in the mandates, the British offered Abdullah an easier prize. He was made amir of Trans-Jordan, the portion of Palestine east of the Jordan River, a largely worthless, mainly desert kingdom from which Abdullah could intrigue to gain the rest of Syria. It is difficult not to believe that he had been bought off, even if one accepts that his forces never could have defeated the French. The amir Faysal, evicted from Syria by the French, was also offered a job by the British. From the time he accepted reign in Iraq he ceased to agitate for a larger Arab kingdom and took little part in Syrian opposition to the French. This was the price for ruling in Baghdad.

Economically, the policies of the mandate governments developed separatism. As will be seen below, Middle Eastern and international trade routes were disrupted by the creation of separate states in what had been one large empire. The mandate governments increased the separation by applying protectionist economic policies in their colonies. In advancing protectionist policies, the mandate governments were neither ill-intentioned nor alone. Protectionism passed for economic orthodoxy among politicians of the time, resulting in policies that worsened the Great Depression. In the Arab world, protectionism had the added effect of further separating economies and peoples.

Nothing showed the real character of the mandates as much as the British actions in Iraq and Trans-Jordan. These two were the least economically developed of the mandate regions. Politically, Iraq and Trans-Jordan could not be called progressive. Large sections of what would be state authority elsewhere were in the hands of tribal leaders. These were exactly the sort of

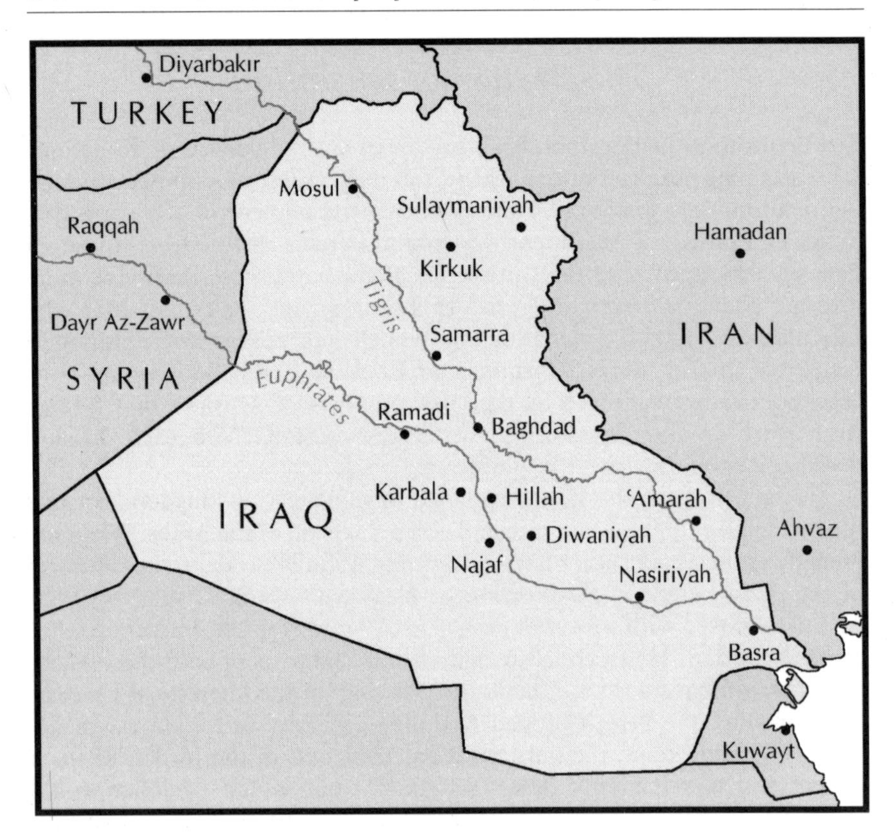

Map 10.3 Iraq

regimes and economies that had been idealistically envisaged in the mandates of the League of Nations as needing 'administrative advice and assistance' by a major power. Yet these were the two regions that were forsaken by their mandatories. The reasons were matters of cold political calculation.

Trans-Jordan was largely worthless to the British. Their sole concern was to keep Trans-Jordan from causing trouble in Palestine. The British, therefore, mainly invested in civil order in Trans-Jordan. They were particularly concerned with ending bedouin incursions into settled areas. Trans-Jordan was also a convenient place to blunt the ambitions of the family of the sharif of Mecca. Amir Abdullah could be offered rule in his desert kingdom if he would not disrupt mandate rule elsewhere.

Iraq proved very early to be an unjustifiable expense in money and lives for the British. The revolt of 1920 cost them heavily in both. They knew that as European conquerors they could expect more of both. The solution was to ensure what they needed in Iraq while paying little or nothing for the rest.

The Anglo-Iranian Treaty of 1920 and military pacts of 1924 made Iraq an independent kingdom, but left overall military control in the hands of the British. A 1930 treaty assured the British two sovereign military bases and the right to use all Iraqi facilities in the event of war. The tax-collector, the policeman, the local judge and the schoolmaster were to be Iraqis, financed by Iraq itself. Iraqis would not see British control in their ordinary lives. Yet the British had ensured that what they most wanted would be kept safe – lines of transportation, British oil companies, and military control.

From the standpoint of subsequent history, the most consequential action of the British in Palestine was the creation of the National Home for the Jews. Sometimes aiding, sometimes hampering Zionist immigration, the British nevertheless oversaw an immigration of 395,000 Jews to Palestine from 1919 to 1945. This was to become the most momentous event in modern Middle Eastern history. Its result was the mass migration of the Palestinian Arabs and the creation of a Middle Eastern state completely separate from those surrounding it in culture, economy, politics and religion. Like the migrations that accompanied the creation of nation-states in the Balkans, the creation of Israel resulted in a *de facto* population exchange, with Jews from other Middle Eastern lands migrating to take the place of the Palestinians.

After initial appeals to Greater Syrian loyalties in the attempt to gain assistance in the fight against Jewish immigration, Palestinian Arabs were forced to turn inward. Syrians were occupied with opposition to the French, Iraqis in coming to a *modus vivendi* with the British. Neither was particularly concerned with the problems of the Palestinian Arabs. Thus Palestinian nationalism increased and was turned inward by its unique problems – opposition to the British mandate and to the Zionists.

It would be a mistake to say that the Arab politicians who developed or flourished during the mandates were not committed to the creation of a greater Arab state. They were usually in favour of such a state, but only if local problems were given precedence and only if the political leadership of the larger state was acceptable to them. Of course, the most acceptable leader is always oneself. With the tradition of the separate mandates behind them, Arab politicians were never to be able to unite. Later attempts at union, such as the Ba'ath party or the union of Syria and Egypt under Nasser, were all to founder because of regional separatism.

Development

The formal intention of the League of Nations in granting mandates to Britain and France was set forth in Article 22 of the Covenant of the League, partly quoted in Chapter 7, in which the mandatories were given their 'sacred trust of civilization'. The Covenant treated the development of the mandates by enjoining the mandatories to advise and assist:

> Certain communities formerly belonging to the Turkish Empire have reached a stage of development where their existence as independent nations can be provisionally recognized subject to the rendering of administrative advice and assistance by a Mandatory until such time as they are able to stand alone. The wishes of these communities must be a principal consideration in the selection of the Mandatory.

The level of hypocrisy in this statement was not particularly unusual for the time. The British and French had undertaken their sacred trust of civilization through military conquest. They did not plan to advise and assist, but to rule. The Arabs, who were in fact never asked their wishes, showed their disbelief in the benevolent intentions of the mandatories through revolts. To the mandatories, 'administrative advice and assistance' meant something close to absolute control. The imperialists of earlier ages, though definitely more cruel in practice, had a more honest credo, the right of conquest. In fact, despite the fiction that the mandates were given and controlled by the League of Nations, they were applications of the right of conquest in the Middle East. The question, then, is not one of intention, which is all too obvious. The question is how well did they carry out their sacred trust?

It is commonly assumed that, whatever the faults of imperialism, at least the imperial powers brought many concrete benefits to the colonized. Those who were ruled became initiated into European technological civilization. They learned the ways of European democratic political life, even if they were not allowed to put their new knowledge to use. Imperialism benefited education, made social life more cosmopolitan, and improved the economy by integrating it with the world market. In the Middle East, it is assumed, all these things were better once the French and British took power. The inhabitants of the mandates might not be happy to be ruled by foreigners, but most aspects of their lives improved. The end of the Ottoman Empire, according to traditional belief, led to a betterment of life that the Arabs could never have experienced had the old empire continued. Is this true?

The question of development and advancement under the mandates is straightforward. Although the Ottomans did successfully begin the reform of their Empire, they were beset with external enemies and internal resistance that damaged their efforts. Frequent nineteenth-century wars with Russia drained the Empire's treasury and added millions of Muslim refugees from conquered lands who had to be fed. Little was left to support reform. In addition, traditional forces within the Ottoman Empire often opposed Europeanizing reforms. While those who resisted reform were ultimately unsuccessful, they undoubtedly slowed the pace of reform. It must be expected, therefore, that the European Powers who conquered Ottoman territories would have been in a far better position to reform the basic conditions of life. They were incomparably richer and by nature not bothered by questions of losing their Arab culture, and perhaps their Muslim souls to European innovations. Did they take advantage of their position to assist the inhabitants of the mandates to live longer, healthier lives?

In comparing the mandates of the French and British and the Ottoman State, a simple model applies:

1 Development in the Ottoman Empire can be assumed to be the base. In the late 1800s the Ottomans built a system which worked, however haltingly, to improve the economy, education and life of the people of Greater Syria and, to a much lesser degree, Iraq. The development success of those who followed the Ottomans should be judged in relation to what went before.
2 The avowed purpose of the mandates was to provide administrative advice and assistance by a mandatory until such time as the nations were able to 'stand alone'. This, one must assume, meant improving living conditions in the affected states. Leaving aside social and cultural factors, the British and French governments were economically and militarily more able to govern than had been the Ottomans, so they should have done better.
3 The mandates should have improved at a faster rate than the Ottoman provinces. The relative rates of improvement in the two periods should be compared. Unless explained by extraneous circumstances such as wars, conditions should have been considerably better in 1930 than in 1910. Indicators such as life expectancy, proportion of students in the population, and trade levels should have been higher in the mandates than in the Empire. But the mandatory governments cannot be considered a success if they merely matched the Ottoman rates of growth in the economy, education, etc. Given their resources, the British and French should have been improving their mandates at a faster rate than did the Ottomans.

To summarize, regardless of one's political or moral judgement of imperialism, if the subjects ate much better, lived much longer, and learned much more, then the mandatories had fulfilled the task they set for themselves.

Population

One of the best indicators of improvement of life is population change. Population statistics are surrogates that indicate economic development. Ideally, they indicate whether conditions actually improved for the individuals in a country by describing the life and death of those individuals. Other economic indicators, which could range from per capita income to gross national product, surely describe economic development, but they do not have the force of life and death. As will be seen below, demographic statistics for much of the mandates territory were less than ideal. However, the statistics do broadly represent real trends in relative development in Syria, Lebanon and Palestine. Comparison of population trends between Ottoman and mandate times in fact provides one of the potentially best evaluations of the status of the inhabitants of the Arab mandates.

With few exceptions, before World War I population increase was directly correlated to better conditions for the inhabitants of non-European regions. Fertility (the number of children a woman would have if she had a sexual partner and lived through her fertile years) did not change much; mortality did. When war was in abeyance and governments properly patrolled the countryside, the resulting civil peace allowed more adults to live and more children to grow to adulthood and raise families themselves. In addition, in traditional societies medical and sanitary conditions were in such a low state that even small improvements, such as providing a few doctors in district capitals or improving the supply of drinking water, caused an improvement in survival. Most importantly, good government and civil order allowed more crops to be grown and to reach markets, necessarily improving health and survival. Population increase is thus a good index of the well-being of peoples.

Unfortunately, the desirability of an index does not affect its availability. Middle Eastern historical population data are deficient and demand careful and detailed evaluation. In Greater Syria, population statistics were barely sufficient for tentative analyses to be made. The availability and accuracy of population statistics are in themselves an indication of the condition of the government. Censuses and population registration must be preceded by government control. If the government does not adequately control an area, it cannot count the people. Moreover, a government that has little concern for the status of its people will not be concerned to assess their social and economic situation. There is no need to discover high child mortality, for example, if you plan to do nothing to improve the situation. Thus adequate population data indicate a certain level of government control and improving data indicates a concerned government, although not necessarily a benevolent one.

Due to a lack of data, it is difficult to chart the course of population change in the Ottoman Empire from the seventeenth to the mid-nineteenth centuries. It is believed that in those two hundred years the population of most of the Empire essentially stagnated. In some areas the population probably decreased. Average life expectancy was less than twenty-five years, in some areas perhaps as low as twenty years. Nearly half of all children died before the age of one. Such numbers were not unusual in Asia before modern times.

It is surely no coincidence that low demographic indicators accompanied a lack of central government control, nor that distinct improvements came with a resurgence of Ottoman control in the Arab provinces. Improvements in civil order and technology meant gains in industry and agriculture. Demographic indicators improved with governmental control and concomitant economic changes. Average life expectancy rose to thirty years or more, in some areas such as Aleppo Province to over thirty-five years. These conditions came about before 1900 and essentially remained the same until the onset of World War I. One can theorize that the demographic plateau represented the level that could be achieved without medical improvements and great investment and change in the economic infrastructure, neither of which could be provided by the Ottoman government.

The French mandates – Lebanon and Syria

According to the theory advanced above, development in mandate Syria and Lebanon should have led to population increase. If life improved under the mandatory regime, the population should have grown at a more rapid rate than under the Ottomans, especially since there were no foreign invasions or major epidemics. Yet the population did not grow at an appreciably greater rate than it had before World War I. It increased at a rate of approximately 0.015 per year from 1878 to 1914 and at 0.017 per year during the French mandate, a minuscule improvement.

If the status of the people is reflected in the growth of their numbers, then the French mandates in Syria and Lebanon were no better than the Ottoman Empire. Indeed, one might expect that with European influence would have come some of the technology and practices that had made Europe a more hygienic place than the Middle East; but the numbers indicate no such improvement. Because French statistics were so deficient, it is impossible to speak with complete confidence of the life expectancy of the people of Lebanon and Syria. However, the growth rates indicate that life expectancy was approximately the same under the French as it had been in the late Ottoman period, an average of approximately thirty to thirty-two years of life from birth. In the most important aspects of existence, life and death, conditions remained just about the same as under the Ottomans.

Palestine

Palestine under the British mandate, while it was unable to satisfy anyone politically (even the British themselves), was a relative success demographically. In all demographic criteria, the people of mandate Palestine enjoyed a distinct betterment of life over Ottoman times. In short, things were demographically as they should have been. One should assume that a strong European power would have been able to improve the conditions of health and civil order that led to population increase. British resources were greater than Ottoman resources and, perhaps most importantly, the British in Palestine were not forced, as the Ottomans had been, to spend money needed for development on defence from external enemies. Therefore, demographic improvement should be expected, and it was indeed present. The figures in Table 10.1 are the official population numbers from the two censuses taken by the British in 1922 and 1931, as recorded and as corrected for slight undercounting. Whereas the data given above for Syria did not include nomads, which the French could not begin to estimate, these figures incorporate a provisional count of nomads in Palestine.

Table 10.1 Rates of population increase in the British Palestine Mandate

Region	Time period	Total yearly rate	Muslim yearly rate
Ottoman Palestine[a]	1878–1914	0.013	0.012
Mandate Palestine	1922–1931	0.028	0.022
Mandate without migration	1922–1931	0.022	unavailable

Source: Justin McCarthy, *Population History of the Middle East and the Balkans*, Istanbul, Isis, 2001.
Note: [a] Kuds, Akka, and Nablus Sanjaks.

The excellent registration system in mandate Palestine says much about the degree of governmental control in Palestine, at least up to the time of the troubles in the late 1930s, when the standard naturally declined. Whether the British could have built their system *de novo* cannot be judged, but the presence of a population which was accustomed to fairly complete registration before World War I must have aided the British registrars. Another factor, which aided both the Ottomans and the British, was the geography of Palestine. Registration was naturally easier in areas like Palestine in which most of the population was close to centres of government control and thus easy for government registrars (and soldiers) to reach. Also, there were no regions of Palestine as remote and difficult to access as were the mountain and desert areas of Syria and Lebanon.

Finally, judged by the rate of population increase, the people of Palestine were demographically more well off under the British than under the Ottomans. Table 10.1 indicates a considerable improvement in the rate of population growth. The rate of increase in Ottoman Palestine was part of the greater Syrian demographic system that held during the Empire and continued in mandate Syria and Lebanon. Under the British, mortality declined greatly. Average life expectancy in Ottoman Palestine had been approximately thirty years as opposed to approximately thirty-seven years under the mandate in Palestine. (For comparative purposes, the Muslim and 'without migration' figures are the most revealing, because they do not include Jewish immigration.) Much of this increase was due to an active programme of inoculation and health care in Palestine. Increase in agricultural production must have also meant better health and thus decreased mortality.

Although consideration of the statistical collection process of government is seldom fascinating, a bit of analysis of the collection of population data by the British and French shows quite a lot about the different level of administration of the two.

The statistical development of Greater Syria was an integral part of the general development of statistical data and procedures in the Ottoman Empire. The patterns of development in Greater Syria were typical of other areas in the Empire: urban areas were first and best recorded and registration gradually improved in rural areas, as well. With an increase in government power came an improvement in population registration. This system applied in Anatolia and the Balkans, as it did in Greater Syria.

One of the most interesting facets of the Ottoman registration system was its integration into the political and social situation of the area registered. For example, the Ottomans realized that in many regions registration of females was difficult, perhaps impossible, because of customary seclusion of women. Therefore, they began by counting only males, enrolling females only when government power was strong enough to force female registrration. Furthermore, the manpower available to the Ottomans was too meagre to allow for a modern census, in which the population was enumerated all at once over a short period, so the Ottomans created a registration system in which available skilled manpower could be used to update registers periodically. In effect, the Ottomans took small censuses in different villages at different times. Their system allowed them to take best advantage of what political power and manpower they had.

The Europeans who conquered the Ottoman domain in Greater Syria chose to bring with them the European idea of a census and updates of population numbers through birth and death registration. In the case of the French, the system was a failure until their last days in Syria and never worked properly in Lebanon. Yet the French kept on with their European system; they updated bad census figures each year by subtracting registered deaths and adding registered births when even they must have known that their figures were meaningless. (Could the French have actually believed that the birth rate in Syria was significantly lower than the birth rate in France? If so, that alone says much about the state of their knowledge.) It was a dogged persistence of ideal over reality that was contrary in practice and spirit to the Ottoman methods. Of the two, one must think that the Ottoman approach was superior.

The British, on the other hand, made the European system work relatively well. Their statistical yearbooks and other governmental statistical reports closely resemble like volumes published each year by Western European governments. How did they do it? In part the British were more successful than the French because Palestine was simply an easier place in which to take a count. Geography made their job easier. (Indeed, the Ottomans had registered the population in Palestine much better than the population in most of Syria. It is instructive that neither the Ottomans, the British, nor the Iraqi kingdom did very well in counting the population of Iraq.) Other factors must be matters of speculation. The British simply put much more into the collection of data than the French were willing or the Ottomans able to do. They surely put more into the publication of the data they collected – for every page of data printed by the French the British printed a hundred. It would be surprising if the expenditure in collecting the data was not correspondingly greater, as well.

Under the Ottomans there was some demographic difference between northern and southern Greater Syria (Haleb, Aleppo Province, seems to have had the lowest mortality), but birth rates, death rates, and the rate of population increase showed little variance throughout the area. With the demise of the Empire, the population in the French mandates continued approximately as it had before, perhaps with very slight improvement. The rate of population growth in the British mandate began to increase. One can speculate as to the causes of this increase. Beyond considerations of civil order, the most likely cause for betterment was an improvement in sanitary standards and medical care. The economic effects of European, primarily Jewish, immigration and financial support may also have had an effect.

Population statistics indicate the demographic success of the British mandate and the relative failure of the French. This is not to say that they also indicate a failure of the Ottomans, due to the relatively worse statistics in Ottoman times. It should be remembered that prior to *c.* 1880 the Ottoman population had not increased – mortality was high and civil order was poor. However, in their final period of rule the Ottomans had begun to create improved conditions that allowed the population to grow. In a demographic sense, conditions had much improved. The British success was a continuation and acceleration of the Ottoman success, as should be expected. The French situation in their mandates was a stagnation.

Education

One of the best indicators of a successful modern state is the state of its educational system, in particular the public education system that educates the masses. In this area, the French improved on the Ottoman record, although at a much slower rate than might have been expected. State-sponsored education had been virtually non-existent until the nineteenth century, left instead in the hands of each religious group (millet). However, when the Ottomans began educational reform they constructed a system of state schools. This was inherited by the French.

The lack of detailed French statistics makes it difficult to compare numbers of students with those in Ottoman times. However, it does seem that the French improved somewhat on the Ottoman public education system. The Ottomans recorded 25,000 Muslim students in state schools in

1895, whilst the French recorded 33,000 Muslim[2] students in *écoles officiels* in 1926. This was a slight improvement in the proportion of Muslims being educated, and the numbers improved in subsequent years. For Christian students the improvements were much greater.

Table 10.2 shows the percentage of the population who were students in mandate Syria and Lebanon. Slightly less than one-third of the population were aged from five to nineteen, so the level of education for any group was not high. It was considerably lower for Muslim and Druze children. If a child were Christian, he or she was three times as likely to be in school. The extent to which this was a conscious policy of preferment for Christians, one of many under French rule, is debated. Cost most definitely was a factor in the difference. The French spent very little on schools. State schools, which could be afforded by those who were not so poor as to need their children's work at home, only educated 34 per cent of the students (1926 figures). Another 58 per cent were in *écoles privées subventionnées*, schools for which the French provided a limited public donation but which were operated by religious communities. Because these private schools were costly to religious communities and individuals, the Muslims were largely dependent on the state schools. Sunni and Shia Muslims made up only 15 per cent of the students in the private schools. A further 8 per cent of students were in 'foreign' schools, operated mainly by Christian missionaries. Muslims were only 16 per cent of their students.

Table 10.2 Syria and Lebanon: percentage of the population in schools in 1926, by religion

Religion	Percentage
Sunni Muslim	4
Shia Muslim	5
Druze	3
Maronite	14
Greek Orthodox	13

Source: Justin McCarthy, *Population History of the Middle East and the Balkans*, Istanbul, Isis, 2001.

For the Muslims of Palestine the availability of education (Table 10.3) was as limited as for their co-religionists in Syria and Lebanon. Once again, the Muslims largely attended state schools (77 per cent), while 87 per cent of the Christians and 99.9 per cent of Jews attended non-governmental schools. The latter were aided by the government, with the remainder of their funding coming from community religious groups and, for the Jewish schools, the Jewish Agency. As might be expected, there was a considerable disparity between the state schools and the others. The Jewish schools approached or exceeded the European standard; the state schools did not.

Nevertheless, there was an incontestable improvement in the numbers of students who had been educated in Ottoman Palestine. More than twice as many students were enrolled in state and private schools in 1926 as had been in 1913. The British had thus improved the educational system they had found considerably more than had the French by 1926. The French, however, did improve their system in the 1930s and always educated a slightly higher percentage of the Muslim population than the British. (Jewish education cannot be compared because of its special circumstances and greater external funding in Palestine.)

Table 10.3 Palestine: percentage of the population in schools in 1926, by religion

Religion	Percentage
Muslim	3
Jewish	18
Christian	19
Other[a]	6

Source: Justin McCarthy, *Population History of the Middle East and the Balkans*, Istanbul, Isis, 2001.

Note: [a] Mainly Druze, some Bahais.

Iraq showed the greatest improvement in numbers of students in any of the Middle Eastern mandates, albeit it from a low base. There were 22,125 students in government primary schools in 1925, four times the number in 1913, and 42,950 students in non-governmental schools that were government-aided. Improvement in numbers, however, hides definite deficiencies. The quality of the education was not great, and the commitment of the government to education was minimal. Almost all of the non-governmental schools were so-called 'mullah schools', traditional Muslim schools with a limited curriculum. Students attended the government primary schools for only four years. A further two years of education were given to a very small number. Actual secondary schools (high schools) were not thought to be needed. The British government noted: 'Whatever may be thought desirable elsewhere, in this country it is neither desirable nor practicable to provide Secondary education except for the selected few. There are at present four government Secondary Schools at Baghdad, Basra, Mosul, and Kirkuk. But there are reasons for thinking that even this limited number may be too large.'[3] Such sentiments may be thought to indicate a certain lack of commitment to Arab education.

One undoubted benefit to the populace in all the mandates was the introduction of Arabic as the language of instruction in state schools. The Ottoman Empire had made Turkish the primary language of instruction in state schools. The intent of creating an empire-wide common literacy in the main administrative language was understandable, but it put a great burden on students and on the supply of teachers. The move to Arabic was popular and successful.

Again, there is the question of the standard to which the French and British should be held. For the Muslims of Syria, Lebanon and Palestine the mandate educational systems did somewhat improve on the past. The Ottoman educational system had also been improving, however, and it can surely be speculated that the mandate improvements were what the Ottomans might have produced in the same period, or perhaps less. What the French did not produce was a system that was a dramatic improvement over the past, except for Christian students. The British cannot be said to have done much better, except for Christians and Jews. Neither occupying power devoted much to the education of the poorer segment of the population, the Muslims. This was sure to exacerbate divisions in society.

Civil order

The preservation of civil order is the first duty of any government. Riots and rebellions against British and French rule caused prominent failures in this obligation. However, when times were less turbulent the mandatories largely succeeded in improving civil order. Police forces showed a marked improvement on Ottoman times.

The greatest success in improving order was the curtailment of bedouin raids on the settled population. Although they were making inroads against bedouin attacks in the final days of the Empire, the Ottomans had never been completely successful in patrolling the desert borders. Their troops were more needed on the Russian border. Utilizing aeroplanes and mobile jeep forces, both the British and French were able to respond quickly to bedouin raids and to keep large bedouin attack forces from forming. In Jordan, the British officer John Bagot Glubb (Glubb Pasha) successfully organized the bedouin themselves into a small army that opposed their brothers. This was a major benefit brought by the mandate governments. Security was a necessary precursor to economic development, not to mention survival of the settled populace.

The economy of the mandates

It is difficult to evaluate the effect of French rule on the economy of Syria and Lebanon. The French did not keep adequate records on the economy. In many ways, their published records were worse than those of late Ottoman date. This in itself is indicative of the lack of French effort in Lebanon and Syria. Adequate record-keeping is a necessary part of a modern economy. The French only had a limited idea of what was transpiring in the economic and social life in the mandates. The British provided much better statistical material.

Trade and commerce

Traditional Middle Eastern trade patterns, dictated by geography and human settlement, had not much changed for centuries when the Ottomans lost their Empire. True, more goods passed between Europe and Asia by sea, and the transit trade from the Red Sea to the Mediterranean was a far less important factor in world trade than in the Middle Ages. Nevertheless, goods still passed from Iraq up the Euphrates, across to Aleppo, and on to Anatolia. Egyptian goods passed by the coast route to Syria, and Syrian goods to Egypt by the same route. Much of this trade was internal, Ottoman provinces trading with each other. There was one integrated system of Middle Eastern trade and commerce.

All of this changed when the British and French divided the Middle East into separate states. Each of these states, as well as Turkey and the independent states in Arabia, put up border crossings, initiated burdensome customs formalities, and instituted tariffs. The effect was an immediate decline in trade among the Middle Eastern regions and the destruction of whole industries. Exports from Syria to Egypt did not return to their 1910 level until 1927, and never went much above that level. Estimates differ, but trade between Syria and Turkey declined by at least one half. Some estimate a two-thirds decline. Aleppo, which had been the trade centre for a vast area which included much of Iraq, Syria and southern Anatolia, fell on hard times. One-third of the famous textile looms of Aleppo disappeared. Two-thirds of the weavers lost their employment. Unemployment struck all the sectors of the economy that had depended on trade with Anatolia, now Turkey.

The combination of customs duties and restricted markets restricted economic growth. What had been gateways to an extensive internal market were now ports opening only onto one smaller region. The port of Beirut, for example, had improved its economic position steadily in late Ottoman times. In 1910, 989 steamships entered the port, but that number was not reached again until the middle 1930s. The port of Iskandarun had been an outlet for the goods of southern Anatolia and the transit trade from Iraq, but it languished when new borders, especially the border with Turkey, ended much of the trade.

As customs duties went up, what had been free internal trade was now international trade, often highly taxed. Syria had a tariff of 11 per cent until 1924, after which the tariff increased to 15–30 per cent. In 1926 it increased to 25–50 per cent. Iraq began to tax imports from Syria at 40 per cent. In other words, the Middle East partook of the tariff madness that also swept the Western nations. Each nation felt that it could aid domestic industries best if it protected them with high tariffs.

All was not disastrous. The Syrian mandates and Palestine mandate eventually adopted a free trade zone that allowed traditional trade patterns to continue between them. Overall Syrian (i.e. Syria and Lebanon) trade with the Middle East thus only declined from one-half of the trade to one-third, much less than if tariffs between Syria and Palestine had been in place. The mandatories realized that the transit trade was suffering from high transit duties of from 15 to 50 per cent. In 1925, they reduced those duties to 1 per cent, and the trade improved. Some traditional trade continued, particularly trade with other mandates and colonies: Palestine, for example, imported and exported approximately the same value to Egypt and Syria as it did to the United Kingdom. However, other Middle Eastern trade languished. Using trade with Britain as a standard, Palestine did twenty-five times as much trade with Britain as with Turkey, fifty times as much as with Greece, Iraq or Iran.

Trade with Europe also increased and offset losses in Middle Eastern trade. All of the mandates greatly diversified their trade with European states. Under the Ottomans trade had overwhelmingly been with large states. The mandates became more integrated with the European market. But the main trading of the mandates, not surprisingly, was with the mandatory countries. In the 1920s, approximately one-fifth of the imports and one-quarter to one-third of the exports (both by value) of Palestine were with the United Kingdom. The trade of Syria and Lebanon was almost mercantilist in its one-sidedness. On average, imports from France were four times greater than exports to France. Among Syrian/Lebanese trading partners, France was in first place for imports, but in fifth place for exports.

One of the effects of the mandates' economic policy was to create actual differences and competition between states. Each new state developed its own industries and internal trade patterns, to the detriment of what had been a broader economy that crossed regional boundaries. Thus economics became a foundation of national separation and, ultimately, nationalism in Syria, Lebanon, Palestine and Iraq. Elites emerged with a stake in the new order; older elites adjusted to it. Trade and commerce, which had been a factor of integration, now became a cause of separation.

Transportation

Lack of proper state attention to the economy in the French mandates meant that opportunities for economic improvement were missed. Far too little was spent on infrastructure. The railroads that were present in the French mandate were those constructed by the Ottomans. Only one relatively short stretch of new track was laid, from Nusaybin to the Iraqi border, not completed until 1935. Some lines were improved, and new rolling stock purchased. However, needed new lines, such as a coast line, were never more than planned. Merchants in Syria rightly called for a continuation of transportation improvements such as those created by the Ottomans. In particular, it was obvious that a railroad was needed to connect the ports of Syria and the Iraqi railroad system, allowing transit goods to pass easily. Plans were made, but the French did nothing to create the railway.

The only rails laid by the French connected the Iraqi railroads to the Turkish railroad system, facilitating an Iraqi–Turkish transit trade. Concessions to operate the existing lines were granted to French companies. Ironically, much of the railroad network of Syria and Lebanon had been constructed and overseen in Ottoman times by French companies. French interests thus were instrumental in speeding communications in the region until the French themselves took charge.

The French did better with roads. An all-weather road was built to connect all the coastal cities from İskandarun to the Palestine border, with similar roads tying the major inland cities to the coast. These were mainly improvements of Ottoman roads, but they allowed a large increase in automobile and truck travel. The major addition to the Syrian transportation grid that was undertaken by the French was a new road connecting Damascus and Baghdad. By 1933, 2000 vehicles a year were taking that route.

In Palestine the British inherited the track of the Hijaz Railway in the west and the railroad from Jaffa to Jerusalem. During and immediately after the war they had built a line from Egypt to Haifa. Mandate authorities rebuilt some lines, and added 15 km of connections. Under the British the railroad track of Palestine increased by 50 per cent and much old track was improved and transformed to standard gauge. This was what was needed in Palestine. The same can be said for road construction and improvement. The emphasis there was on upgrading roads for motor transport, which built a limited system of trunk roads in Palestine.

The British made a major transportation effort in Iraq. As advisers to the Iraqi kingdom they were in fact in charge of transportation. Needs of the military position and of the British-controlled Iraq Petroleum Company drove the British to considerable effort. The rail line from Basra to the northern border, planned by the Ottomans, was completed. With a short section built in Syria the railroad connected to the Turkish grid and on to Europe, the final step in the Berlin to Baghdad Railway envisaged decades before under the Ottomans. This was the only mandate railroad construction that could rival construction in the Ottoman times.

Agriculture

Agriculture improved markedly under the Palestine mandate. Although always hampered by lack of funds, agricultural bureaux did advise farmers on new crops and on improving old ones. Production of most crops

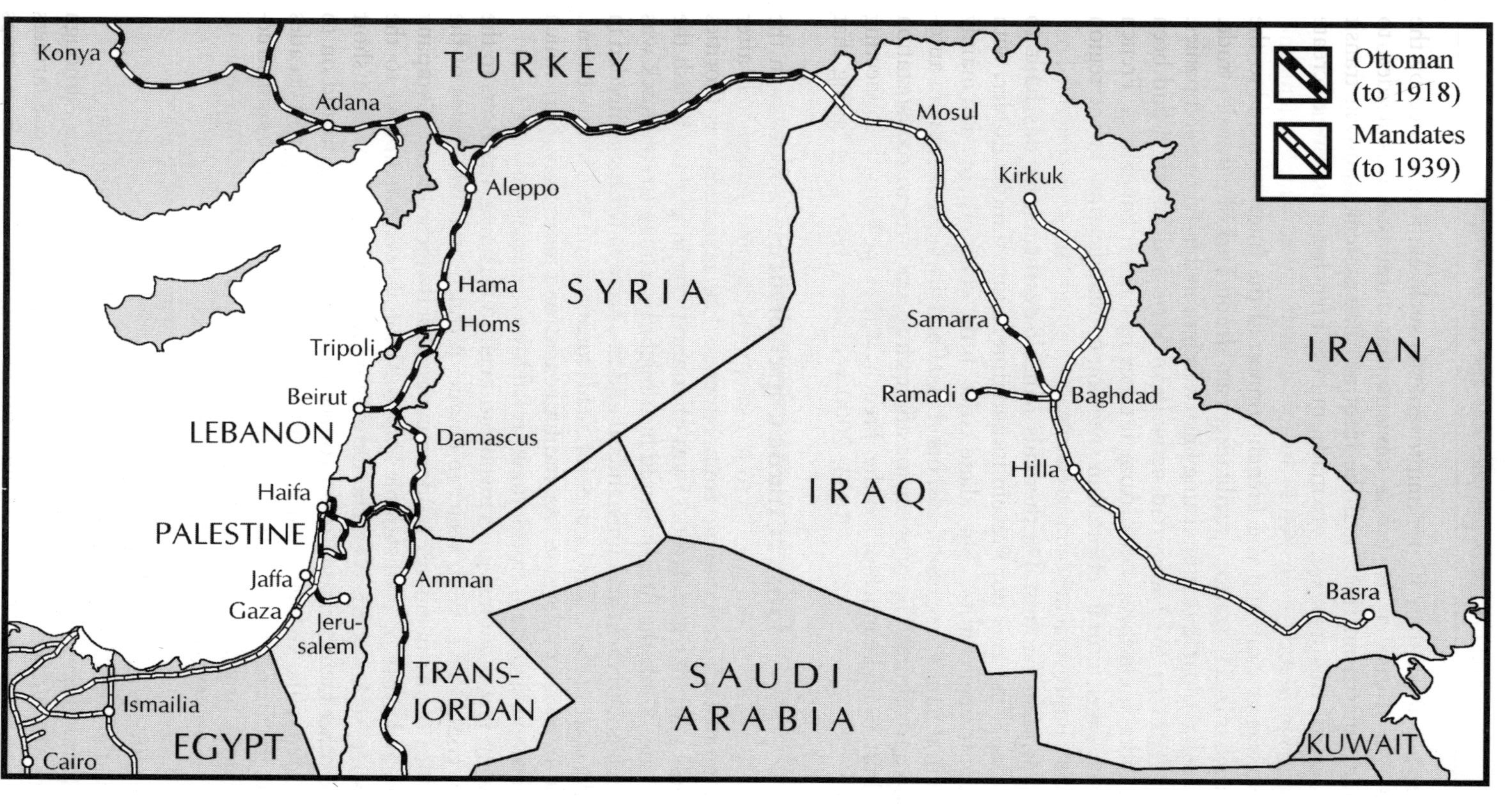

Map 10.4 Middle Eastern railroads

increased by more than 50 per cent from 1921 to 1926. By the outbreak of World War II cash crops such as olives and oranges had increased more than ten times from their 1921 production. Zionist industry provided a good deal of this increase, especially in the later years, but yields were growing significantly even before major Zionist investment. Agricultural increase was general, and was a shining point of the Palestine mandate. In Iraq, mechanized irrigation greatly increased the amount of cultivable land. The British estimated that land so irrigated in Iraq increased from 72 square miles in 1921 to 2670 square miles in 1927 (almost all of which unfortunately ended up in the hands of large landowners and tribal chiefs).

French agricultural effort, on the other hand, was insignificant. Significant improvement seems to have come only in cash crops intended for export, especially cotton. On the other hand, the silk industry died, due to international markets not French mishandling. Some state lands were distributed to cultivators, but there was little progress in developing agricultural banks, irrigation, and other state activities that were needed to develop agriculture. The problem was financing; too little was allocated to agriculture to make much of a difference.

Government expenditure

The largest block to economic advancement in the mandates was finance. The policy of the mandatories was that each territory should be self-supporting. While the British and French might be willing to run deficits in their own government accounts, they would not do so in the mandates, even after the start of the Great Depression. This meant that it was impossible to borrow in order to develop. As the Ottomans had seen, such borrowing could become a curse if not done wisely. However, without some level of borrowing few economic enterprises can begin. Of course, the British and French could have kept their economic policies and still helped the economies of the mandates by donating the funds themselves, as part of their sacred trust of civilization. This was not viewed as an acceptable alternative, so funds always remained extremely limited.

Two other factors further restricted the funds available. The first was the need to repay the Ottoman public debt. Debt payments took up 12–14 per cent of the mandate budgets. The Treaties of Sèvres and Lausanne had accepted the principle that the Ottoman debt would be apportioned among the successor states, so these sums had to be paid.

The largest state costs were not debt repayment; they were the costs of policing the populace. To use the French as an example, in 1926, 864 French and 10,793 local residents were part of the gendarmerie (primarily rural, paramilitary police), the 'mobile guards', and auxiliary troops; 758 were in the urban police. The numbers of French 'sûreté' police, not included in these figures, were not given in French reports. These figures can be compared to the Ottoman policing forces, which numbered approximately 3500 in the Ottoman Syria, Beirut and Aleppo Provinces, a larger area than the French mandate in Lebanon and Syria. (Neither the Ottomans nor the French counted regular troops in their figures for police.) To pay for this level of policing, the gendarmerie, police and courts took up 30 per cent of the mandate budget.

Public safety costs in the British mandates were similar. From 1919 to 1939 the Palestine government spent an average of 29 per cent on public safety. In 1923, the last year for which the British had been wholly responsible for drawing up the budget in Iraq, 31 per cent was allocated to police, defence and the Ministry of Justice.

Administrative costs were also high, especially since European salaries had to be paid to so many administrators. From 1919 to 1939, the government of Palestine spent 29 per cent of its revenue on administration. (The published budgets for the other mandates do not separate administrative expenses.)

These figures should be compared to other governmental expenses to understand the condition of the mandates. The British in Palestine, who spent 58 per cent on policing and administration, spent only 11 per cent on health and education. (In Britain itself, by contrast, the government spent 50 per cent of its revenue on education, health, welfare, and national insurance.[4]) The 1923 Iraq budget allocated 4 per cent to health and 4 per cent to education. The 1925 Syria and Lebanon budget gave 8 per cent to education and 4 per cent to health and public assistance.

Contributions from the home countries were made, but for military purposes: the French army's costs in putting down rebellions were mainly covered by France; the British government made a small contribution to the Palestine budget, approximately 4 per cent during the 1920s, almost all of which went toward defence of Trans-Jordan.

Given the level of expenditure demanded by the police, the military and administration, it is no surprise that so little was left for education or other public welfare. The expenditures for security, in particular, must be understood in the light of the political situation. Palestine, Syria and Lebanon were not threatened by external foes. High security expenditures were necessitated by the fact that the mandatories had to defend themselves and their governments from internal enemies. The fact that the British and French were unwanted made such expenditures necessary. The nature of the mandates meant that very little would ever be available for education.

The record of the mandates

The British in Palestine and to a lesser extent in Iraq were more successful than the French in the most meaningful sphere of government, bettering the lives of the populace. Population increase in Palestine demonstrates this better than any other indicator. Transportation and communication were also more improved by the British. Educational improvements were insufficient in any of the mandates. Overall, only in Palestine can the general economy be said to have improved more than what might have been expected if the Ottoman Empire had continued. Such comparisons are only guesswork. They do indicate, however, that the rule of the British and the French was a disappointment.

Politically, evaluation of the mandates depends on the central question of the desirability of an Arab state. There can be no question but that the mandates through their policies of political, economic and religious segregation aggravated divisions within the Arab world and encouraged separatism. Again, what would have been the result if a large Arab state had been created is unknowable. In the light of the history of the mandates and what followed them, it seems likely that, whatever the possible failings of an Arab state, the peoples of the Middle East would have benefited from its existence.

11

The Turkish Republic

In terms of both mortality and physical destruction, the events that overtook Anatolia between 1912 and 1922 were among the most disastrous in history. In Anatolia, out of a pre-war population of 17.5 million, nearly 3 million Muslims, nearly 600,000 Armenians, and slightly more than 300,000 Greeks were lost in World War I and the Turkish War of Independence that followed.

It is impossible to identify ethnic or linguistic groups in Ottoman statistics, because the Ottomans kept population records only by religion. Nor is it possible to differentiate in which regions non-Muslims suffered worse mortality. This is due to the process of estimating mortality, which is to take the number who were in a province before the wars and subtract from it the number present in the province at wars' end, the result of which is 'population loss', not strictly mortality. Muslims, who ultimately won the Anatolian wars, were present in their Anatolian provinces at wars' end; Greeks and Armenians, who were counted mainly as refugees, were not. Therefore, one can only give total mortality figures for Christians, but can be more specific for Muslims. Because of this, the descriptions below are primarily of Muslim suffering. The Christians suffered in much the same way and in the same places, largely because the Christians and Muslims killed each other.

Map 11.1 is drawn by subtracting the Muslim population in 1922 from the population in 1912. It does not include immigrants from the Balkan Wars, although the figure of almost 3 million Muslims lost does so. The mortality in some provinces was staggering: in Van Province, 62 per cent of the Muslims who were present before the wars were gone by the end of 1922; in Erzurum Province, 31 per cent were gone; in Bitlis, 31 per cent; in Hüdavendigâr (capital, Bursa), 10 per cent; in Aydın (capital, İzmir), 10 per cent. By comparison, in what became the USSR, 8 per cent of the population disappeared in World War I and the Russian Revolution. France lost 1 per cent of its population in the world war. The populations of Germany and Great Britain did not decline during the war.

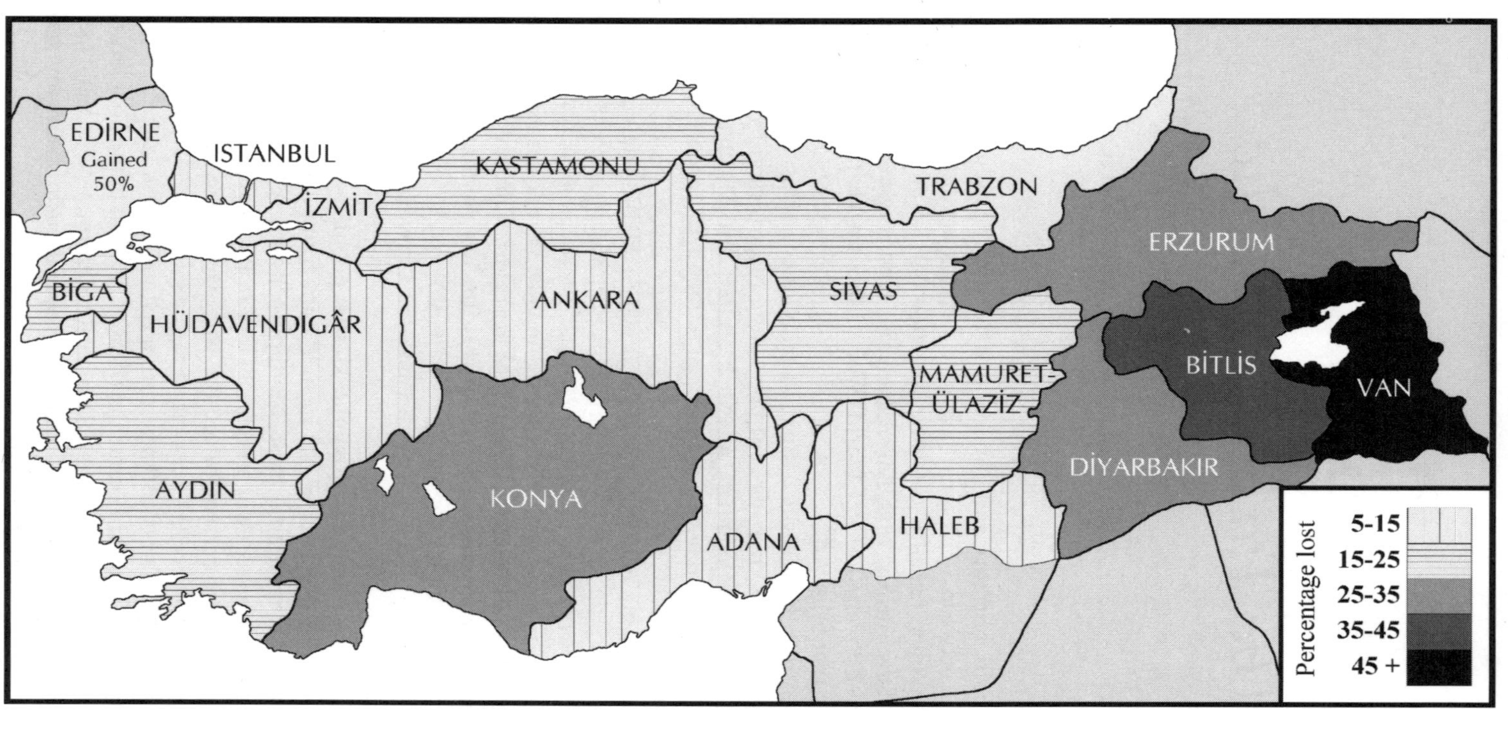

Map 11.1 Mortality in Anatolia, 1912–1922

The effects of mortality and migration

After the wars, the Turkish Republic was a new state, made up of Ottoman Anatolia, the regions of Kars and Ardahan, which had been in Russia, and what little was left of Ottoman Europe – eastern Thrace and Istanbul. Those who remained in the Turkish provinces were not only the natives of Anatolia and eastern Thrace who had survived the wars. Waves of immigrants had come to Anatolia and eastern Thrace, adding more misery to regions in which there was not enough food for those already there. Some 414,000 Turks had been expelled to Turkey (i.e. what was to become the area of the Turkish Republic) from the Balkan countries during the Balkan Wars. Nearly 300,000 Muslims had fled from the southern Caucasus, primarily from Armenia, during World War I and the Independence War. A further 431,000 more came to Turkey after the wars, primarily from Greece. Approximately 10 per cent of the post-war population of Turkey had migrated from other lands. They had arrived as refugees, without possessions, dependent on the charity of a destitute land and people.

Table 11.1 indicates the scale of the 'international immigration' (i.e. from regions that had been part of the Ottoman Empire until conquered) to those Turkish Republican provinces that accepted the greatest number of refugees from the Balkans. Reliable statistics are unavailable on the refugees from the Armenian Republic to eastern Anatolia. The actual proportions in 1922 were somewhat smaller than indicated in the table, because some of the migrants had died, especially in the Independence War. The population of the area of the Ottoman Edirne Province, occupied in both the Balkan Wars

Table 11.1 In-migrants to Turkey, 1912–1927

	1912–20 refugees	**1921–27 migrants**	**1922 population**	**Proportion**
Edirne	132,500	125,420	476,069	0.54
Ankara	16,148	8,150	1,158,376	0.15
Aydın	146,723	56,912	1,400,949	0.15
Biga	4,033	10,856	140,715	0.11
Hüdavendigâr	66,041	79,482	1,437,971	0.10
İzmit	6,771	20,470	259,712	0.10
Istanbul	11,109	35,487	510,648	0.09
Sivas	10,805	37,195	1,015,887	0.05
Konya	8,512	30,207	1,123,889	0.03

Source: Justin McCarthy, *Muslims and Minorities*, New York, New York University Press, 1983.

and the Independence War, must have died in great numbers. Nevertheless, in-migration assured that Edirne actually gained population in the wartime period – the only Turkish region to do so. It became a province in which half the inhabitants were newcomers. Newcomers also made up for some of the population loss in the western Anatolian provinces.

Large numbers of internal migrants added to the international refugess in the Anatolian provinces. During the Independence War, more than 1.2 million Turkish refugees fled from the Greek invasion. In the east, there were more than 1 million Muslim refugees from the Russians and Armenians. When the wars were over, many of these refugees returned to their home provinces, but many did not. Many, of course, had died while exiled. Map 11.2, which records the percentage of Turks who were living in their district (*kaza*) of birth, indicates that the greatest proportions of immigrants were found in the provinces that had been occupied by Russians and Armenians (the east), the French and the Armenians (Cilicia), and the Greeks (the west).

Most of the migrants in the Turkish provinces had come to their new homes from some distance. This is demonstrated by the numbers who had come from other provinces or other countries (Table 11.2). The figures in the table are for 1935, because Turkey did not include data on birth district in the earlier 1927 census. If earlier data had been available, they would have shown even higher proportions of residents born elsewhere, because of deaths of migrants and new births from 1927 to 1935. This has the effect of adding numbers born in the districts and subtracting some migrants. Had 1922 figures been available, the percentage of migrants in the populations might have increased by 25 per cent or more. (For example, the proportion of migrants in Edirne Province in 1922 was probably at least 50 per cent.)

Table 11.2 Turkish provinces in 1935: resident population born elsewhere

Province	Percentage not born in same district	Percentage not born in same province
Edirne	41	40
Kırklareli	50	48
Tekirdağ	48	46
Ağrı	39	33
Kars	24	17
İzmir	39	35
Bursa	29	26

Source: 1935 Turkish census.

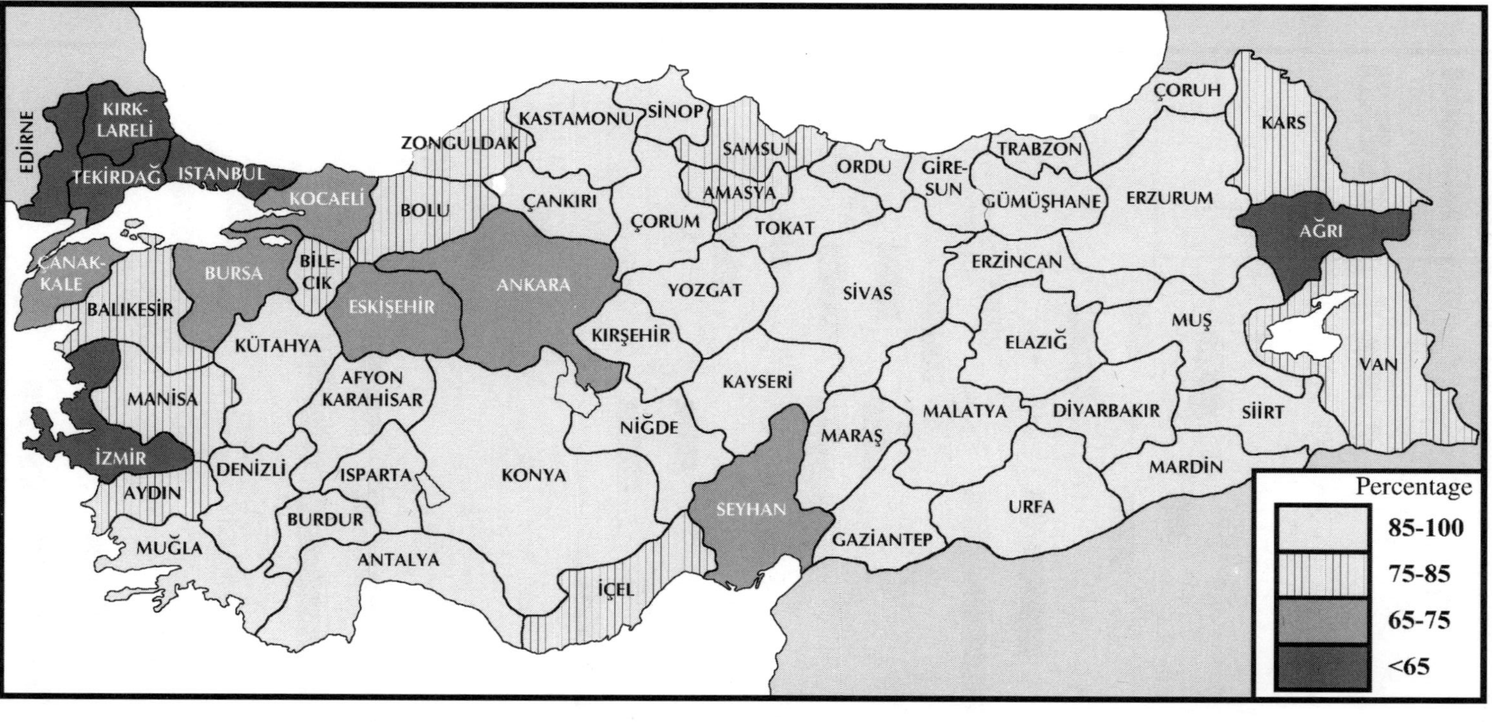

Map 11.2 Population living in district of birth

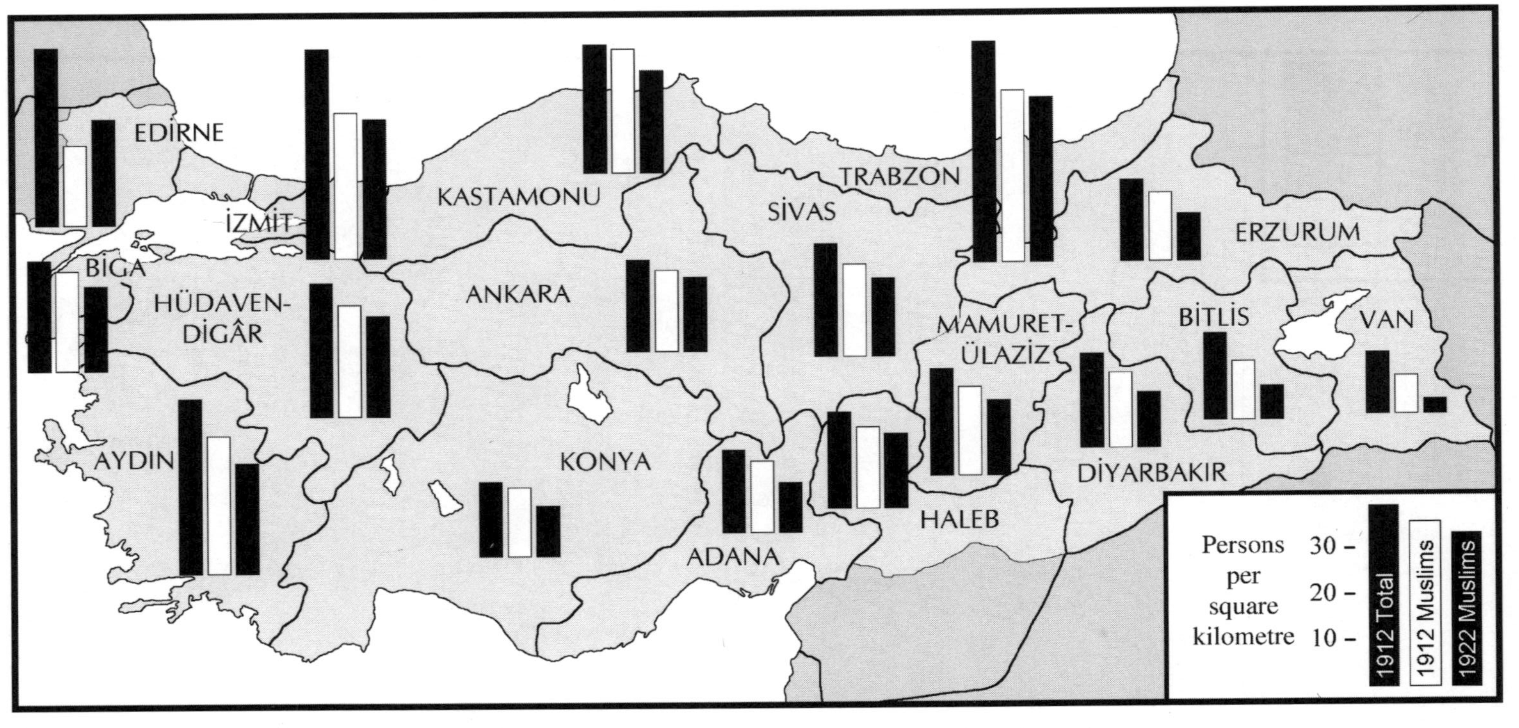

Map 11.3 Population by province, 1912 and 1922

Prior to the wars, the Anatolian Turks had primarily been a settled people. Despite often temporary migration for work and military service, most Anatolian Turks continued to live in the same regions as their forefathers. This was especially true of women. Now masses of people had moved permanently. For many, as will be seen below, their old homes and villages were destroyed, so living in new regions was to be expected and perhaps welcomed.

The mortality and migration of the Muslims changed the relative demographic importance of the Turkish provinces. Map 11.3 indicates a shift in importance from the east to the west. While northern and western Anatolia had for centuries been more densely settled and more economically developed than eastern Anatolia, the comparatively greater destruction in the east and migration to the western provinces exacerbated this condition after the wars. This undoubtedly contributed to the much more rapid advancement of the west in Republican times. Where population is more dense, education and the economy are more easily developed.

Many Turkish cities lost population in the wars (Map 11.4). They were reduced in size and changed in character. The Christian populations of most were gone. The cities of Van and İzmir were largely destroyed. In İzmir, however, the natural attractiveness of the region seems to have drawn thousands, who rebuilt quickly. This was not true of Van, which had become a small city in a ravaged province.[1]

Judged by its population, Anatolia was a much changed land in 1922. Except in Istanbul, the Greeks and Armenians were gone. The Turks had experienced great mortality and they now lived in different places. Demographic relationships between provinces, between regions, and between the rural and the urban had all changed. This was particularly noticeable in eastern Anatolia. Not only had the population greatly decreased in the east, but many of the cities that had been the centres of trade and communication with other regions were partly or wholly destroyed.

Devastation

Map 11.4 cannot adequately reflect the scope of the changes that faced the Turks. In numbers, the city populations do not appear much different. There were still significant populations in the Anatolian cities. Those populations, though, were often living in ruins. Wartime destruction of western Anatolian cities meant that many city populations lived in rough housing, in tents, or roofless dwellings.

In western Anatolia most destruction was done by retreating Greek soldiers and civilians. Some of this destruction was what might be expected: those who knew the history of forced migration in the Balkans might have known that they would never be returning to their villages; they destroyed their homes rather than have them pass to their enemies. This was not the

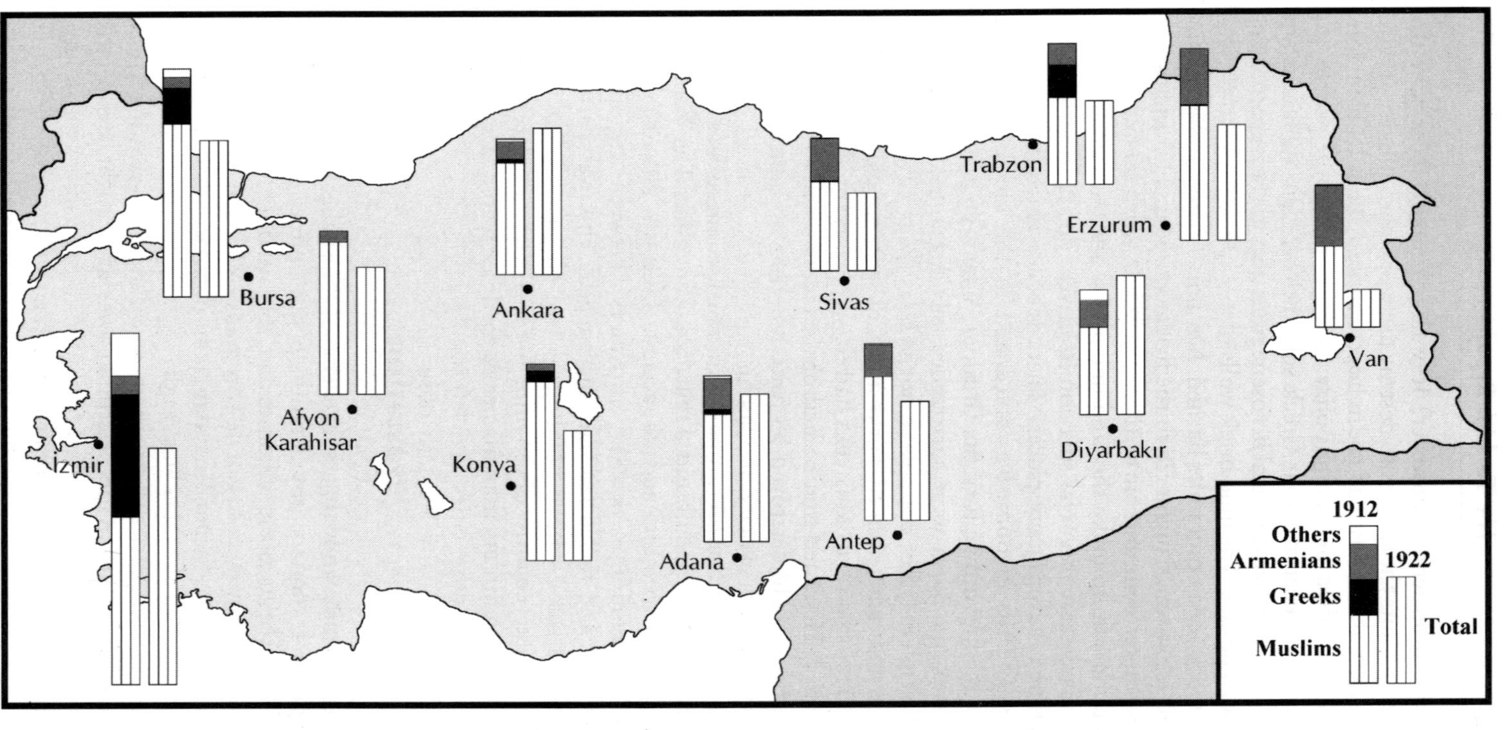

Map 11.4 Central districts: population by religion, 1912 and 1922

main cause of destruction, however. It was probably too difficult for villagers or merchants themselves to destroy all that they had. Regardless of their past history, there must have been hope of return. The actual cause of most destruction was a deliberate policy of the Greek army. British and American observers reported that Greek soldiers with dynamite destroyed buildings and whole towns. Special kerosene pumps were used to spread fire among wooden houses. The mud brick walls of village houses were knocked down and their wooden roof poles burned. Livestock could seldom be taken away quickly, so it was slaughtered in the fields. Trees were chopped down or sprayed with kerosene and burned.

The intention was to make the land uninhabitable, and in many towns and rural areas the intention was successfully carried out. Only the speed of the Greek retreat saved many places. There was too little time to do an effective job. The city of Bursa was saved, for example, by Allied officers who stopped the first attempts of the Greek army to destroy the city. Soon after, the Greeks in Bursa were surrounded by Turkish troops and were forced to surrender. Other cities were not spared: the American consul at İzmir, Park, a man who disliked Turks and had completely supported the Greek cause, reported that the Greeks had destroyed everything they could as they retreated. He stated that he had observed the results in four cities, and that the Greeks had destroyed 90 per cent of the cities of Manisa and Kasaba, 70 per cent of the city of Alaşehir, and 65 per cent of the city of Salihli. He described the murder, rape and torture of thousands of Muslims as the Greeks retreated, and observed that 'The burnings of these cities was not desultory, not intermittent, not accidental, but well planned and thoroughly organized'.[2]

Careful statistics compiled for the Turkish delegation at the Lausanne Peace Conference listed 54,200 buildings destroyed by the Greeks in the cities, 88,000 in the countryside. Aydın, Nazilli, Bilecik and other cities were totally destroyed. Less than 10 per cent of the buildings in Manisa, Alaşehir, Kasaba and other cities were left standing. The level of destruction was remarked on by many Western observers, including an enterprising reporter from the *Chicago Tribune*, who toured western Anatolia immediately after the Greek occupation and reported that the Greeks had left cities uninhabitable and villages levelled.

There were no accurate statistics on the destruction in the war zone of eastern Anatolia. The numbers of houses and shops had not been accurately counted before World War I. But it is known that the destruction was massive. Some of it can still be seen today. For example, the old city of Van, the Muslim quarter of the city, was totally destroyed and has never been rebuilt on the old site. After the war the new population left it almost as a great shrine to the lost. It resembles nothing so much as a moonscape with a few surviving buildings.

The best description of the destruction in the east came from two Americans, Emory Niles and Arthur Sutherland, who were sent by the

American government to examine conditions in the east. They were virtually the only Westerners to visit the region immediately after the war. (Their report was suppressed by the American government until recently, when it was found in the American Archives.)

Niles and Sutherland reported that the north of the region was worst affected. People in the land between Erzurum and Beyazit were forced to live on wild grasses. Cattle were gone, so there was little milk. Much starvation was expected there in winter, since people were already starving in summer. They had not seen the region of Erzincan and Kars, but they theorized from what they had heard and seen that the situation was as bad there as at Erzurum. Oddly, the region of Van and Bitlis, which had suffered the worst wartime mortality, had little starvation in 1919. Two-thirds of the former population was gone, so land was plentiful. Therefore, while the population was ill-housed and hungry, it was not starving.

Table 11.3 Population and houses in the cities of Bitlis, Van and Beyazit

	Population		Houses intact	
	Pre-war	August 1919	Pre-war	August 1919
Bitlis				
Muslim	30,000	4,000	6,500	0
Armenian	10,000	0	1,500	1,000
Van				
Muslim	43,000	5,000	3,400	3
Armenian	35,000	160	3,100	1,170
Beyazit				
Muslim	5,000	2,460	960	600
Armenian	1,000	0	190	90

Source: United States, National Archives, 184.021/175, 'The Report of Captain Emory H. Niles and Mr. Arthur E. Sutherland, Jr. on Trip of Investigation through Eastern Turkish Vilayets'.

Table 11.4 Villages in the province of Van and sub-province of Beyazit

	Van			Beyazit	
	Pre-war	Intact 1919		Pre-war	Intact 1919
Muslim	3,400	350	Muslim	448	243
Armenian and mixed	299	200	Armenian	22	33

Source: United States, National Archives, 184.021/175, 'The Report of Captain Emory H. Niles and Mr. Arthur E. Sutherland, Jr. on Trip of Investigation through Eastern Turkish Vilayets'.

Destruction of agriculture and the economy

It is difficult to estimate the extent of agrarian loss in Anatolia. Statistics are non-existent for much of the east, and changing borders make it impossible to compare Ottoman and Republican statistics accurately, even in some provinces for which data exists. Map 11.5 and Table 11.5 identify Republican provinces for which comparative data is available. The table illustrates widespread destruction of livestock. When one considers the need of horses, donkeys and mules for sowing and taking crops to market, the loss of so many animals must have put an incredible burden on agriculture. Moreover, the figures do not consider the lack of seed grain or other factors such as the almost complete destruction of olive trees in many provinces. Such loss would have contributed greatly to agricultural disaster. The conclusion to be drawn is obvious: not only were the Turks without homes to live in, they were without food to eat.

Table 11.5 Livestock in the Western Anatolian war zone before and after the wars

	Horses		Donkeys and mules		Sheep	
	1913	Lost	1913	Lost	1913	Lost
İzmir	42,711	20,774	25,068	13,962	429,752	166,031
Aydın	24,008	7,126	18,186	4,830	188,424	29,581
Denizli	12,013	1,832	31,210	3,314	191,046	28,249
Bursa	17,015	3,730	21,815	630	322,989	39,916
Afyon	14,223	528	40,711	954	621,157	28,260
Manisa	21,893	24,502	28,079	13,170	394,101	86,137
Eskişehir	—	28,202	—	15,796	—	1,120,009

Source: Great Britain, Public Record Office, Foreign Office 371-9061, no. E969, 'Mémorandum relatif aux dévestations grecques en Asie Mineure' by İsmet Paşa (İnönü), Lausanne, 20 January 1923.

Economic loss in Turkey matched other losses. Indeed, losses of farms, city buildings, animals, and human beings were all economic loss. Industrial loss was also great, as exemplified by İzmir. Prior to the wars, as enumerated in 1910, İzmir had contained 27 per cent of the grain mills in Anatolia – 30 per cent of the grain milling capacity.[3] It was a major textile manufacturing centre, the main centre of box making, a major centre of production of food commodities, printing, and publishing, and contained all four of the biggest Ottoman oil companies (petroleum and vegetable oils). Aydın Province, of which İzmir was the centre, paid more taxes than

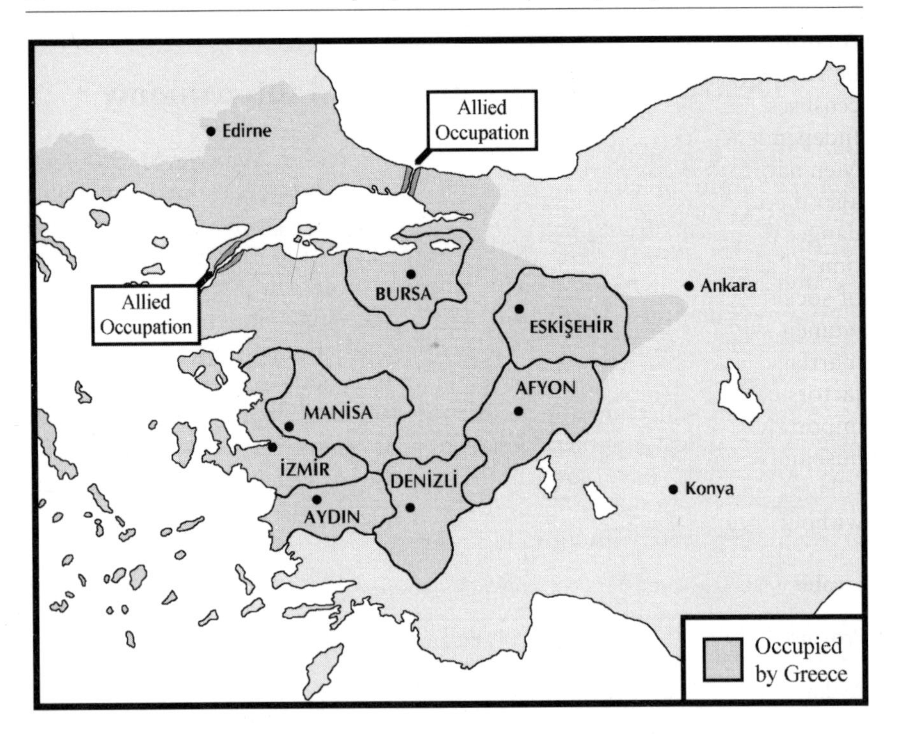

Map 11.5 Destruction of agriculture

any other province in Anatolia. It was the centre of the latest technology, housing, for example, almost half of the steam-powered mills in Anatolia. In most areas of manufacturing, İzmir was second only to Istanbul in the Ottoman Empire. Now it was all destroyed, burnt to the ground.

Other western Anatolian cities naturally showed less destruction of manufacturing potential – there was less to destroy. However, it can be noted that 42 per cent of the grain mills in Anatolia had been in cities that were largely destroyed, as were a similar percentage of other industries.

Personal loss

The most difficult of the Turkish losses to understand and explain is personal – psychological and social loss. It is impossible to quantify sorrow for the dead, the anguish of seeing villages and homes destroyed, or the fear that you and your children will soon die of starvation. Yet, next to death itself, it was probably the worst of all the losses.

Table 11.6 explains social loss with a simple statistic – the greater number of adult females in the post-war population. Aydın, Hüdavendigâr and Erzurum provinces were scenes of most of the worst fighting in

Anatolia. In a normal population, the numbers of males and females would be roughly equal. Indeed, females were undercounted in all early Turkish censuses, so the numbers of males appeared to be higher. After the Independence War, however, the numbers of females were much higher. Men naturally died in greater numbers because they were the soldiers. They also died because young males were singled out for murder. They were a danger that could be eliminated, as was to be seen later in Bosnia in another time of atrocities. The economic effect of the loss of a most productive part of society is obvious. There must also have been a high psychological loss: women without husbands in a traditional society that expected universal marriage, and children without fathers. The fact that such psychological factors cannot be quantified in a statistical pattern does not diminish their importance. To that must be added the fact that these women without husbands and children without fathers were often refugees returning to villages and cities that had been destroyed, beginning life again, often without food and shelter, on their own.

Table 11.6 Turkey in 1927: female population as percentage of male population

Province	Female percentage of population
Aydın	123
Hüdavendigâr	130
Erzurum	140

Source: 1927 Turkish census.

The effect of the ruin of Anatolia

It is impossible to appreciate properly the real difficulties facing the Turks or to evaluate their success in meeting them unless one understands the desolate state of Turkey at the beginning of the Turkish Republic. The task that faced the survivors of the wars was immense. The success of the Turkish people in rebuilding is thus all the more impressive.

Others also suffered during the war years. Greeks, Armenians and others went through the torments of those awful times, and they too went on to rejuvenation. But they did not do it alone. The world assisted them. Americans alone gave more than $100 million to Armenians, creating orphanages, schools, agricultural programmes and industries. The Greeks, who accepted great numbers of refugees, but whose land had not been destroyed in the wars, received donations from America, Switzerland, Holland, Britain and other countries, as well as loans on favourable terms, as seen in Chapter 9. Except for a very few charitable organizations with limited resources, no one helped the Turks.

The Turkish Republic

The Turkish Republic was proclaimed by the Turkish parliament, the Grand National Assembly, in Ankara on 29 October 1923. From its beginning, the Republic was led by Mustafa Kemal, given the name Atatürk ('Father Turk') by the Assembly when Turks adopted surnames. Atatürk and the Assembly set upon a programme of radical reforms. Women were given the vote and elected to the Assembly. Islam was disestablished, making Turkey a secular state. Completely new secular law codes were written, to be enforced by purely secular courts. These laws shattered the old traditions of the Ottoman state. While the Tanzimat and its successors had slowly altered governance and law, their reforms were never truly radical, because the forms of the past were left to coexist side by side with the new. Now all was changed.

The basis of Turkish foreign policy became neutrality and a rejection of irredentism. Most states claim they have no territorial ambitions in the lands of their neighbours, but enforcing that policy in Turkey was a task. The survivors of the Ottoman Empire included hundreds of thousands who had been forced from what was now Greece, Bulgaria, Yugoslavia and the Soviet Union. Mustafa Kemal Atatürk had himself been born in Salonica, now in Greece. Aided by a deep war weariness and his own control of the state, Atatürk was able to submerge feelings and get on with the business of rebuilding the Republic. In 1926, Turkey submitted to a League of Nations Council decision and relinquished the province of Mosul to Iraq. Turkey signed the Balkan Pact in 1934 with Romania, Yugoslavia and Greece, guaranteeing the territorial integrity of all signatories.

Development in the Republic

The achievements and failures of the Turkish Republic must be judged in the light of the devastation of war. No other country, not even Russia in the Revolution, suffered so much loss of life, physical destruction, and dislocation of people in the wars. The Turks were rebuilding a ruin, not simply starting where they had left off before the wars. There was a deficiency of capital, machines, skilled labour, and even buildings, which had been destroyed in the Independence War and World War I.

There was also a deficiency in business skills. In Ottoman times, international trade and much industry had been in the hands of minorities. The CUP government had attempted to enlarge the Turkish middle class just before the outbreak of World War I. The policy was heavy-handed, based on actively discouraging Greek enterprise and transferring it to Muslim hands. Discouragement of minority commerce through boycott of Greek goods and extortion was successful, but development of Muslim industry and entrepreneurship largely unsuccessful. Would-be Turkish businessmen, many of whom only had political connections to recommend them, had scant knowledge of business methods, few connections in the European mercantile community, and little time to learn before the war broke. The Republic renewed the policy in a far different environment. Outside of Istanbul, there were no longer any minority businessmen to compete. The Republic had to create a business class.

Table 11.7 indicates the relative economic success of the Republic in its first years. Since there was a long-standing practice of hiding production from the government, actual figures were surely higher. It must be remembered that these statistics began at a very low base, the war-ravaged economy of 1923. It is generally outside the scope of this study to examine economies beyond the first years of the Ottoman successor states. The second column in Table 11.7 has been included, however, for comparison. The figures for the period after 1929 partly demonstrate the difficulty of keeping up such rates of growth and mainly the effect of the Great Depression. Other statistics show that the expansion of the economy was significant in certain sectors. For example, in 1925, factories produced 7000 tons of cement, 41,000 in 1927, and 100,000 in 1930. The Istanbul Electric Company produced 36,000 kw in 1925, 48,000 in 1928, and 69,000 in 1931. The cloud that always hung over the economy was state finance. To avoid the economic dependency that afflicted the Ottomans, Turkey bought out foreign owners of utilities and transportation systems, which was expensive. Railroad extensions and other infrastructure improvements also had their cost. Since the government was unwilling to borrow beyond its means, another Ottoman sin, many sectors such as education were underfunded.

Table 11.7 Average annual rates of growth (%) in Turkey, 1923–1939

	1923–29	1929–39
Gross National Product	10.3	5.2
GNP per capita	8.4	3.0
Agricultural output	13.6	4.4
Manufacturing output	7.2	5.2
Total industrial output[a]	10.2	5.7

Source: Roger Owen and Şevket Pamuk, *A History of Middle East Economies in the Twentieth Century*, Cambridge, Mass., Harvard University Press, 1999, p. 244.

Note:
[a]Including construction.

The greatest success in the post-war economy was the agricultural sector, which within ten years approached the level of per capita production that had been reached in 1912. The government improved the situation of farmers by radically altering the Ottoman tax system in 1924. A tax of 10 per cent on agricultural production, which had in fact been higher because of collection methods, was replaced with a land tax. The new tax brought in less government revenue, but encouraged production, because peasants could maximize their yields without incurring new taxes. Cash crops were favoured by the government to bring in foreign exchange. Tobacco production, for example, was 49 million kg in 1913. That amount was exceeded by 1924. The growth in agriculture was more impressive because so much of the agricultural production of the most fertile land, western Anatolia, had been badly damaged. No amount of government support could quickly replace the olive trees cut down in the Greek retreat.

Transportation

The Turkish Republic finished the Anatolian railroad grid begun by the Ottomans. In the Ottoman Empire, 3200 km of track were laid in Anatolia between 1863 and 1917. The Republic laid 3000 km between 1925 and 1934. For the first time eastern Anatolia was brought into the system. The dream of the Ottomans, a railroad that connected Istanbul to the Iraqi border and on to Baghdad, was completed by the Turks and the British. An average of 287 km of new roads were constructed each year between 1928 and 1934. An average of forty-five bridges were built in the same period.

Transportation was an area in which the Republic far exceeded the Empire. It was a labour that caused hardship, both financial and social. Much of the road network was built with corvée labour. Yet the transportation system was essential to the new economy that was to arise after World War II. It also allowed the government to project power easily from the centre, with a corresponding benefit to civil order.

Education

The educational system of the Republic cannot be said to have been a great success numerically, but given the lack of financial resources, the Republic made strides in improving the provision of schools. In 1926, 466,000 students were registered in all schools, 3.4 per cent of the total population. This compared to 265,000 in state schools in 1913, when the population was higher. (Private schools, which educated mostly Christians, have been excluded from the Ottoman data.) Nevertheless, the proportion of children being educated in the Republic was small. The limited funds available and the modest percentage of state funding allocated for education (4–5 per cent in the 1920s) was one reason for this. Another was the lack of teachers, partly due to the great wartime mortality in the young adult age group, from which teachers were drawn.

Radical reform

The political discontinuity between the Republic and the Empire was not as great as it has often been portrayed. On the highest level, there is a fundamental difference between a democracy and an empire. Even if flawed, a democracy proclaims that the people can and should rule. Compare this to the European mandates in the Arab world, whose colonialist ideology was predicated on the assumption that the people could not rule.

Mustafa Kemal unquestionably was the master of Turkey as long as he lived, although he stressed the forms of democratic government. The Republican political system inherited much from the tradition of the Committee of Union and Progress. As in the days of the CUP single-party government, there was one dominant ruling party, now the Republican People's Party. The party was ubiquitous in localities through the country, where it cooperated with and fitted into local power structures.

From the days of the Independence War, Turkey was in theory ruled by a parliament, the Grand National Assembly. Major decisions depended on the agreement of the president, but the parliament was not a negligible body. It did not have the power to name ministers, which was the president's prerogative, but could refuse to accept the president's choices. It also could vote to dissolve the government. Neither of these took place, of course. Real power was in the hands of the Republican People's Party, which expressed its power through the Assembly. The party, in turn, represented the wishes of local elites to the centre.

The existence of the forms of democratic government was not unimportant. The value in their existence and training in democratic forms became evident after World War II, when Turkey evolved into a genuine democracy. Democracy is always a preferable system, but authoritarian rule can speed reform. Atatürk's authority surely did so. He had a firm commitment to westernization as the only proper path, a dislike of what he felt were the failed ways of the past, and the will and power to change the traditional system.

The greatest break with Ottoman tradition was religious and cultural. Since the reign of Mahmud II, the Ottoman Empire had set itself on a path of Europeanizing reform, but reformers had never taken the final radical steps in any area but the military. Old institutions had been allowed to exist alongside new. Islamic schools continued, as did the entire panoply of the Islamic legal system. Millets still existed even when many of their functions had begun to be taken up by the state. Each of these institutions had its conservative defenders, and these were always a threat to reforms and even to the state itself. A power such as Abdülhamit II could arise, ally himself to reactionary forces, and frustrate some (not all) reforms. Separatism as expressed by the very existence of the millet system was a threat to all attempts at Ottoman unity. It was one of the factors that hindered the development of Ottoman nationalism. Separatism was also a prime contributor to the development of minority nationalism.

The only Ottoman institution that developed without a traditional counterpart was the military. Mahmud II had ensured this when he forcibly dissolved the Janissaries. Even in the military unity and reform had been impeded by traditional officers who opposed many changes and resented the new ideas of the young, educated officers who graduated from the military schools. Nevertheless, the military was able to reform itself more successfully than other institutions. This eventually led to the revolt of the CUP, the reforming government that followed, and the pivotal place of the military in the War of Independence and the Republic.

The Republic removed the formal structures of reactionary power. First the sultanate was abolished (1922), then the caliphate (1924). Although religious groups continued to provide welfare and education, the millet structures were abolished. (In theory, the separate millets themselves renounced their privileges, which had been partly guaranteed in the Treaty of Lausanne.) The Republic ended the predominance of Islam. In 1928 the Republic was declared to be a secular state. Islamic Law was not just modified, as it had been in the Empire, it was abolished. From 1924 to 1926, the basis of law in the Turkish Republic changed: law codes drawn primarily from European examples took the place of the Holy Law, and secular judges took the place of Islamic ones. Muslim schools were closed, and state schools were forbidden to teach religion. Secularism in the Turkish Republic was aggressive: the Republic forbade all dervish orders and closed their lodges; traditional religious garb was outlawed; various practices abhorrent to the Orthodox, such as mandating that the Call to Prayer be given in Turkish, not Arabic, became the law. In general, the leaders of the Republic made it clear that expressing Orthodox Islamic views was the way of the past, and not the path to success in the new age. Strict secularism, espoused in the spirit of becoming more European, was enjoined.

In the place of the millets and Islam came the state. The parliament (Grand National Assembly) passed secular laws based on European models. All schools were ordered to teach according to a common educational programme promulgated by the Ministry of Education. In themselves, these reforms can be seen as continuations of Ottoman reforms. Unlike Ottoman reforms, however, they stood alone. The Republican law was now the only law. Republican judges were the only judges. All students were to be exposed to the secular curriculum, at least once there were enough schools and teachers to teach it.

The Republic went far beyond the ordinary scope of government in making radical reforms. Potential traditionalist opposition was rooted out. Some of this was private action – vocal opponents of the new Republican way were soon unemployed or made to know that their attitudes would not be tolerated in schools or the media. Members of the outlawed derviş mystical brotherhoods were not all against the new system, but they represented an alternative loyalty for a sizeable portion of the populace, and thus were viewed as a possible rival to the state. The brotherhoods ran afoul of the Republic's sense of the importance of symbols. The Republic was above all to become a modern European society. 'Oriental' was a term of ridicule. Therefore, government initiatives encouraged and sometimes forced the Turks to relinquish symbols of the Middle Eastern and Ottoman past, such as Muslim religious garb, veils for women, old-style peasant clothing, and fezzes. The European calendar was adopted. Polygamy was abolished. The Arabic/Persian alphabet was replaced by Roman characters. Everyone was made to adopt a surname such as Europeans all had. (Mustafa Kemal was given the name Atatürk, 'Father Turk', by the parliament.)

This was not the stuff of liberal democracy. Personal choice was not a consideration in the new system. Yet Atatürk's policies recognized that reform was much more than a matter of laws. He intended to change the basic culture of the Turks, under the theory that a people who dressed, wrote and voted like Europeans would eventually come to think like Europeans. As anyone who has walked down main streets in Ankara, the Turkish capital, can attest, the campaign had a great success. In the villages the success was more mixed, and took much longer. It was the elites who were first and most convinced that change was needed. But no one can argue that the Turks did not radically change their culture, nor that this made them more receptive to Europeanizing reform. In short, the Turks became much more European. One of the signs of European culture was nationalism.

Turkish nationalism

The War of Independence left behind the first mass Turkish nationalism, forged in a war in which Turks were forced to stand as Turks against enemies who saw them as a national group. Atatürk and his followers believed that it was essential to develop that nationalism, both to unite the people and to stand against the nationalism of others. No thought was given to continuing the Ottoman non-national tradition of religious identity; that had not worked.

There were difficulties. Unlike the Greeks, Bulgarians and others, the Turks were made up of various groups with different histories. Most were descendants of the Turks who had arrived long ago from Central Asia or those who had joined with the Turks in early days and had linguistically and ethnically become Turks themselves. The two groups were mingled and indistinguishable. They would be the base of ethnic nationalism. Many others had been added to the mix, however: Circassians, Abhazians and Laz from the Caucasus, Kurds in the east, Arabic-speakers in the south,

Pomaks who had emigrated from Bulgaria, Georgian Muslims, Sephardic Jews, and many other groups. Any Turkish nationalism would have to be in some way inclusive. Yet the Turks, like peoples of the Balkans and most of the rest of the world, had been infected by the 'racial' concept of nationalism – the belief that something genetic or spiritual tied together the nation. They felt they needed something more than loyalty to an inclusive state. The attempt to combine an inclusive nationalism, a nationalism that would include the diverse ethnic groups of Turkey, with the 'racial' nationalism that the Turks had inherited from Europe led to a peculiar nationalist ideology.

Perhaps the ideal form for nationalism to take would have been an inclusive nationalism such as that which developed in North and South America. The basis of such nationalism was identification with national ideals, citizenship and a common culture. Those from many different cultures could join and often became the most fervent of nationalists (although far from perfect beliefs might exclude some groups, such as those of African descent, from their Nation).

An inclusive nationalism would have been historically and practically proper for the Turks. No one who looked at Turks in all their genetic complexity from east Turkistan to the Balkans could call them a homogenous 'racial' grouping. The Turks had been inclusive since early times; the way to become a Turk was to want to be one and to become a Muslim, and even Islam was not necessary for all Turks. Someone who spoke Turkish and said he or she was a Turk was a Turk. In the nineteenth century, millions of refugees came into the Ottoman Empire. Some of these, such as the Crimean Tatars, were Turkish-speaking Muslims. Others, such as the Laz, Circassians and Abhazians, were definitely not ethnic or linguistic Turks. Yet no observer of modern Turkey could say that their descendants did not become Turks – linguistically, culturally, and usually nationalistically.

The other type of nationalism, called racial nationalism here, was the type of nationalism seen in German law and practice. A German was someone whose forebears lived in Germany or partook of Greater German Culture, a vague criteria that was in practice defined by looking into one's ancestry. Thus German-speakers from Munich or Berlin were considered German, but so were non-German-speakers whose ancestors had gone to Russia centuries before. There were excellent reasons for Turkish nationalism to adopt racial criteria for membership. Today some of these reasons are difficult to understand. In the first half of the twentieth century, however, much was made of the need for nations to occupy their ancestral homes, no matter who was living there at the time. Zionism was obviously based on this sentiment. In the various Balkan nationalisms, much attention was given to 'returning' ancestral homes to national groups (a practice which with the Serbs, for example, has brought much tragedy). The victorious Europeans were bent on giving western Anatolia to Greeks and eastern Anatolia to Armenians. One of the justifications for this total blindness to demographic realities was that those peoples had been there before the Turks.

To counter this reasoning, the Turkish Republic adopted an unusual combination of racial and inclusive nationalism: the people of Anatolia and eastern Thrace, including those ethnically not Turkish, were the descendants of Turks. The Hittites and other ancient peoples, the first dwellers in Anatolia, had been Turks, their languages a form of Turkish. Schools taught generations of Turks that they were a people like the peoples of Europe, defined by an ancestry that went back to pre-history. The Turks, therefore, had more historic right to Turkey than did anyone else.

The beneficial upshot of this concept was that the Turkish Republic simply refused to listen to any of the arguments of those who said that Anatolia was really theirs. Separatist voices inside the Republic and the claims of Greeks and Armenians outside could be ignored, because their cultures were declared to have been only intermediate steps between ancient and modern Turkish cultures. The various peoples in the Republic were told that they were all Turks, and not simply because they were citizens of Turkey. They were Turks because their ancestors had been Turks. The negative upshot was the enforcement of this ideology. Non-Turkish ethnic expression was suppressed. For most of those with non-Turkish heritage this was little problem. They were already well along the road to assimilation. The main problem was the Kurds. For many Kurds, nationalistic Turkish ideology was not unwelcome. It reinforced the assimilationist tradition of the Turks, which was beneficial to them. These Kurds became ethnic Turks and full partners in the governing of the Republic. Generals and even presidents of the Republic were to come from Kurdish stock. For many Kurds, however, Turkish nationalism presented problems which were to give focus to the later development of a separate Kurdish nationalism and ensuing rebellion.

The people's will

The question is why did the Turks go along with truly radical change? Atatürk and the Republican People's Party unquestionably controlled the army and other instruments of state power. Press censorship, or more precisely the closing of newspapers, was an instrument of government control. The army was used to put down a rebellion among tribal Kurdish followers of a leader of the Nakşibendi movement, Şeyh Sait, in 1925. The rebellion was put down fairly easily, and most Kurds did not support it. In 1926, four opponents of Mustafa Kemal were executed and a number imprisoned after an attempted assassination of the president. Other opponents, ex-members of the CUP, were discredited as possible conspirators. Yet these actions cannot be seen as part of any general rebellion of either Kurds or Turks. What might have been expected, popular revolt against radical changes that threatened Islam and traditional values, never took place. In general, the army was not needed to implement reform. Atatürk's Turkey, while authoritarian, was not a state in which government power was omnipresent and oppressive. This is especially true when Turkey is compared to the authoritarian states of Europe at the time or to the European mandates in the Arab world.

It is interesting to compare the expenditures on civil order in Turkey and the mandates. As a percentage of its budget, Iraq spent more than twice as much as Turkey on its police and gendarmes; Syria and Lebanon spent more than three times as much. Different states counted such expenditures differently, but the differences are great enough to be significant no matter what the accounting practices. It is doubtful whether Turkey had fewer crooks, but it did have less to worry about from popular disaffection or from rebels.

Why, then, were radical reforms accepted in Turkey? The answer may lay in the shock of the death and destruction that had been visited on the Turks in the wars. Their suffering had caused the Turks to want peace above all else. This Atatürk gave them, peace derived from civil order and an end to the wars. He might change many of the bases of their old lives and destroy elements of religion and culture that they respected, but their crops could get to market, their children could go to new schools, no one destroyed their homes or killed their families, and their sons were not killed in wars. Given the experience of the recent past, these were great gifts that could overcome any number of disliked reforms.

How great was dislike of the reforms? No opinion polls were taken and the answer will never be known. It should be considered that the recent disaster may have caused a sea change in the attitudes of the Turks. The old ways, particularly the old ways of government, had failed abysmally in the most important duty of a state – protecting its people. How seriously could the Turks have taken calls to return to the 'good old days' when all knew that the old days had been awful? The Ottoman reforms had largely depended on a constituency first in the bureaucracy and later in a small middle class and the army. How much would the farmers of the Empire have seen the benefits of reform? Markets were better. Civil order was greatly improved. The increase of population in late Ottoman times indicates that life as a whole was improved. These were gradual improvements. It is doubtful if the populace as a whole equated incremental improvements with the benefits of reforms. Against the benefits stood losses in wars and the gradual cutting off of Ottoman territory. The prestige of the reforming Ottoman state must necessarily have suffered when it could be seen by all as too weak to defend itself. The presence of more than a million refugees in the Ottoman dominions cannot have aided the government's image. That sort of public image does not build a constituency in support of reform. Nor could the ideals of Ottoman democratic reform have had much effect on the common consciousness. It is doubtful if the grand ideas of the reformers were ever understood by the masses.

The disasters of 1912–22 could be easily understood by all. It is not a great leap of logic to assume that the Turkish people knew that change was necessary, no matter what their lack of education or lack of political understanding. Things had to change. For the first time there was a constituency for reform among the people.

There was one more factor in building a constituency for change in the Turkish Republic, something that can only be understood emotionally. Atatürk had made the Turks proud. In recent Ottoman times there had been little to be proud of. Under Mustafa Kemal, the Turks had saved themselves when all were against them. It must have made good sense to the Turks to put themselves in the hands of the man who had given them that.

12
Legacy and consequences

The political legacy the Ottomans left to their successors was much less than might have been expected from an empire that had lasted so long. The states of the Balkans did not want anything from 'the Turk'. They rejected the Islamic and imperial traditions of the Empire, especially the Ottoman ideal of a state encompassing many ethnic groups. The Arabs might have wished to keep much that had been Ottoman, but they were not their own masters.

Even the Turks rejected Ottoman traditions so that they could more completely become a part of the West. It was the fundamental ideology of the new Turkish state that the Republic had begun anew and owed little to the Ottomans. Nevertheless, the reforms of the Turkish Republic were the culmination of those begun a century before by Mahmud II. The governmental ideas of the CUP were the intellectual antecedents of the reforms of the Republic, even though Republican reformers were more thorough, more committed, and more successful. In the Republic, reform was continued under new and improved management. Not until very recently have the Turks begun to glory in the achievements of their ancestors.

The bureaucratic tradition of the Ottomans did continue in the Middle East. Centrally directed reform remained the ideal in Turkey and the Arab world. The exceptions were countries such as Iraq in which bureaucrats and politicians would have liked to control society and economy, but could not. Military control over civilian government, such as seen in the CUP, was to be seen in later Middle Eastern states, as well, but this was more a function of the nature of power than an emulation of Ottoman methods.

This was not much of a political legacy for one of history's greatest empires to leave behind. The destruction of the Ottoman Empire was too complete a conflagration for more to remain.

Britain and France, although charged by the League of Nations to teach Western ways to their charges, were the ones who most kept to Ottoman religious practices, while abandoning the spirit of Ottoman religious reform. Islam, rejected as a principle of state in the Balkans and Turkey, retained much power and influence in the mandates. The Ottoman Mecelle legal code remained as the law of personal relationships. Islamic pious foundations remained under control of the religious hierarchies in the mandates long after being taken over by the state elsewhere. The Islam of the mandates was not the Islam of the Ottomans, however. Nineteenth- and twentieth-century Ottoman Islam had been open to change; not so in the mandates, where Ottoman law was frozen. The Ottomans had whittled away the power of Islam, but Islam was to become more political in the Middle East of the mandates. The British in Palestine, for example, engineered a political system in which Muslims were primarily represented to the government through religious leaders, a return to a system left behind by the Ottomans. The character of the Palestine mandate, set at its creation when Jews were politically separated from others, was in its essence a division of peoples. The millet system was more alive in the Palestine mandate than it had been at the end of the Ottoman Empire.

The Balkan successor states all substituted a Christian state religion for the Ottoman Muslim state religion, but this was in no way a continuation of Ottoman tradition. In each, religion had become the province of national group – the antithesis of Ottoman tradition. Islam also became more politically important in the Balkans, as the only self-identification legally allowed to Muslim peoples. To accept inhabitants of their states as Turks or Albanians would have been to accept that there was more than one 'nation' in their state.

Only the Turks overturned Islamic law completely and gave Islam no formal place in their state. But this complete rejection was also a repudiation of the changing Islam of the later Ottomans. That Islam was not to appear again. The upholders of Islam and secularist reformers were henceforth to harden their positions, to become antagonists who recognized little middle ground.

There were Ottoman economic practices that no one would wish to become a legacy, government financing chief among them. A system in which a minority controls commerce is a tradition that has proved to be disastrous in many places, as it was in the Empire. Beyond the finances of state, the Ottoman government actually intervened little in the economy, at least little by the standards of Europe. It could not afford it, and had only limited ideas of what could be done. The greatest effect on the economy came from its increasing integration into the world market. The reforms of the government opened the door to this integration, but could not ensure its success. European intervention in the local economy was, in its way, an unfortunate Ottoman tradition, but was too global to be viewed as an Ottoman legacy.

The beneficial economic legacy of the Ottoman Empire lay in the creation of a transportation and communications infrastructure. The Ottomans left behind themselves a legacy of physical development upon which the successor states could build. In 1850 the internal communications and transportation infrastructure of the Ottoman Empire was not much different from what it had been 400 years before. The basic means of transportation were the camel, the horse, donkey caravans and sailing ships. What communications passed between cities or provinces went by something akin to the Pony Express of the American West – horse riders who carried only the most important messages, most of them governmental. Much changed before the Empire's demise. Sometimes at a prohibitive cost, the Ottomans had built roads, railroads and telegraph lines. The construction programme had begun to knit together provinces that had been separated by distance and travel time. Turkey and Iraq were to make great efforts in completing the Ottoman transportation system, usually working to Ottoman plans, but they built on an Ottoman base.

One thing that was assuredly not a legacy of the Ottomans was the separation of peoples and religions that has led to so much of the strife in the modern Balkans and Middle East. That was a legacy of nationalism and of European military power.

The Ottoman system was one of religious separatism within a political unity. There was a cost to the Ottoman polity. One religious group, the Muslims, asserted their authority. Non-Muslims were politically second-class subjects of the sultan, despite their freedom of religion. While the political system was rapidly evolving toward political equality, the Ottoman state was still an Islamic Empire at its end, and Muslims were still the undisputed leaders of the state. Yet it is important to note that non-Muslims were not economically second-class. The concept of political subordination usually brings to mind a picture of inferiority in all things, as in the examples of African-Americans in the Old South, serfs in Russia, or indigenous peoples in most of the New World. This was not the case in the Ottoman Empire. On the contrary, in nineteenth-century Anatolia, the Balkans and coastal Syria it was Christians who developed economically while Muslims were left behind. Educationally, the Ottomans allowed a separate educational system that offered better education to Christians, funded both from the Christians' own efforts and by American donations to the great enterprise of missionary schools. Muslims might have been politically superior, but Christians were richer and better educated. That was definitely not the intention of the government, but it was accepted.

Until the final years of the Ottoman Empire, peoples of different religions lived together who have been unable to live together since. The ultimate marks of what was lost with the demise of the Ottoman Empire are the national divisions of the twentieth century. Expulsion of peoples and population exchange were the ultimate result of nationalism in the Ottoman domains. Once nationalism had begun its reign, those who had lived together for centuries could do so no longer. Some of the population exchanges were peaceful, because they were the result of treaties following wars that exhausted the protagonists. The exchanges that followed World War I were of this sort: Turks and Greeks and Greeks and Bulgarians each were exchanged peacefully, if forcibly. Other forced migrations of peoples were not peaceful. Expulsions of Balkan Muslims were accompanied by mass murder. The exchanges between Armenians and Muslims in eastern Anatolia and Transcaucasia were inhuman disasters. And the expulsion of peoples has continued to our day.

Mustafa Kemal of Turkey and Venizelos of Greece were wise to exchange their populations peacefully, because, failing a peaceful exchange, they would eventually have been exchanged in war: after the events of the Balkan Wars and the Turkish Independence War, Greeks and Turks could never again live together in peace. This says much of their wisdom as leaders, but it also speaks to the nature of nationalism. Nothing that leads to such results can be considered good.

Despite the inexorable forces that destroyed it, the question can still be asked, should the Ottoman Empire have continued? If it would have evolved more rapidly away from the separatism of the millet system and toward democracy, yes, but who can tell if that evolution would have continued? If the Empire were to be divided, an Arab state encompassing the Ottoman Arab provinces would probably have been beneficial to its inhabitants. Perhaps a division of the Balkans along ethnic and religious lines should have taken place. It could have been made along the lines suggested in Chapter 3, displacing a relatively small number of people. A planner looking at a map in 1912, much as the victors of World War I were to look at their maps, but with more humanity and less greed, could have arrived at many possible divisions of the Middle East and the Balkans. What a compassionate planner would never have designed was a sequence of events in which millions were driven from their homes, millions more were killed, and the powerful divided the spoils without regard for the wishes of the populace. No change, no matter how potentially beneficial or desirable to nationalists, the planner might have thought, could be worth that.

The indelible legacy of the imperialism and nationalism that ended the Ottoman Empire was the loss of opportunities – the chance for peoples to continue to live together in the Balkans and Anatolia, the chance for the Arabs to join together and determine their own fate, and the chance for the millions of dead simply to survive. The Ottomans, who could not reform their Empire quickly enough to save it, have a share of responsibility for those lost opportunities, but guilt falls mainly on the nationalists and imperialists, who did not count the cost when they destroyed the Ottoman Empire.

Notes

Chapter 1

1 The name Anatolia, or Asia Minor, is used here to describe the region that is today Asiatic Turkey.

Chapter 2

1 The term Syria as used in this and following chapters means the large region that included roughly the areas of today's Lebanon, Syria, Israel, Palestine and Jordan. The actual Ottoman province of Syria (Suriye Vilâyeti) had different borders and was smaller than today's Republic of Syria. Syria as the term is used here included that province, the provinces of Beirut (Beyrut Vilâyeti), Mount Lebanon (Cebel-i Lübnan Sancağı), Jerusalem (Kuds-i Şerif Sancağı), and the southern half of Aleppo Province (Haleb Vilâyeti). Later Syria, created by the French after World War I, will be referred to when it arises in Chapter 10.
2 This information is taken from Carter Vaughn Findley, *Ottoman Civil Officialdom: A Social History*, Princeton, Princeton University Press, 1980, Chapter 3.

Chapter 3

1 Carnegie Endowment for International Peace, *Report of the International Commission to Inquire into the Causes and Conduct of the Balkan Wars*, Washington, 1914.

Chapter 4

1 The so-called Six Vilâyets (provinces) of Bitlis, Diyarbakır, Erzurum, Mamuretülaziz, Sivas and Van.
2 Descriptions of the Armenian revolutionary organizations have been drawn from

Louise Nalbandian, *The Armenian Revolutionary Movement*, Berkeley and Los Angeles, University of California Press, 1963.

3 Quoted in William L. Langer, *The Diplomacy of Imperialism, 1890–1902*, New York, Knopf, 1960, pp. 157 and 158.

4 An offshoot sect from Shia Islam, with its own sacred book and law. Druze are regarded as heretics by both Sunni and Imami Shia (the Shias of Iran and Iraq) Muslims.

Chapter 5

1 Great Britain, Public Record Office, Foreign Office 371–1762, Young to Bax-Ironside, Cavalla, 21 December 1912.

Chapter 7

1 From Article 22 of the Covenant of the League of Nations, quoted in H.W.V. Temperley (ed.), *A History of the Peace Conference of Paris*, vol. VI, London, Froude, 1924, p. 561.

2 Quotes and descriptions of these treaties and agreements are taken from J.C. Hurewitz, *Diplomacy in the Near and Middle East: A Documentary Record, 1914–1956*, vol. II, Princeton, Van Nostrand, 1956. Some agreements were drawn up in correspondence that spanned a length of time, which explains their dates.

3 A honorific indicating he had married into the imperial family.

4 David Lloyd George, *The Truth about the Peace Treaties*, vol. II, London, Victor Gollancz, 1938, p. 1013.

5 Ibid., p. 1015.

Chapter 8

1 Aydın, Hüdavendigâr, Biga and İzmit provinces.

2 Harold Nicholson, *Peacemaking: 1919*, New York, Harcourt, Brace, 1919, p. 136.

3 Great Britain, Public Record Office, Foreign Office (FO) 371–4218, no. 91491, Mallet (for Balfour) to Curzon, Paris 1919, enclosure no. 3, the statement of Donald Whittall, Smyrna, 18 May 1919.

4 FO 371–4218, no. 91491, Mallet (for Balfour) to Curzon, Paris 1919, enclosure no. 9, 'Commanding Officer USS *Arizona* to Senior Naval Officer, Constantinople', Smyrna, 18 May 1919.

5 FO 371–4218, no. 86551, 'Cable from A.C.O. Smyrna, 18th May 1919', in Calthorpe to Curzon, Constantinople, 24 May 1919.

6 France, Ministère de la Défense, Etat Major de l'Armée du Terre, Service Historique, Général (CR) du Hays, *Les Armées Françaises au Levant, 1919–1939*, vol. I, Paris, 1939, p. 122.

7 A. Rawlinson, *Adventures in the Near East, 1918–1922*, London, A. Melrose, 1924, p. 227.

Chapter 9

1 Great Britain, Public Record Office, Foreign Office 388/11, no. 457/43, Intelligence Report for 6 May 1920, Sofia, 8 May 1920.

Chapter 10

1 'The Mandate for Palestine', in J.C. Hurewitz, *Diplomacy in the Near and Middle East*, vol. II, Princeton, Van Nostrand, 1956, pp. 106–11.
2 This includes all groups the Ottomans counted as Muslims – Sunni, Shia, Alawi, Ismaili and Druze.
3 *Report by His Britannic Majesty's Government on the Administration of Iraq*, League of Nations, Geneva, 1927, p. 115.
4 This analogy was pointed out by Nachum Gross in *The Economic Policy of the Mandatory Government in Palestine*, Jerusalem, Maurice Falk Institute, 1982, pp. 7 and 8.

Chapter 11

1 Note that it was only possible to enumerate the populations of central districts (*kazas*), not cities themselves, because Ottoman statistics recorded kaza populations only. Figures on cities in the Ottoman period are usually lacking.
2 United States, National Archives, 767.68116/34, J. Loder Park to Secretary of State, Smyrna, 11 April 1923.
3 *Osmanlı Sanayii 1913, 1915 Yılları Sanayi İstatistik*, ed. Professor A. Gündüz Ökçün, Ankara, Devlet İstatistik Enstitüsü, 1997.

Suggested readings

Allen, W.E.D. and Paul Muratoff, *Caucasian Battlefields*, Cambridge, Cambridge University Press, 1953.

Brown, L. Carl (ed.), *Imperial Legacy: The Ottoman Imprint on the Balkans and the Middle East*, New York, Columbia University Press, 1996.

Crampton, R.J., *Bulgaria 1878–1918: A History*, East European monographs no. 138, New York, Columbia University Press, 1983.

Danforth, Loring M., *The Macedonian Conflict: Ethnic Nationalism in a Transnational World*, Princeton, Princeton University Press, 1995.

Findley, Carter V., *Bureaucratic Reform in the Ottoman Empire: The Sublime Porte, 1789–1922*, Princeton, Princeton University Press, 1980.

Fisher, Sidney N. and William Ochsenwald, *The Middle East: A History*, 5th edn, New York, McGraw-Hill, 1997.

Fromkin, David, *A Peace to End All Peace*, New York, Avon, 1989.

Haddad, William and William Ochsenwald (eds), *Nationalism in a Non-national State: The Dissolution of the Ottoman Empire*, Columbus, Ohio State University Press, 1977.

Helmreich, Paul C., *From Paris to Sèvres: The Partition of the Ottoman Empire at the Peace Conference of 1919–1920*, Columbus, Ohio State University Press, 1974.

Hourani, Albert, *A History of the Arab Peoples*, Harvard, Harvard University Press, 1991.

Jelavich, Barbara, *History of the Balkans*, vols I and II, Cambridge, Cambridge University Press, 1983.

Kayalı, Hasan, *Arabs and Young Turks*, Berkeley, University of California Press, 1997.

Khalidi, Rashid, Lisa Anderson, Muhammad Muslih and Reeva S. Simon (eds), *The Origins of Arab Nationalism*, New York, Columbia University Press, 1991.

Khoury, Philip S. (Philip Shukry), *Syria and the French Mandate: The Politics of Arab Nationalism, 1920–1945*, Princeton, Princeton University Press, 1987.

Langer, William L., *The Diplomacy of Imperialism, 1890–1902*, New York, Knopf, 1960.

McCarthy, Justin, *Death and Exile: Ethnic Cleansing of the Ottoman Muslims, 1821–1922*, Institute of Turkish Studies Series, Darwin Press, 1995.

McCarthy, Justin, *The Ottoman Turks*, London, Longman, 1997.

Marr, Phebe, *The Modern History of Iraq*, Boulder, Colo., Westview, 1985.

Nalbandian, Louise, *The Armenian Revolutionary Movement*, Berkeley, University of California Press, 1963.

Owen, Roger, *The Middle East in the World Economy, 1800–1914*, London, Methuen, 1981.

Owen, Roger and Şevket Pamuk, *A History of Middle East Economies in the Twentieth Century*, Cambridge, Mass., Harvard University Press, 1999.

Özkırımlı, Umut, *Theories of Nationalism: A Critical Introduction*, New York, St Martin's Press, 2000.

Pamuk, Şevket, *The Ottoman Empire and European Capitalism, 1820–1913: Trade, Investment, and Production*, Cambridge Middle East Library, Cambridge, Cambridge University Press, 1987.

Poulton, Hugh, *The Balkans: Minorities and States in Conflict*, 2nd edn, London, Minority Rights Publications, 1993.

Salibi, Kamal, *The Modern History of Lebanon*, New York, Caravan, 1965.

Shaw, Stanford J. and Ezel Kural Shaw, *History of the Ottoman Empire and Modern Turkey*, vol. II, Cambridge, Cambridge University Press, 1977.

Tibawi, Abdul Latif, *A Modern History of Syria Including Lebanon and Palestine*, Oxford, Oxford University Press, 1966.

Todorov, Nikolai, *The Balkan City, 1400–1900*, Publications on Russia and Eastern Europe of the School of International Studies, University of Washington; Seattle, University of Washington Press, *c.* 1983.

Todorova, Maria, *Imagining the Balkans*, Oxford, Oxford University Press, 1997.

Yalman, Ahmed Emin, *Turkey in the World War*, New Haven, Yale University Press, 1930.

Yapp, M.E., *The Making of the Modern Near East, 1792–1923*, London, Longman, 1987.

Yapp, M.E., *The Near East Since the First World War*, London, Longman, 1991.

Zürcher, Erik J., *The Unionist Factor*, Leiden, Brill, 1984.

Zürcher, Erik J., *Turkey: A Modern History*, 2nd edn, London, I.B. Tauris, 1998.

Index

Abdullah 170, 173, 174
Abhazia and Abhazians 2, 21, 68, 109, 211, 212
Adana 105, 121, 127, 130, 140
Aegean region 47, 120, 123, 124, 131, 132, 135, 151, 152, 154, 155, 157, 159
agriculture 12, 33, 80, 110, 136, 154, 180, 188, 190, 203, 207, 208
Alawites 171, 172
Albania and Albanians 1–3, 53, 56, 57, 60, 87, 92, 94, 115, 124, 125, 149, 151, 154, 162
Aleppo 32, 77, 82, 164, 171, 179, 182, 186, 191
Algeria 89, 139
Ali, Mehmet Emin 16, 25
Allenby, Edmund 104
Allies (Entente)
  World War I 98–9, 102, 112, 165, 166
  Turkish War of Independence 128–32, 134, 135, 137–40, 143, 145, 147, 151, 154
America and Americans 8, 18, 19, 34, 55, 57, 69, 71, 74, 79, 80, 83, 103, 111, 113, 114, 117–22, 129, 131, 134, 161, 201, 202, 205
Anatolia 3, 33, 35, 42, 63, 74–8, 85, 86, 90, 96, 104, 105, 115, 116, 118, 120, 121, 127, 129, 138–41, 161, 165, 181, 186
  eastern 47, 66, 67, 70, 72, 92, 97, 99, 103, 106–11, 116, 121–3, 126, 127, 129, 131, 141, 143–5, 171, 195, 199, 201, 208, 213, 219
  western 85, 86, 123–7, 130–2, 134–7, 145–8
  see also Turkish Republic
Ankara 138, 140, 145–7, 195, 203, 206, 211
Arab Middle East and Arabs 19, 23, 28, 33, 35, 39, 73, 74, 76–83, 85, 86, 116, 117, 118, 120, 136, 138, 149, 163–6, 168–73, 175, 176, 178, 192, 209, 214, 216, 219
  Bedouin 78, 80, 83–6, 166, 169, 174, 185
  see also by region or state
Arab state 78, 79, 84, 115, 116, 163–6, 173, 175, 192, 219
Arabia 115, 116, 127, 166, 186
Arabic language 3, 75, 77, 79–81, 83, 164, 184, 185, 211
Armenia and Armenians 2, 63, 86, 106–12, 116, 119–23, 126, 129, 130, 138–41, 143–5, 148, 195, 196, 199, 202, 205, 212, 213, 219
  deportation 110–12
Armenian revolutionaries 66, 68–73, 106–12
  Armenakan Party 70, 72
  Dashnaktsuthian Party (Dashnaks) 71
  Hunchakian Revolutionary Party (Hunchaks) 70–2
armies
  Arab 166, 169
  British 103, 104, 118, 165, 166, 171, 175, 191
  Bulgarian 91, 93, 155
  French 118, 168

armies cont.
Greek 61, 62, 123, 132, 134, 156, 201
Iraqi 171
Ottoman 13–16, 23, 26, 30, 31, 42, 43, 45, 46, 61–3, 70, 72, 76, 81, 92, 93, 95, 96, 103, 104–9, 111, 112, 118, 123, 127, 129, 130
Russian 48, 67, 107, 108–11
Serbian 88, 92
Turkish Nationalist/Turkish Republican 137, 139, 143, 145, 213, 214
armistices 47, 109, 146, 155
Mudros 109, 125, 128–32, 135, 139, 169
Austria–Hungary and Austrians 6, 20, 48, 73, 95, 97, 103, 108, 112, 120, 153
Ayans 12, 14, 33, 42, 43, 52
Azerbaijan and Azeris 2, 67, 108, 109, 111, 143, 144

Baghdad 77, 103, 104, 127, 164, 166, 173, 184, 188, 208
Baku 67, 109
Balkans 1–3, 6, 14, 35, 38–40, 42, 43, 47, 48, 51–3, 60, 67, 75, 80, 84, 85, 90, 91, 94, 113, 118–20, 130, 131, 135, 136, 147, 149, 152, 159, 163, 175, 181, 195, 199, 212, 216–19
bandits 12, 42, 44, 80
banks 22, 25, 28, 30, 73, 161, 190
Basra 103, 164, 166, 184, 188
Batum 47, 67, 68, 96, 106
Bessarabia 43, 47
Bitlis 66, 67, 107, 109, 144, 193, 202
Bosnia and Bosnians 1, 2, 6, 25, 45–8, 73, 74, 149, 153, 205
Bristol, Mark 60, 135
Britain and the British 6, 15, 20–2, 32, 34, 46, 47, 61, 67, 72, 73, 81, 84, 85, 89, 91, 95, 96–9, 102–5, 112, 115–18, 120–2, 124–7, 130–2, 134–6, 138, 139–41, 143, 145–7, 154, 156, 161, 164–6, 168–71, 173–7, 179, 180–2, 184–8, 190–3, 201, 205, 208, 216, 217
British mandates, government and politics 165, 170, 180, 187, 188, 190, 217
basic law 170, 175
finance 174, 183, 186, 187, 190, 191, 214
Jewish Agency 170, 183
League of Nations 166, 170
representation 170–2, 175
see also economy; education; nationalism and nationalists
Bulgaria and Bulgarians 1, 2, 6, 18, 21, 22, 25, 32, 39, 42, 45–51, 53, 55, 56, 58–60, 66, 67, 71–3, 87–94, 99, 112, 123, 131, 136, 149, 151–62, 206, 211, 212, 218
Allied administration 155, 156
Bulgarian revolutionaries 45–7, 87–9, 92

capitulations 21, 22, 24, 33, 34, 76, 127, 147
Caucasus region 21, 68, 108, 109, 211
See also Transcaucasia
Cemal 32, 35, 81, 82, 98, 128
Christianity and Churches 2, 6, 8, 44, 46, 53, 69, 72, 79, 82, 94, 119, 132, 147, 166, 171, 217
Armenian Gregorian 66, 67, 69, 138
Bulgarian Orthodox 49–51, 55, 56, 87, 88, 91, 93, 94, 162
conversion 69, 93, 94, 119, 151, 156
Greek Orthodox 49–51, 53, 57, 68, 88, 124, 138, 156, 158, 160
Maronite 82, 118, 171
Protestant 19, 69, 119
See also missionaries
Serbian Orthodox 51, 158
Uniate Catholic 82, 118, 138, 171
See also Christianity and Churches: Maronite
Churchill, Winston 99, 102, 105, 106
Cilicia 102, 121, 127, 130, 138–41, 145, 196
Circassia and Circassians 21, 46, 68, 77, 109, 211, 212
civil order and public safety 6, 21, 33, 50, 51, 61, 66, 88, 111, 134, 158, 174, 178, 179, 182, 185, 191, 208, 214
Clemenceau, Georges 118
commerce, *see* trade and commerce
commissions of control, control officers
Albania 153, 154
Bulgaria 155
Turkish Republic 130, 134, 135, 137, 141, 143

communications 9, 79, 96, 103, 108, 164, 188, 217, 218
conferences and treaties
  Agreement of Saint Jean de Maurienne 115
  Alexandropol 144
  Anglo-Iraqi 175
  Berlin 68, 96
  Bucharest 43, 91
  Budapest Convention 47
  Constantinople 91, 93
  Constantinople Agreement 115
  Convention of Akkerman 43
  French–Turkish 140, 145
  Greek–Ottoman 62
  Lausanne 146–8, 160, 190, 201, 203, 210
  London 115, 154
  Neuilly 154, 155, 157
  Niš 158
  Ottoman–German 98
  Paris (Crimean War) 47, 48, 113
  Rapallo 120
  San Remo 122, 166, 169
  San Stephano 47, 68
  St. Germain 120
  Sèvres 126, 127, 129
  Soviet–Turkish 145
  Sykes–Picot Agreement 116, 118, 122, 125, 127, 166
  Versailles (Paris) 113, 114, 117–27, 129, 131, 132, 137, 159, 166
  Vienna 8, 113, 114
Constantine I 123
Crete 61, 62
Croatia and Croats 1, 149, 159
Curzon, George 121, 134
Cyprus 22, 97, 124, 125

Damascus 77, 78, 82, 105, 164, 166, 169–71, 188
democracy 23–7, 30–2, 34, 75, 138, 209, 211, 219
disease 92, 110, 131
Disraeli, Benjamin 46
Diyarbakır 144
Dobruja 157
Dodecanese 90, 115, 120, 124, 125, 127
Druze 82, 83, 170–2, 183, 184

Eastern Rumelia 47
economy
  British mandates 164, 168, 170, 173–5, 179, 180, 182, 186–8, 190, 192
  Bulgaria 152, 154, 155
  French mandate 164, 168, 179, 181, 185–8, 190
  Greece 161, 162
  mandates 163–5, 168, 173, 175–8, 181, 185–7, 190, 192
  Ottoman 3–6, 12, 16, 17, 20–3, 28, 33, 34, 40, 69, 76, 80, 83, 87, 96, 103, 127, 168, 176–9, 186, 203, 204, 206, 207, 214, 217, 218
  Serbia/Yugoslavia 150, 159
  Turkish Republic 165, 186–8, 199, 203–8, 214, 216
education 8, 9, 15–19
  American missionary 69, 79, 119, 218
  Armenian 69, 70
  British mandates 183–5, 192
  Bulgarian 49, 158, 159
  French mandates 182, 183, 185, 192
  French missionary 79, 83
  Greek 49, 159
  Islamic 16, 209
    See also education: Ottoman
  nationalist 49, 51, 87
  Ottoman 15–19, 35, 79–81, 218
  Serbian/Yugoslavian 49, 158, 159
  Turkish 75, 76, 207–10
Egypt 2, 6, 15, 18, 22, 32, 44, 61, 84, 89, 104, 111, 115, 118, 164, 165, 175, 186–8
England 6, 43, 60, 62, 97, 161
Enver 32, 35, 76, 95, 96, 98, 103, 105, 106, 108, 109, 128, 137
Erivan (Yerevan) 66, 67, 109, 141
Erzurum 47, 67, 109, 112, 137, 144, 193, 202, 204, 205
Ethnike Hetairia 61, 88

Faysal 84, 166, 169, 173
Ferit, Damat Mehmet 120, 121, 127–9, 137
Fourteen Points 118, 119, 121
France and the French 21, 44, 46, 73, 81–3, 85, 93, 95–8, 112, 114–18, 120–2, 125–7, 131, 136, 138–41, 145–7, 155, 156, 164, 166, 168–73, 175–7, 179–88, 190–3, 196, 216

French mandate, government and politics 179, 180, 183, 190
  basic law 171
  finance 183, 186, 187, 190, 191
  League of Nations 166
  representation 171, 172
  see also economy; education; nationalism and nationalists

Gallipoli 99, 102–4, 106, 111, 130, 137
Georgia 2, 67, 111, 143
Germany and Germans 40, 42, 45, 47, 73, 89, 95–8, 102, 103, 105, 108, 114, 115, 118, 123, 154, 193, 212
Gladstone, William Ewart 46
Glubb, John 185
Gourad, Henri 140
Great Depression 173, 190, 207
Greece and the Greeks 1, 6, 23, 30, 32, 33, 39, 40, 42–5, 47–53, 55–62, 76, 82, 85–8, 90–4, 97, 112, 117, 118, 122–7, 129–38, 140, 144–62, 187, 193, 195, 196, 199, 201, 205, 206, 208, 213, 218, 219
  Anatolian Greeks 130, 131, 134, 147, 148, 159, 160, 161

Hamidiye cavalry 63, 66, 72
Harrington, Tim 136, 146
Hatt-ı Hümayun of Gülhane 16, 19, 34–6
Hijaz 80, 83, 105, 116, 127, 173, 188
Husayn 81, 83–5, 115, 116, 127, 166, 170, 173, 174

imperialism 3, 7, 8, 21, 43, 97, 110, 117, 126, 165, 166, 168, 176, 177, 219
  economic 20–2, 33, 34, 76, 97
  see also capitulations
India and Indians 99, 103, 117, 125, 168
industry 5, 20–2, 159, 168, 178, 190, 206
Iran (Persia) and Iranians 67, 82, 96, 99, 103, 107, 111, 117, 168, 187
Iraq and Iraqis 2, 3, 63, 78–80, 82, 84, 96, 99, 102–4, 107, 115–18, 120, 126, 147, 164–6, 168–71, 173–5, 177, 182, 184, 186–8, 190, 191, 206, 208, 214, 216, 218
  see also British mandates
İskenderun (Iskandarun, Alexandretta) 80, 169, 171, 186
Islam 7, 16, 24, 35–7, 39, 73–81, 85, 164, 169, 206, 209, 210, 212, 214, 216–18
  see also Ottoman government and politics: Ulema; laws: Islamic Law and judges
Istanbul 13–15, 20, 25, 28, 31, 35, 42, 47, 50, 58, 70–3, 75–9, 84, 90, 95, 97, 99, 102, 108, 109, 115, 121, 126–30, 132, 135–8, 146–9, 156, 158–60, 195, 199, 207, 208
Italy and Italians 21, 32, 89, 90, 104, 115–17, 120, 124, 125, 127, 129, 130, 131, 141, 147, 153, 154
İzmir 125, 132, 134, 201

Janissaries 12–14, 42, 43, 78
Jebel Druze 170
Jerusalem 32, 104, 164, 188, 191
Jews 2, 57, 60, 69, 115, 116, 126, 135, 151, 155, 164, 169–75, 180, 182–5, 217
  see also Zionism and Zionists

Karabekir, Kâzim 143, 144
Kars 47, 68, 96, 141, 143, 144, 195, 196, 202
Kosova (Kosovo) 1, 53, 92, 152, 153, 159
Kurds 3, 63, 66, 72, 73, 76, 77, 85, 86, 104, 107, 108, 110, 111, 138, 141, 164, 171, 213, 214
Kut al-Amara 103

laws 16–19, 21, 22, 24, 26, 27, 32, 34–6, 38, 55, 61, 75, 82, 83, 115, 129, 137, 138, 147, 170, 206, 210–12, 217
  Islamic Law and judges 16, 18, 24, 35–7, 210, 217
  Mecelle 36, 217
League of Nations 114, 147, 160, 161, 166, 170, 174–6, 184, 216
Lebanon and Lebanese 32, 79, 82, 83, 115, 118, 126, 164–6, 168, 169, 171–3, 178–81, 183, 185–91, 214
  Maronites 79, 82–4, 118, 164, 168, 171, 173, 183
Libya 32, 89, 104

Liman von Sanders, Otto 95, 102, 105
Lloyd George, David 117, 121, 124–6, 132

Macedonia and Macedonians 30, 31, 42, 48, 49, 53, 55–60, 62, 87–94, 149–53, 155, 157, 158, 159, 162
mass murder 1, 21, 44–8, 61, 72, 88, 91–3, 107, 110–12, 125, 126, 130, 132, 134–40, 143–7, 152, 153, 201, 202, 205, 219
Mehmet Cavit 35
middle class 30, 35, 37, 159, 206, 214
missionaries
  American 19, 69–72, 79, 83, 119, 121, 122, 183, 218
  French 83, 118, 183
Montenegro and Montenegrins 32, 45, 47, 90–2, 153, 154
Mosul 63, 104, 120, 147, 164, 166, 169, 170, 184, 206
Muhammad Ali 15, 44, 61
Muslims 1–3, 6, 21, 25, 36, 40, 42–8, 53, 56, 58–63, 66–9, 71–5, 78–80, 82–8, 90–4, 97, 107–12, 125, 126, 130, 131, 134, 139–41, 143–6, 149–53, 162, 164, 171, 173, 180, 182–5, 193, 195, 199, 201, 202, 212, 217–19
  Shia 78, 82, 164, 183
  Sunni 36, 78, 82, 138, 164, 171, 183
Mustafa Kemal (Atatürk) 102, 105, 137, 138, 143, 145, 146, 206, 209, 211, 213, 215, 219
Mustafa Reşit 16, 25

nationalism and nationalists 1–3, 7, 20, 30, 38–40, 42, 43, 47–53, 55–62, 73, 74, 86, 88, 90, 91, 94, 106, 126, 159, 162–5, 169, 173, 175, 187, 210, 218, 219
  Albanian 152, 153
  Arab 75–85, 163–5, 169, 173, 175, 187
  Armenian 64–73, 85, 106, 110
  Bulgarian 40, 45, 50, 51, 53, 55–9, 87, 94
  Greek 44–6, 49, 50, 53, 55–62, 85, 88, 94, 159, 162
  and history 39, 40, 52, 57, 73–5, 124, 163
  and language 38–40, 50, 52, 53, 55, 57–61, 74–6, 79, 80, 151, 163–5, 184, 213
  Ottoman 152, 153
  pan-Slavism 45, 46
  Serbian 40, 53, 55, 56
  Turkish 28, 73–7, 80, 136–8, 211–13
navies 96, 98, 99, 102, 104, 127, 155, 168
Nestorians, Assyrians 108, 171
newspapers 19, 24, 25, 46, 49, 81, 87, 102, 213
Niles, Emory 202
North Africa 89
  see also Egypt; Libya

oil 99, 103, 117, 118, 165, 168, 175, 203
Ottoman government and politics
  bureaucracy 12, 14–19, 22–5, 28, 30, 31, 35–7, 72, 75, 79, 81, 88, 89, 107, 111, 125, 128, 129, 130, 134, 137, 138, 159, 214, 216
  Committee of Union and Progress 30–2, 35–7, 66, 75–7, 80, 89, 120, 128–31, 136, 153, 206, 209, 210
  Constitution 24–7, 30, 34–7, 74
  Council of Ministers 17
  councils 17, 18, 23, 36
  finance 9, 12, 16, 17, 19, 21–3, 25–8, 33, 34, 45, 78, 95, 127, 153, 203, 208, 217
  Finance Ministry 17
  Foreign Ministry 17, 35, 36, 70, 191, 210
  governors 9, 18, 23, 33, 42, 61, 78, 79, 81, 83, 120, 132, 171
  grand vezirs 12, 13, 17, 18, 25, 26, 31, 32, 35, 98, 120
  Interior Ministry 6, 17, 32, 35, 61, 92, 111, 130, 164
  Liberals and the Liberal Union 27, 31, 32, 98, 128, 129
  millets 9, 16, 17, 19, 39, 49, 74, 82, 182, 209, 210, 217, 219
  ministries 15, 17, 35, 36
  Parliament 16, 26, 27, 31, 32, 35, 37, 81, 106, 118, 126, 138, 206, 209–11
  provincial government 18
  Tanzimat 16–20, 23–5, 27, 28, 30, 34, 36, 74, 79, 87, 206
  traditionalists 13–15, 17, 20, 26, 27, 31

Ottoman government and politics cont.
Triumvirate 32, 95, 96, 98
Ulema and religious affairs 36, 37
vezirs 12, 13, 17, 18, 25, 26, 31, 32, 35, 98, 120
Young Ottomans 24, 25, 28, 30, 74
Young Turks 28, 30
see also economy; education; nationalism and nationalists

Palestine and Palestinians 2, 81, 99, 104, 105, 115, 116, 126, 164–6, 168–71, 173–5, 178–81, 183–5, 187, 188, 190–2, 217
Balfour Declaration 115, 116, 126, 171
see also British mandates
peace conferences, *see* conferences and treaties
Pious foundations (vakıfs) 36, 75, 217
police and gendarmerie 5, 17, 27, 66, 72, 89, 96, 107, 111, 127, 134, 137, 154, 185, 190, 191, 214
Pomaks 40, 94, 155, 212
Pontus 147, 161
population and demography 1–5, 18, 21, 33, 35, 48, 55, 58–61, 63, 66, 72, 76, 79, 82, 85–7, 90–4, 107, 109–13, 115, 116, 122–6, 129–31, 135, 138, 143, 144, 146, 147, 149–52, 155–60, 164, 165, 171, 173, 175, 177–85, 191, 193, 195, 196, 199, 202, 204, 205, 208, 214
censuses 158, 178, 180, 181, 205
fertility 178
migration 21, 38, 44, 47, 60, 66, 69, 82, 91–3, 97, 110, 141, 143, 144, 146, 149–51, 158, 160, 165, 170, 175, 180, 182, 195, 196, 199
see also population and demography: population exchanges; refugees
mortality 7, 25, 46–8, 72, 92, 93, 125, 126, 135, 139, 140, 144–7, 151, 157, 159, 161, 165, 178, 180–2, 193, 195, 196, 199, 202, 204, 208
see also mass murder
population exchanges 2, 68, 93, 94, 109, 144, 147, 149, 156, 157, 160, 175, 218, 219
see also migration
Prizren 152
propaganda 69, 112, 113, 121, 122
Public Debt Commission 22, 28, 33

race and racism 8, 38, 40, 56, 57, 59, 75, 116, 119, 212, 213
railroads 28, 34, 80, 83, 105, 187, 188, 208
rebellions, revolutions 2, 5, 8, 9, 14, 24, 25, 27, 30–2, 39, 42–6, 48, 50–2, 61–3, 68, 69, 70–2, 74, 77, 78, 80–2, 85, 87–9, 92, 104, 106–11, 113, 115, 117, 138, 153, 166, 169–71, 174, 176, 193, 206, 210, 213, 214
Bosnia 45
Bulgaria 45, 48
Crete 61, 62
Greek Revolution 43, 44, 52, 61
Greek War of Independence 51
guerrillas 32, 45, 72, 87–9, 103, 106–8, 110, 152, 155
Macedonia 88, 89, 152
partisan bands 1, 30, 45, 71, 72, 88, 92, 106, 107, 111, 134, 136, 139, 140, 152, 155, 156, 158
Sasun 72
Young Turk 30, 32
Zeytun 70, 72, 106
see also Armenian revolutionaries; Bulgarian revolutionaries
reform and reformers
mandates 176, 177
Ottoman 8, 12–28, 31, 33, 34, 36, 37, 45, 47, 68, 75, 78, 152, 176, 182, 209–11, 214–17, 219
Ottoman military 95, 96, 98
Turkish Republic 206–11, 214–16, 219
refugees
1877–78 Russo-Turkish War 45, 48
Balkan wars 92, 93, 130, 131, 135, 136, 150, 154, 156–8, 195
Caucasian, Transcaucasian 68, 212, 214
Lebanon 82
Turkish War of Independence 132, 135, 136, 138, 140, 141, 143, 144, 147, 159, 160, 161, 193, 195, 196, 205
World War I 109–11, 130, 131, 138, 140, 155–8, 160, 195, 205
Romania and Romanians 6, 21, 44, 45, 67, 91, 206

Russia and Russians 4, 6, 9, 20, 21, 25, 43–8, 51, 67–73, 75, 76, 82, 89, 91, 95–9, 103, 106–12, 114–17, 137, 138, 140, 141, 143, 153, 161, 165, 176, 185, 195, 196
  Russian Revolution 109, 111, 143, 193, 206
  see also Soviet Union

Sait Halim 32, 98
Salonica (Selanik, Thessaloniki) 53, 58, 87, 90, 91, 123, 152, 161, 206
Sarajevo 96
Serbia and Serbs 1, 2, 7, 21, 30, 32, 39, 40, 42–9, 51, 53, 55–7, 59, 60, 87, 88, 90–4, 97, 112, 121, 123, 149, 151–5, 157–9, 212
Sivas 67, 96, 106, 137, 144, 195
Skopje (Üsküp) 53
Slovenia and Slovenians 159
Soviet Union, Bolsheviks 123, 128, 143–5, 206
Stamboliski, Alexander 155, 156, 158
starvation 92, 110, 131, 140, 159, 202, 204
Suez Canal 99, 104, 117, 168
Sultans 1, 2, 12, 23, 26, 36, 42, 169, 210
  Mahmud II 14–16, 37, 209, 210, 216
  Mehmet II 15
  Mehmet V 31
  Mehmet VI 1, 128
  Murat V 26
  Mustafa IV 13, 14
  Selim III 12–15, 43
  Süleyman I 15
Sutherland, Arthur 202
Syria 69, 77–84, 96, 99, 102–4, 109–11, 115, 116, 118, 126, 130, 137, 138, 140, 164–6, 168–73, 175–83, 185–8, 190, 191, 218
  Greater Syria 110, 164, 166, 175, 177, 178, 180–2
  see also French mandate

Taurus Mountains 96, 139
telegraph 28, 34, 96
textiles 20, 33, 34, 186, 203
Thessaly and Epirus 47
Thrace
  eastern 47, 90–3, 125, 126, 128–30, 135, 138, 146, 151, 156–9, 161, 195, 213
  western 1, 93, 97, 118, 148–52, 154–8, 160
Tiflis 71, 143
trade and commerce 5, 6, 8, 16, 17, 21, 22, 40, 63, 84, 118, 138, 150, 156, 157, 161, 163–5, 168, 173, 177, 186–8, 199, 206, 217
  transit trade 164, 186–8
Transcaucasia 106–9, 141, 143, 144
  Transcaucasian Federation 111
Trans-Jordan 164, 166, 170, 173, 174, 191
transportation 5, 6, 22, 28, 96, 107, 108, 127, 164, 175, 187, 188, 208, 217, 218
  railroads 3, 5, 28, 34, 80, 83, 87, 96, 104, 164, 187, 188, 207, 208
  roads 3, 5, 28, 32–4, 80, 81, 87, 96, 108, 164, 188, 208
Treaties, *see* Conferences and Treaties
Tsars 2, 46, 70, 97
  Catherine the Great 9, 97
  Peter the Great 9
Tunisia 6
Turkish Republic, government and politics 206, 209, 213–15
  ethnic groups 211–13
  finance 203, 207, 208, 214, 217
  Grand National Assembly 138, 143, 145, 206, 209–11
  reform 209, 210, 214
  Republican People's Party 209, 213
  see also economy; education; nationalism and nationalists
Turkish nationalists 75, 137, 140–7
  National Pact 137, 138, 140
  see also Turkish Republic, government and politics: Grand National Assembly
Turkish Republic 33, 160, 193–216, 219
Turks 1, 2, 9, 21, 40, 44, 48, 53, 55, 56, 59, 60, 66, 71, 74–7, 79, 80, 86, 87, 93–5, 106, 108, 109, 112, 117–19, 121, 123–32, 134–49, 155, 156, 159, 160, 193, 195, 196, 199, 201, 203, 205, 206, 208, 211–19

unemployment 37, 186
Urfa 107, 127

Van 63, 66, 67, 70, 72, 107, 108, 110, 115, 143, 144, 170, 193, 199, 201, 202
Venizelos, Eleftherios 123–6, 132, 159, 160, 219
villages and villagers 3, 12, 19, 23, 24, 39, 42, 44–6, 48, 61, 71, 72, 75, 77, 82, 87–9, 91, 92, 107, 108, 110, 112, 134, 136, 138–40, 143, 152, 154, 169, 171, 181, 199, 201, 202, 204, 205, 208, 211

wars 6, 9, 14, 21, 27, 28, 33, 35, 43–5, 51, 61, 67, 68, 70, 72, 73, 76, 78, 84, 97, 113, 114, 176
  Balkan wars 2, 32, 55, 56, 59–61, 75, 76, 81, 87, 90–5, 97, 99, 127, 130, 131, 134, 135, 146, 148, 149, 151, 153, 154, 158, 160, 162, 193, 195, 219
  Crimean War 6, 22, 46, 97, 113
  destruction 7, 27, 28, 43, 71, 88, 89, 92, 111, 134, 135, 137, 143, 186, 193, 199, 201, 203, 204, 206, 214, 216, 217
  Greco-Turkish War of 1897 61, 62, 88
  Russo-Turkish War of 1828–29 43, 44, 67
  Russo-Turkish War of 1877–78 27, 45, 47, 48, 61, 68, 91
  Tripolitanian War 89, 90
  Turkish War of Independence 28, 61, 128, 130–41, 143–8, 193, 195, 196, 199, 201–6, 208, 214
    see also Allies; Commissions of Control
  World War I 27, 28, 32, 76, 79–81, 84–6, 89, 93–9, 102–11, 114–16, 119, 120–3, 129–31, 137, 138, 141, 145, 146, 149–52, 154, 156–8, 161, 165, 166, 169, 171, 178–80, 188, 193, 195, 199, 202, 214
    see also Gallipoli; Kut al-Amara; Allies; Commissions of Control
  see also armies
waterways
  Black Sea 6, 47, 91, 96, 98, 99, 111
  Danube 3, 18, 47
  Dardanelles and Bosphorus 20, 72, 73, 90, 99, 102, 115, 116, 146, 147, 157
  Euphrates 80, 186
  Marmara 99, 115
  Mediterranean Sea 20, 80, 97, 104, 117, 118, 120, 121, 125, 131, 154, 157, 168, 186
Wilhelm II 123
William of Wied 154
Wilson, Woodrow 114, 119–22, 125, 126, 128, 129

Yugoslavia 1, 2, 57, 120, 149, 154, 155, 157–9, 206

Zionism and Zionists 2, 81, 115, 170, 171, 175, 190, 212
Ziya Gökalp 75, 76